LETTER SOUNDS

VOL. 2 Teacher Resources for Blended Learning

Teacher Resources for Blended Learning

Vol. 1
Print Concepts & Phonological Awareness

Vol. 2
Letter Sounds

Vol. 3
Decodable Words, Sight Words & Spelling

Vol. 4
Reading Comprehension: Grades K-1

Vol. 5
Reading Comprehension: Grades 2-3

Vol. 6
Reading Comprehension: Grades 4+

Vol. 7
Grammar, Vocabulary, Speaking & Listening

Available at imaginelearning.com/bookstore

Developed and published by Imagine Learning, Inc.

September 2016 Edition

ISBN 978-1-945460-01-2

CONTENTS

LETTER SOUNDS

This volume includes activities, resources, and lessons to help students learn letter-sound relationships for consonants, long and short vowels, blends, and digraphs.

Using Imagine Learning in the Classroom

Blended Learning with Imagine Learning

Along with the lessons and activities in this volume, Imagine Learning offers a wealth of digital instructional activities. Used together, the offline and online teaching materials provide teachers more flexibility to teach language and literacy within a blended learning environment.

Implementation Options

Offline lessons and online resources can be used for whole group lessons, small group interventions, or individual coaching sessions. Imagine Learning's individualized learning paths also allow students to learn independently at their own individual levels.

TEACHER-LED INSTRUCTION

Because Imagine Learning activities teach key language and literacy skills, teachers can select desired lessons for focused whole-class instruction, practice, and review. Projecting activities or using them with an interactive white board makes it easy for everyone to participate.

ONE-ON-ONE INSTRUCTION

Teachers can use the Action Areas Tool to gain insight on where individual students are struggling and use that information to provide focused instruction. This data is especially helpful as you create an RTI plan and work on skills remediation. Teachers can also extend learning by reviewing student recordings and written responses to offer direct feedback.

SMALL-GROUP INSTRUCTION

The Action Areas Tool pinpoints where groups of students are struggling and immediately creates skill-based intervention groups. The tool also suggests online activities and reteaching lessons that allow for targeted intervention.

COMPUTER BANK OR LAB ROTATION

Imagine Learning provides each student with an individualized learning path by providing systematic, adaptive instruction. This makes it ideal for independent student learning—whether it be at an in-class station or in a computer lab.

Digital Imagine Learning Activities

Teachers can access Imagine Learning's engaging digital activities through the Activity Menu. The Activity Menu is organized by curriculum area. For digital activities that match the skills in this volume, click the corresponding curriculum area. Use the functions below to find the best settings for your class.

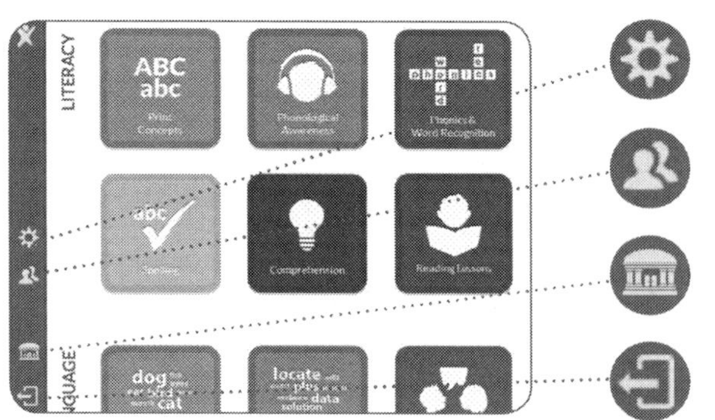

Change **program settings,** including first-language support.

Launch the **Imagine Learning Portal** to find reports, management functions, and additional resources.

Enter the **Imagine Museum** to preview performance-based student engagement features.

Log out of the Activity Menu and return to the **login page.**

Reports and Tools

Tools for setting up the program and monitoring student progress and growth are provided to teachers and administrators. Reviewing data regularly, as well as analyzing student recordings and writings, drives program efficacy and success.

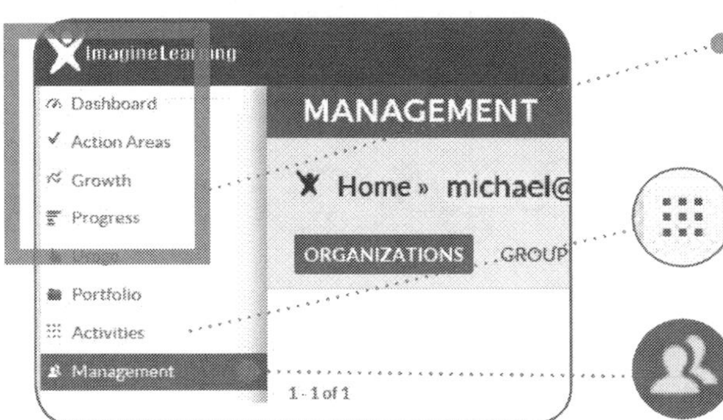

Review group and individual student data, and listen to student recordings.

Launch Activity Menu and Teacher Resources.

Manage classroom and student account preferences (session time, student passwords, etc.).

Action Areas Tool

Use data from the Action Areas Tool to identify individual students or groups of students that struggle with a particular skill. Action Areas will also suggest online activities that can be used to help struggling students.

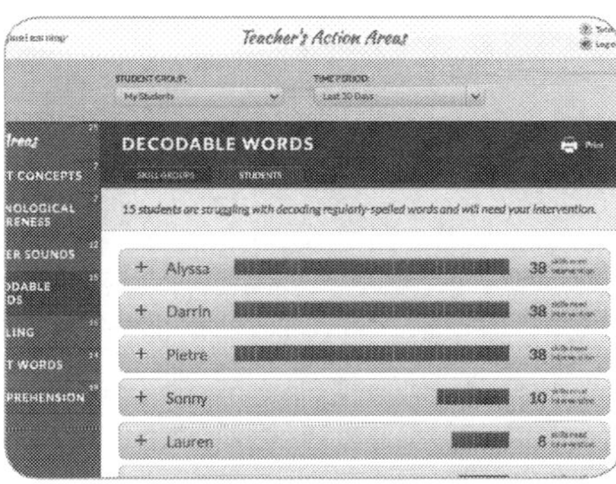

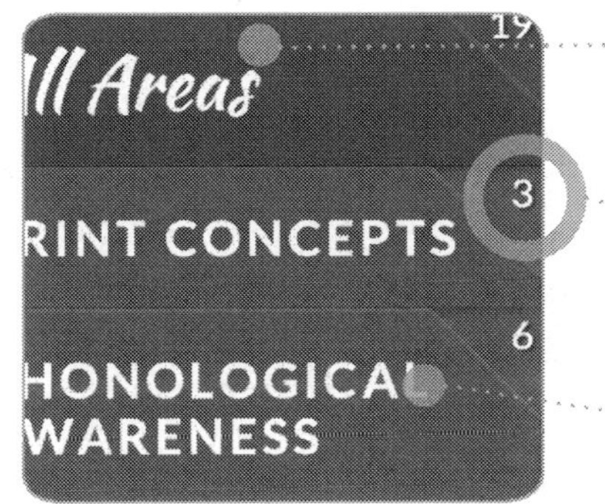

The left navigation pane lists all curriculum areas.

This number denotes how many students are struggling in a curriculum area.

Click a curriculum area and click **Intervention Tools** to view details, suggested activities, and printouts.

Teacher Resources

All Classroom Activities and Reteaching Lessons included in this volume can also be found in the Teacher Resources section online.

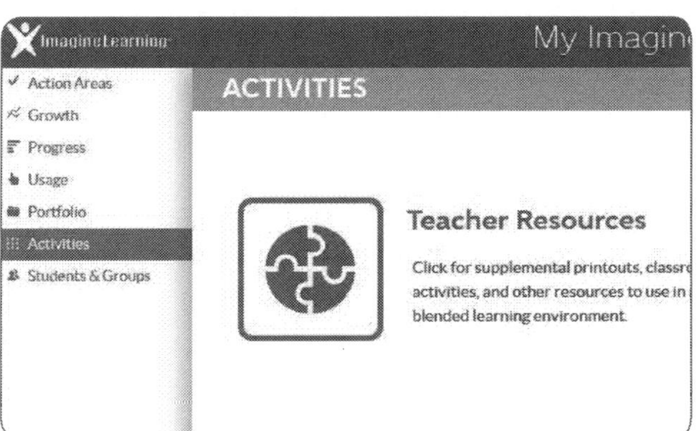

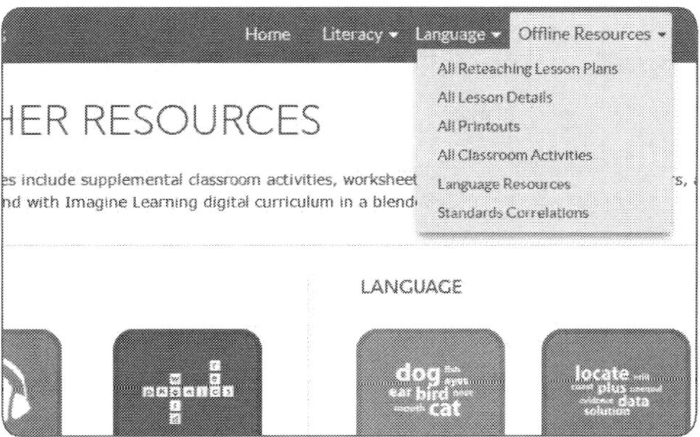

LETTER SOUNDS

CLASSROOM ACTIVITIES

Classroom activities include engaging and active whole-class lesson plans that promote interaction and help students develop knowledge of letter-sound correspondences. The instruction and practice reinforce what students have learned from the Imagine Learning online curriculum and provide opportunities for students to actively respond and demonstrate knowledge. Also included in this section are a variety of activities print-ready resources that can be used to plan lessons for a variety of instructional needs and settings.

- Flexible format that can be adapted to fit different student needs and classroom settings
- Movement and interaction involve students with language in an enjoyable way
- Blackline masters for illustrated letter sound flash cards

Clap Your Hands

CCSS.RF.K.3a-b
TEKS 110.11.3.A

LEARNING OBJECTIVE: Demonstrate letter-sound knowledge by identifying a letter and producing the letter sound.

LANGUAGE OBJECTIVE: Identify the target letter and produce the letter sound when shown a visual grapheme.

Activity Overview

Students look at five letters and match one of them with the letter sound provided by the teacher.

Materials

- Whiteboard or chalkboard
- Markers or chalk

Explain

Introduce the activity: ***This game is called Clap Your Hands. I'll write five letters on the board. I'll say a letter sound. You'll look at the five letters on the board and point to the one that matches the letter sound. If you are right, everyone will clap once andthen we'll all say the letter sound together twice.***

Play

1. Write five letters on the board.
2. Say the letter sound of one of the letters on the board.
3. Have a student come to the board and point to the letter that matches the sound. If the student is correct, all the other students clap once and repeat the letter sound twice. (/m/, /m/) The student at the board erases the letter.
4. Write a new letter on the board so there are always five letters.
5. Repeat steps 2–4 as time allows.

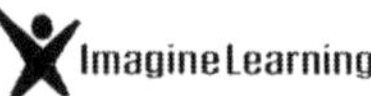

Letter Sounds

Beach Ball Alphabet

CCSS.RF.K.3a-b
TEKS 110.11.3.A

LEARNING OBJECTIVE: Demonstrate letter-sound knowledge by producing the most common sounds for each letter, blend, digraph, or silent consonant.

LANGUAGE OBJECTIVE: Produce the letter, blend, digraph, or silent consonant sound when shown a visual grapheme.

Activity Overview

Students will play a game with a beach ball and say the name and sound of letters, blends, digraphs, and silent consonants.

Materials	Preparation
• Inflatable beach ball	• Write letters, blends, digraphs, and silent consonants all over the beach ball.

Explain

Introduce the activity: ***This game is called Beach Ball Alphabet. When you catch the beach ball, grab it with both hands, then look at your right thumb. Find the letter closest to your thumb, then tell us the letter and the letter sound, like this: letter* m, /m/, /m/, /m/.**

Play

1. Toss the ball to a student.
2. Have the student find the letter closest to his or her right thumb and then say the letter name followed by the letter sound three times.
3. Have the student toss the ball to a classmate.
4. Repeat steps 2–3 as time allows.

Suggested letters, blends, digraphs, and silent consonants:

- Letters a–z
- Blends: st, sk, pr, gl, fl, cr, fr, pl, tr, dr, br, bl, sl, sn, scr, sw, sp, sc, cl
- Digraphs: ch, sh, ph, th, wh
- Silent consonant blends: kn, wr

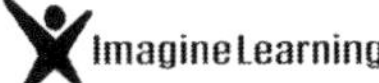

Letter Sound Scramble

CCSS.RF.K.3a-b
TEKS 110.11.3.A

LEARNING OBJECTIVE: Demonstrate letter-sound knowledge by identifying the corresponding letter, blend, or digraph after hearing the sound for the letter, blend, or digraph.

LANGUAGE OBJECTIVE: Identify the target letter, blend, or digraph after hearing the letter, blend, or digraph's phoneme or phonemes.

Activity Overview

Students will find a word card that matches the letter, blend, or digraph sound they hear.

Materials	Preparation
• Word Cards, set 1 • Word Cards, set 2 • Tape	• Cut out Word Cards set 1 or 2, depending on which letter sounds you want to practice. • Tape the cards all over the floor or walls in a large, open space.

Explain

Introduce the activity: ***We are going to play a game called Letter Sound Scramble. I'll say a letter sound and you will walk around and look at the words on all these cards until you find one with that letter sound.***

It's called a scramble because you will be moving around, but it is a silent scramble. There is no running allowed. Walk quietly and when you find a word with the right letter sound, don't say anything. Just stand quietly by the card.

Let's practice walking quietly. I'll give you just a moment now to move silently around the room and look at some of the word cards.

Allow students to look at the word cards for 20 to 30 seconds, then begin the game.

Play

1. Have students start walking around the room.
2. Call out a letter sound from the letter sounds bank below, such as /s/ /s/ /s/.
3. Have students walk quietly to a word card that includes the target letter sound.
4. Repeat the activity as time allows.

Word bank set 1: *bed, car, dug, hum, jam, lid, mop, rug, fix, hen, van, yes, quiz, kiss, wax, vet, joy, zip, way, ask, fox, lot, cub, job*

Letter sounds bank set 1:

- Letters a–z

Word bank set 2: *chop, show, phone, that, when, stop, skip, press, glue, flow, crab, frog, trip, drip, brush, black, slip, snap, scrub, swim, spin, scan, clip, small*

Letter sounds bank set 2:

- Digraphs: ch, sh, ph, th, wh
- Blends: br, bl, cr, cl, dr, fl, fr, gl, pr, st, sk, sl, sm, sn, scr, sw, sp, sc, tr

NOTE: To use this activity with the whole class or with a larger group, add additional word cards with blends, digraphs, and less common letters.

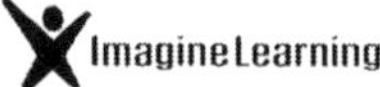

bed	car
dug	hum
jam	lid
mop	rug

fix	hen
van	yes
quiz	kiss
wax	vet

joy	zip
way	ask
fox	lot
cub	job

chop

show

phone

that

when

stop

skip

press

glue	flow
crab	frog
trip	drip
brush	black

slip	snap
scrub	swim
spin	scan
clip	small

Word Cards, set 2

Circle the Alphabet

CCSS.RF.K.3a-b
TEKS 110.11.3.A

LEARNING OBJECTIVE: Demonstrate letter-sound knowledge by producing the most common sound for each letter.

LANGUAGE OBJECTIVE: Produce the sound for the target letter when shown a visual grapheme.

Activity Overview

Students stand in inside-outside circles and practice identifying letters and letter sounds.

Materials	Preparation
• Letter Sound Flash Cards	• Cut out flash cards.

Explain

Introduce the activity: ***This game is called Circle the Alphabet.*** Show students the Letter Sound Flash Cards. ***I will give each of you one letter sound card. Then we will stand in two circles, one inside the other. The student facing you will be your partner. Take turns saying your letters and letter sounds. After you've both had a turn, trade cards and practice saying your new letter and letter sound. Then we'll rotate the circle and you'll say the new letter and letter sound to your new partner.***

Play

1. Give each student a Letter Sound Flash Card.
2. Have students form two circles, one inside the other. Have students face each other, the outside circle facing in and the inside circle facing out.
3. Have each student pair show each other their flash cards and say the letters and letter sounds. (Letter d, /d/, /d/, /d/.) If students do not know the letter sounds, they can ask for help.
4. Have partners trade cards and practice saying the new letter and letter sound.
5. After students have practiced their own letter and their partner's, have the students in the inner or outer circle move to the right or left.
6. Repeat the activity as time allows.

NOTE: To help young children form inside-outside circles, have them stand in two lines. Have the students in one line follow you as you walk in a circle. When all students are in a circle, have them stop and stand in place. Repeat with the second line, forming a circle surrounding the first circle. Have all students turn to face the student across from them in the other circle. Have them point to show they know who their partner is. Have any students who do not have a partner raise their hand.

EXTENSION ACTIVITY: Ask students to tell their partner a new word that starts with the letter shown on their card.

A-A-A Alphabet

CCSS.RF.K.3a-b
TEKS 110.11.3.A

LEARNING OBJECTIVE: Demonstrate letter-sound knowledge by producing the most common sound for each letter.

LANGUAGE OBJECTIVE: Produce the letter sound when shown a visual grapheme.

Activity Overview

Students will say the letter sound when presented with a Letter Sound Flash Card.

Materials	Preparation
• Letter Sound Flash Cards	• Cut out flash cards.

Explain

Introduce the activity: ***This game is A-A-A Alphabet.*** Pronounce the name as "/a/, /a/, /a/, alphabet." ***I'm going to hold up a card. If you know the letter sound it makes, I'll have you stand up quietly and say it three times, like this: letter* j*, /j/ /j/ /j/. When you say the letter sound, tap your desk three times.***

Play

Practice:

1. Show a flash card to students.
2. Tell students to stand up quietly if they know the letter sound.
3. Have standing students say the name of the letter followed by the letter sound three times. Have students tap their desks each time they say the letter sound.
4. Encourage students who are not standing to join in saying and tapping the letter sound and letter.

Letter Sound Flash Cards

Resource Overview

This flash card set includes blackline masters of 52 half-page cards for teaching and practicing letter sounds.

- 26 Individual Letter Sounds: a–z
- 19 Blends: bl, br, cl, cr, dr, fl, fr, gl, pl, pr, sc, scr, sk, sl, sn, sp, st, sw, tr
- 5 Digraphs: ch, ph, sh, th, wh
- 2 Silent Consonants: kn, wr

How to Use This Resource in the Classroom

- Hold up a Letter Sound Flash Card and tell the students to think about what sound the letter makes. Give them a cue (thumbs up, point to the letter card, etc.) and have the students say the letter sound in unison. Repeat exercise until you have gone through the entire stack of cards. Repeat letter cards students struggled with as necessary.
- Display a Letter Sound Flash Card. Show the students the example picture on the card. Review the letter and its sound, and then ask students to think of other words they know that include the same sound. For example, the flash card Tt has a picture and word for turtle; other words that include the same sound are teacher or table. If the students struggle, look together around the classroom for objects that include the same sound.
- Have students form pairs and give each student a Letter Sound Flash Card. Tell students to not look at their cards. Have students hold their card in front of them so their partner can see it. Instruct students that partner 1 will say what picture is on partner 2's card. After hearing the word, partner 2 will say what letter is on partner 2's card, based the word he or she heard. Then have the partners switch roles.

  Example:

  Ali: Kenny, there is a picture of a turtle on your card.
  Kenny: The letter is t.
  Ali: That's right! T says /t/.
- Have students form a circle and assign all but one student a Letter Sound Flash Card. Have the student without the flash card stand in the middle of the circle. Say the letter sound of one of the student's letters. The student in the middle of the circle points to the flash card that matches the sound. If the student is correct, all the other students stomp each foot once (for a total of two stomps) and simultaneously repeat the letter sound twice (/t/ /t/). Give the student in the middle of the circle a new flash card and have the student switch places with the student holding the correct flash card. The student who was holding the correct letter card then goes to the middle of the circle. If the student points to an incorrect flash card, prompt the student to try again. Repeat the activity as time permits.
- Spread a selection of Letter Sound Flash Cards across the floor and do any of the following activities to get the students moving.

  a) Hand a student a bean bag. Tell the student to toss the bean bag on the card that stands for the sound /p/.

  b) Call out a student's name and then say a letter sound and have the student hurry to the corresponding card.

  c) Hum or play music and have the students walk from card to card. Stop the music and call on a student to say the letter sound of the card he or she is standing next to. Have the student think of a word that begins with the sound.

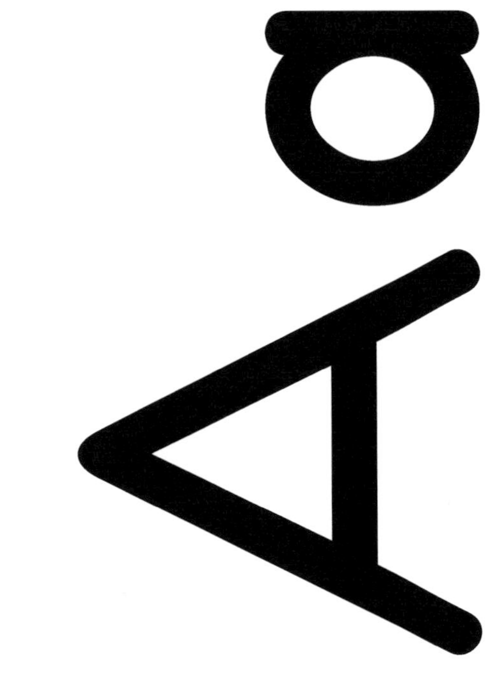

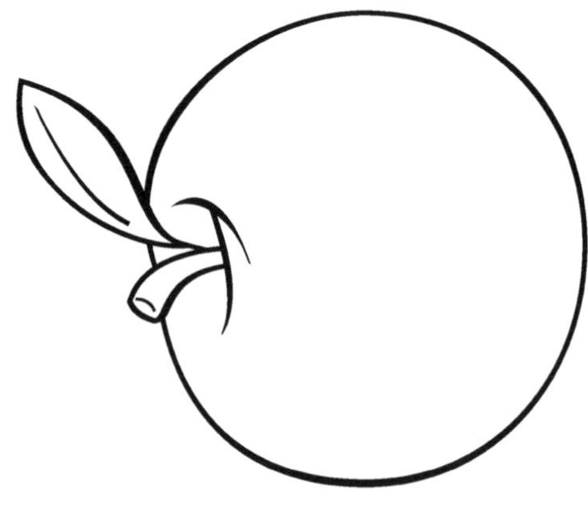

apple

Bb

bee

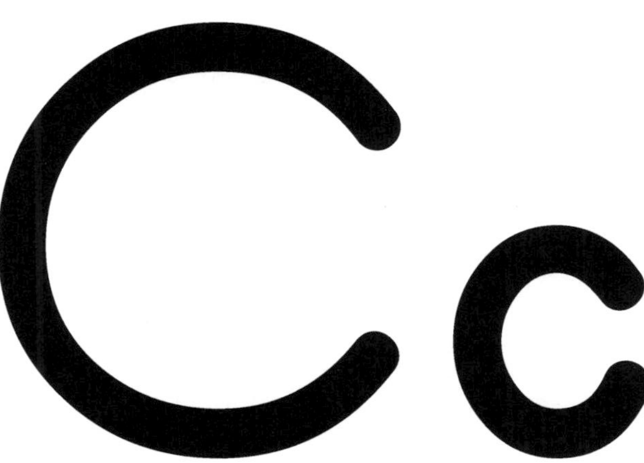

cactus

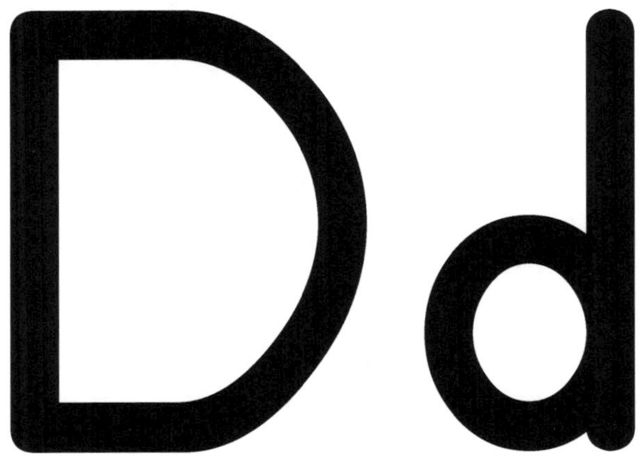

dinosaur

elephant

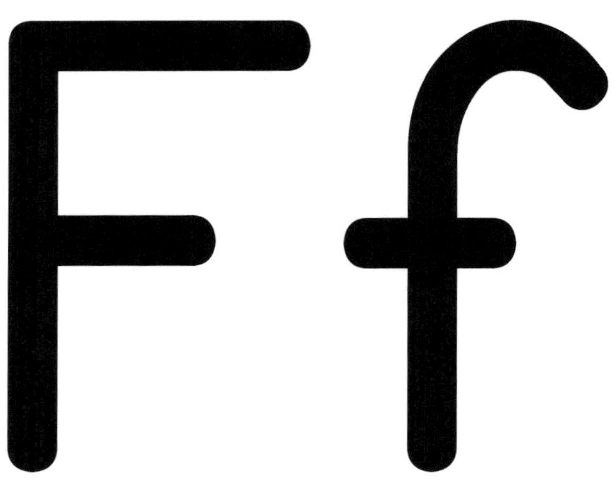

fish

Gg

gecko

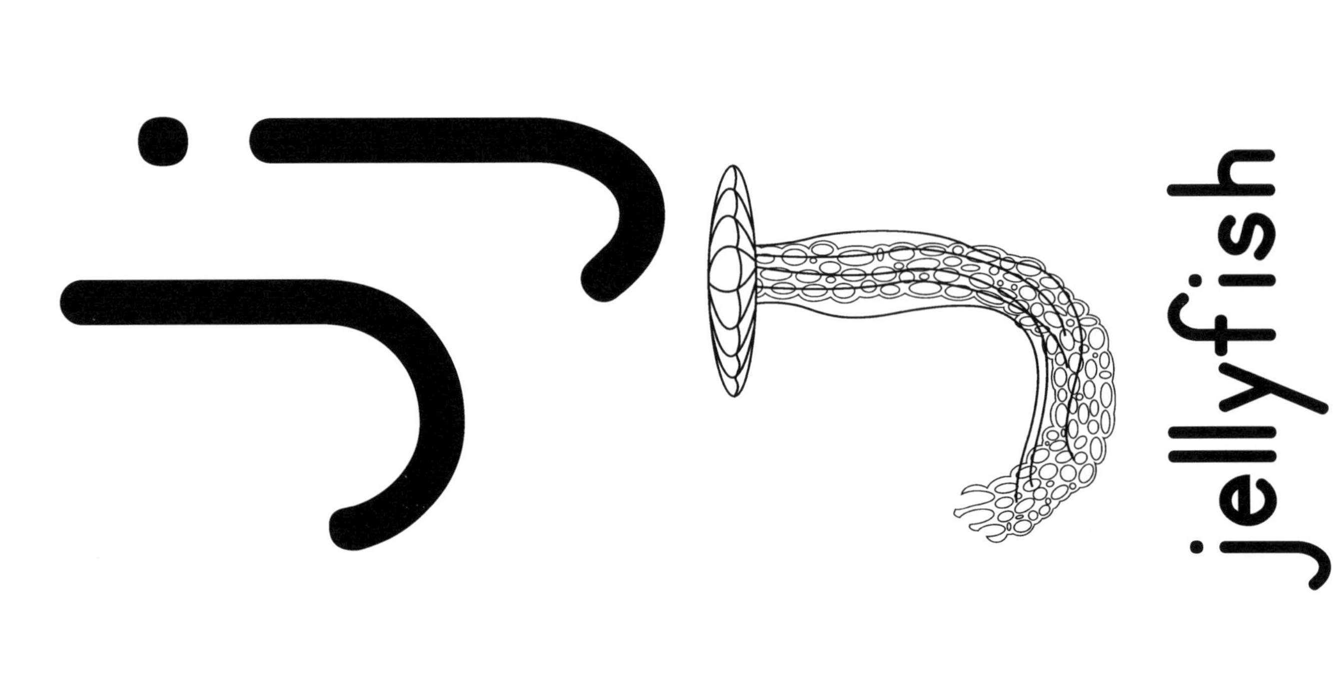

jellyfish

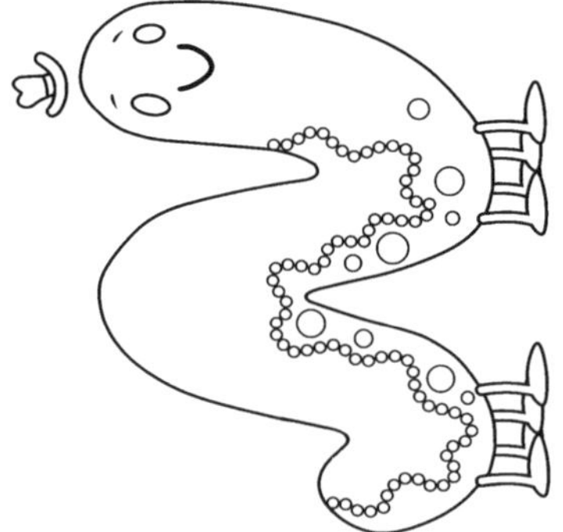

inchworm

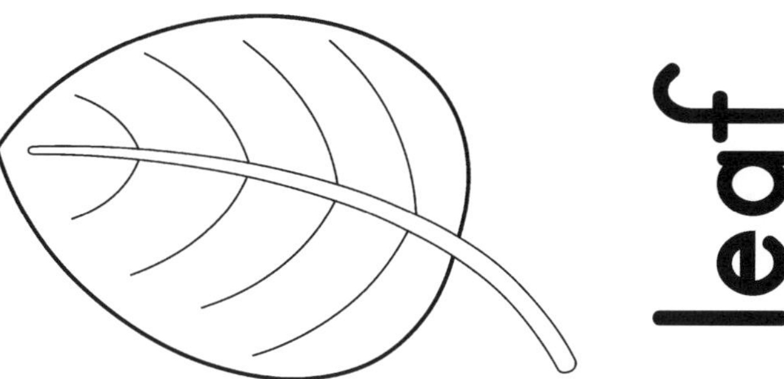

leaf

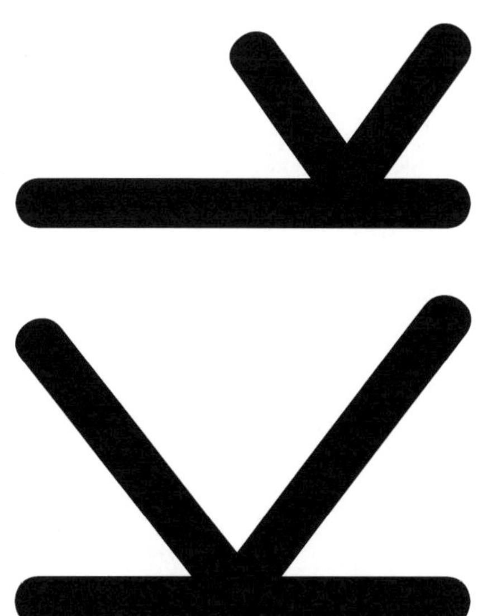

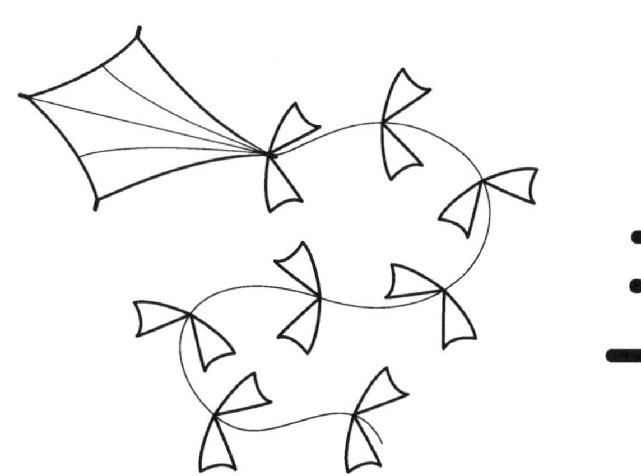

kite

Nn

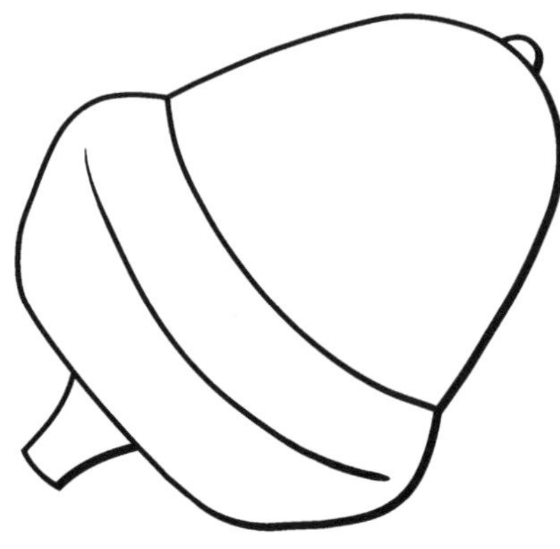

nut

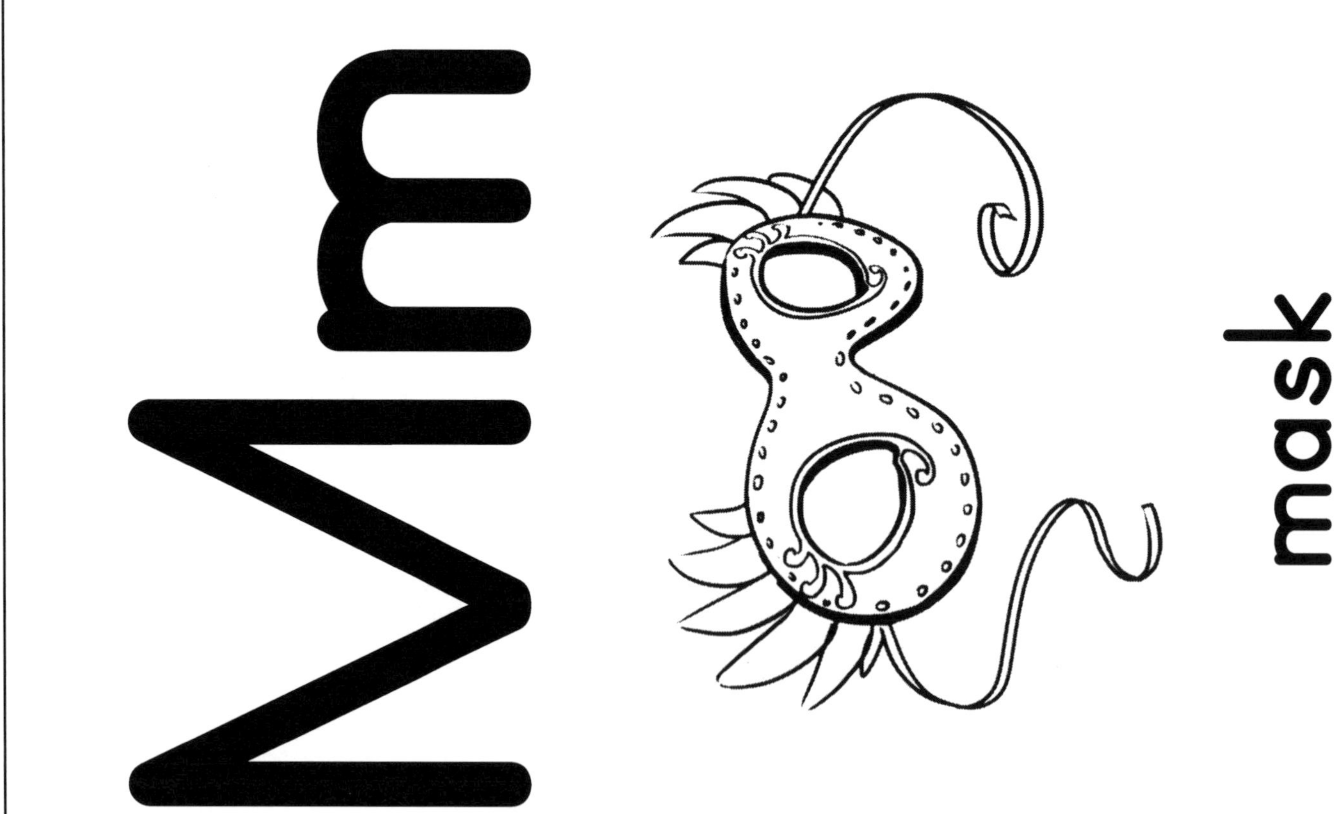

Pp

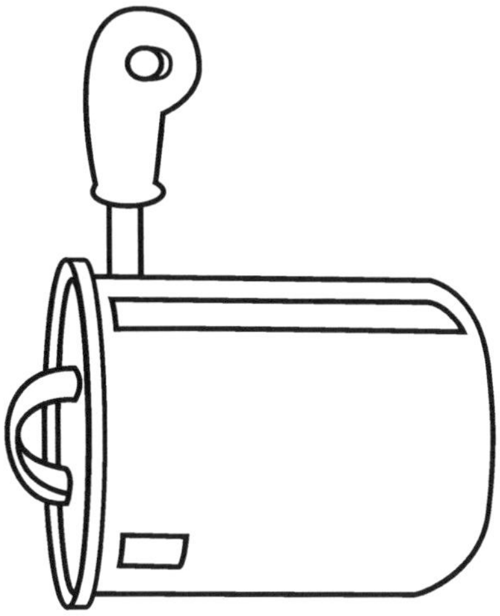

pan

Oo

octopus

Qq

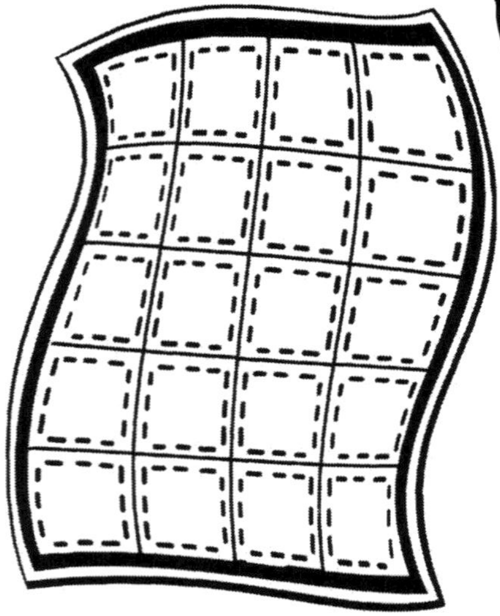

quilt

Rr

rabbit

Ss
seal

Tt
turtle

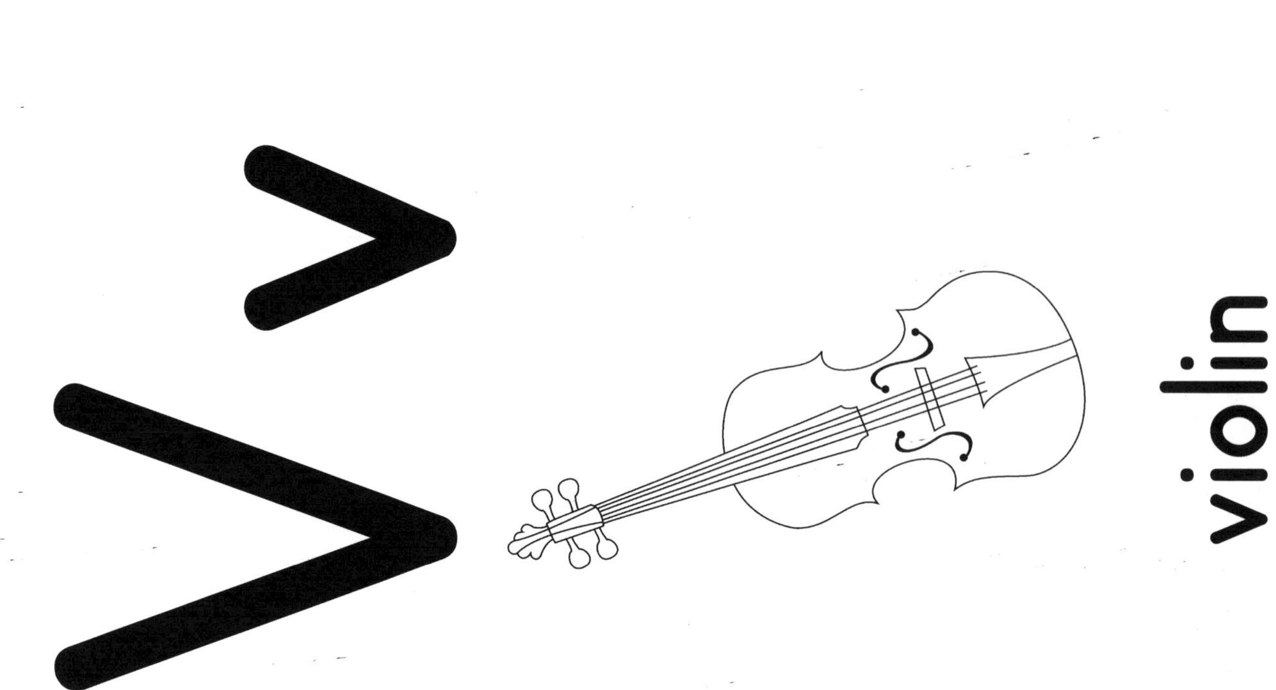

Uu

umbrella

Xx

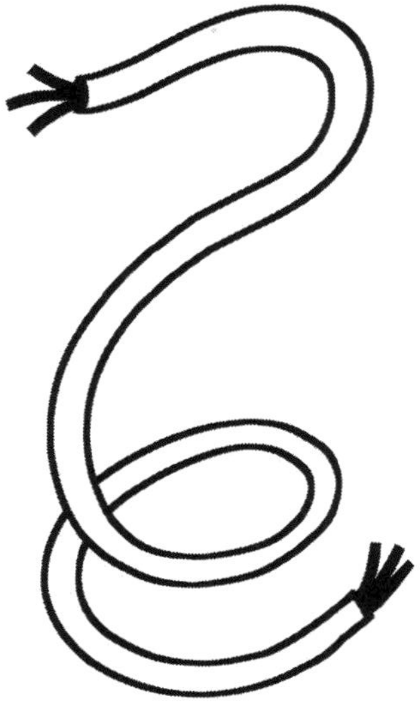

x ray

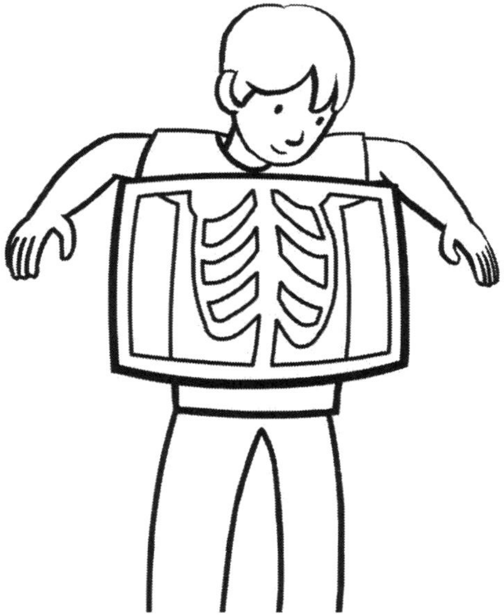

Ww

wire

Z z

zipper

Y y

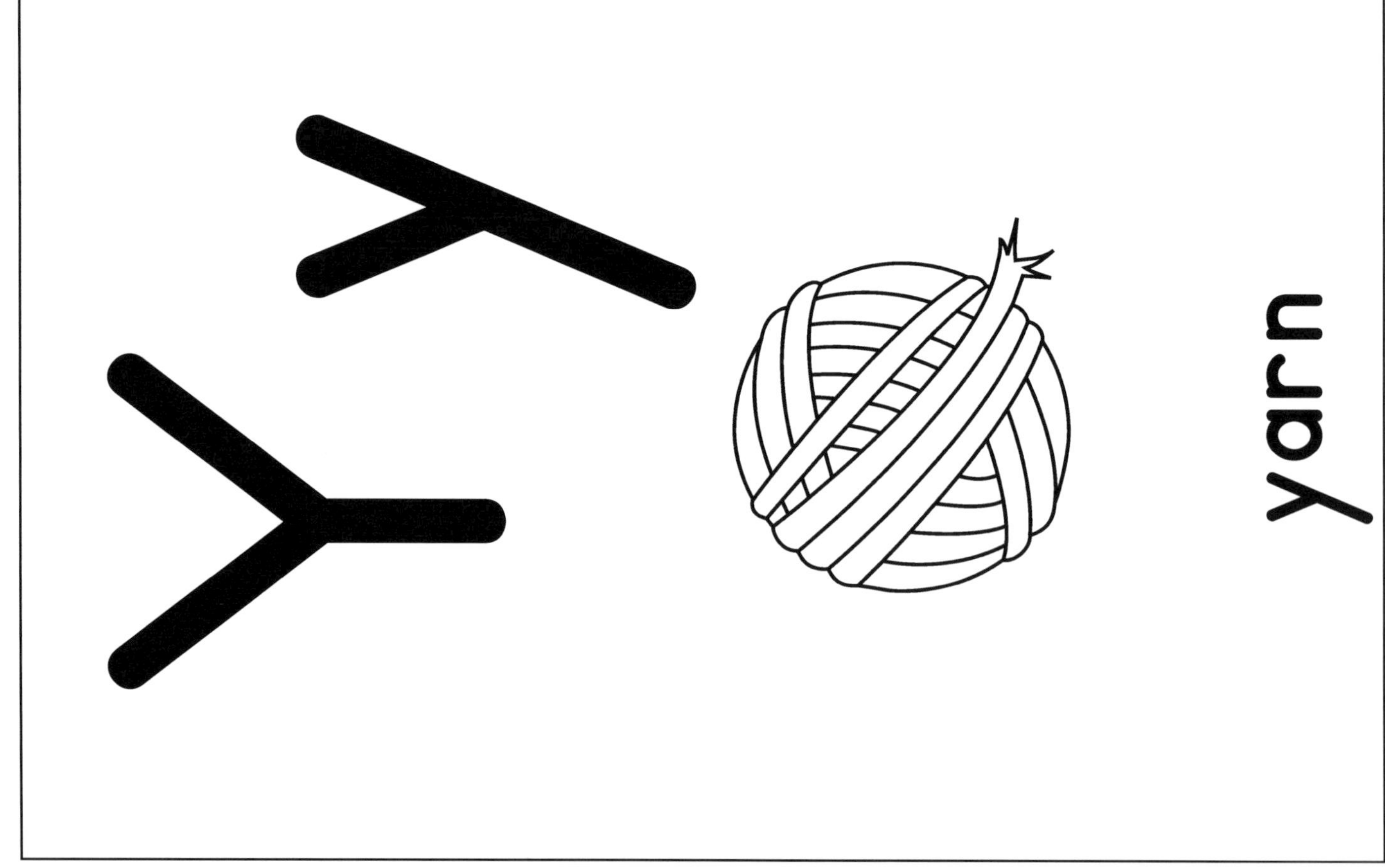

yarn

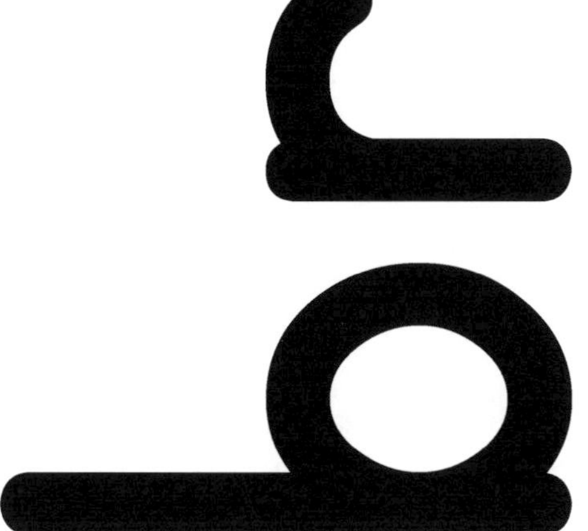

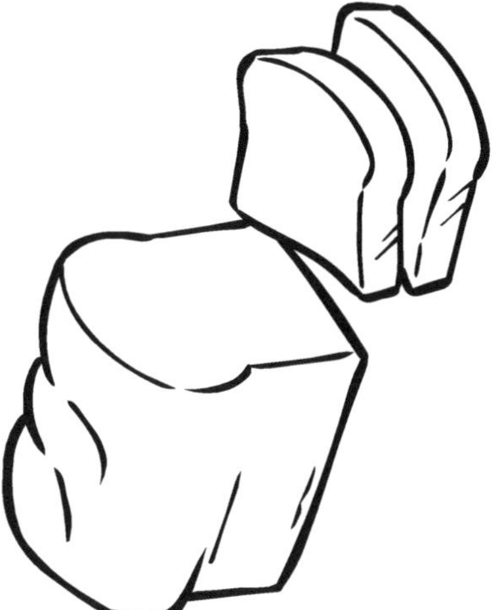

bread

bl

block

cl

clown

ch

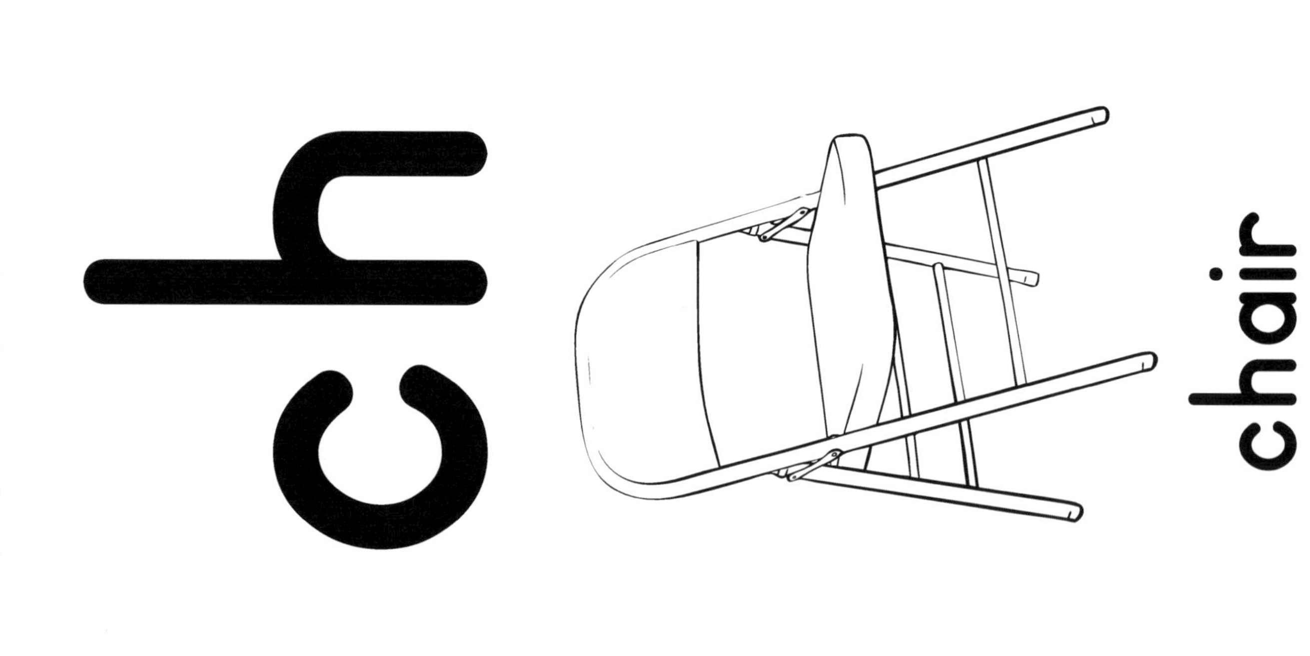

chair

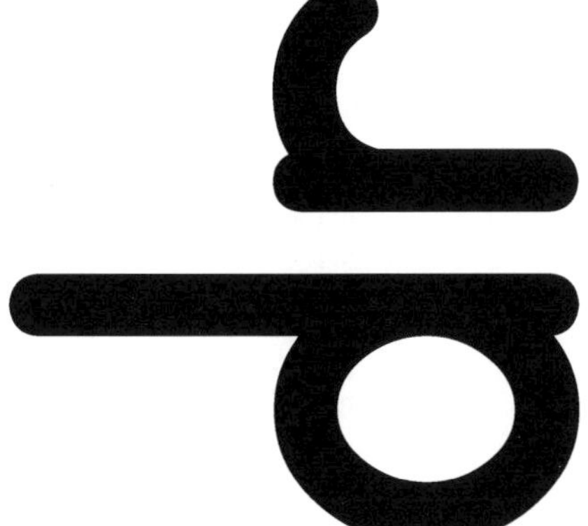

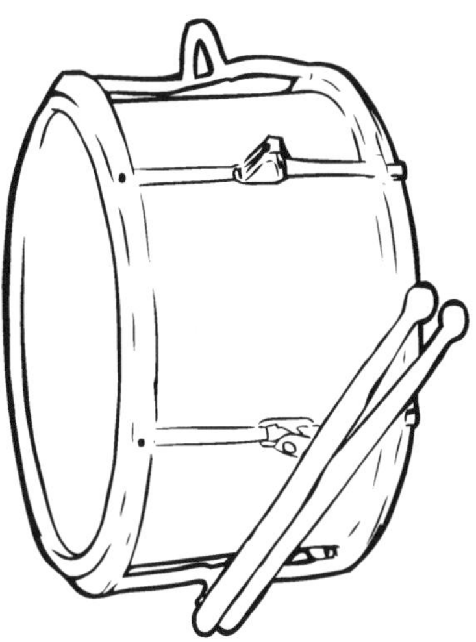

drum

cr

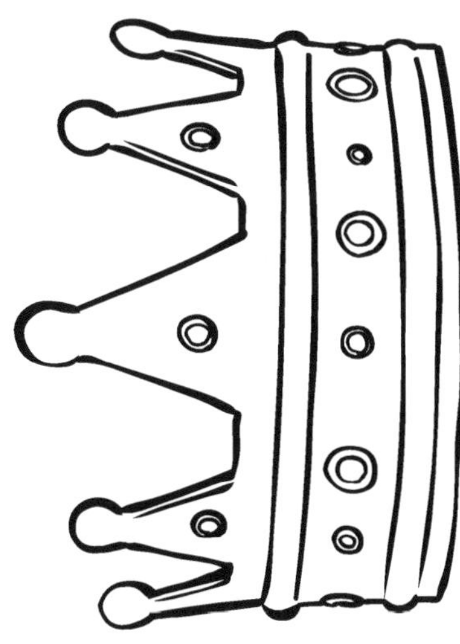

crown

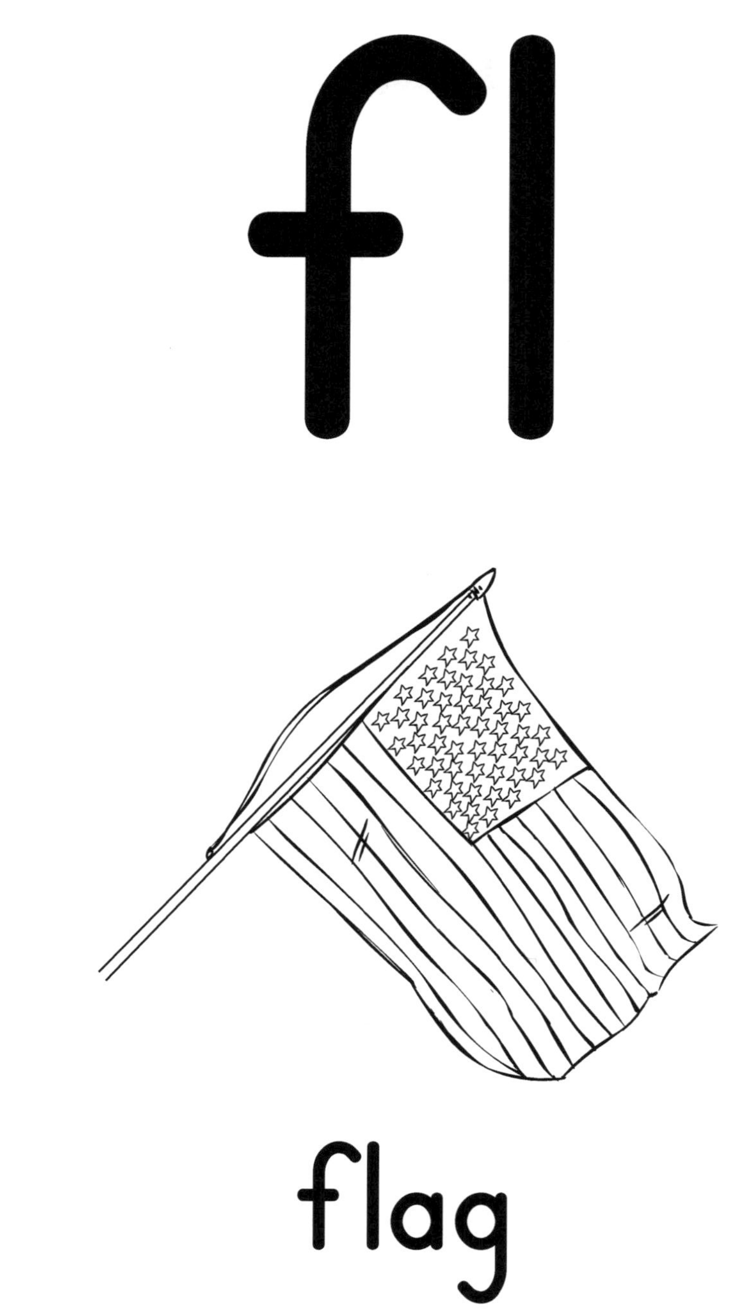
fl
flag

fr
fruit

kn

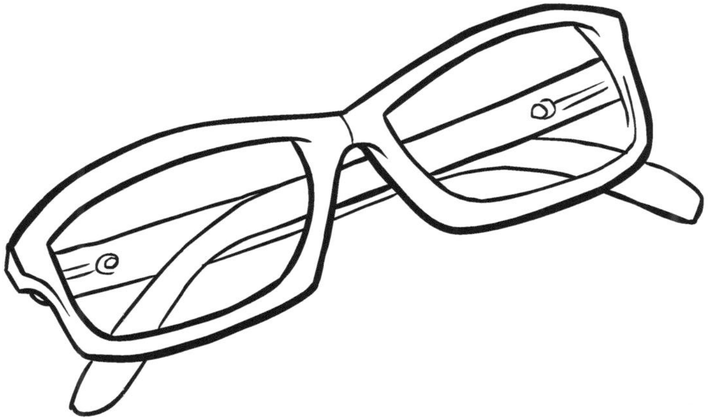

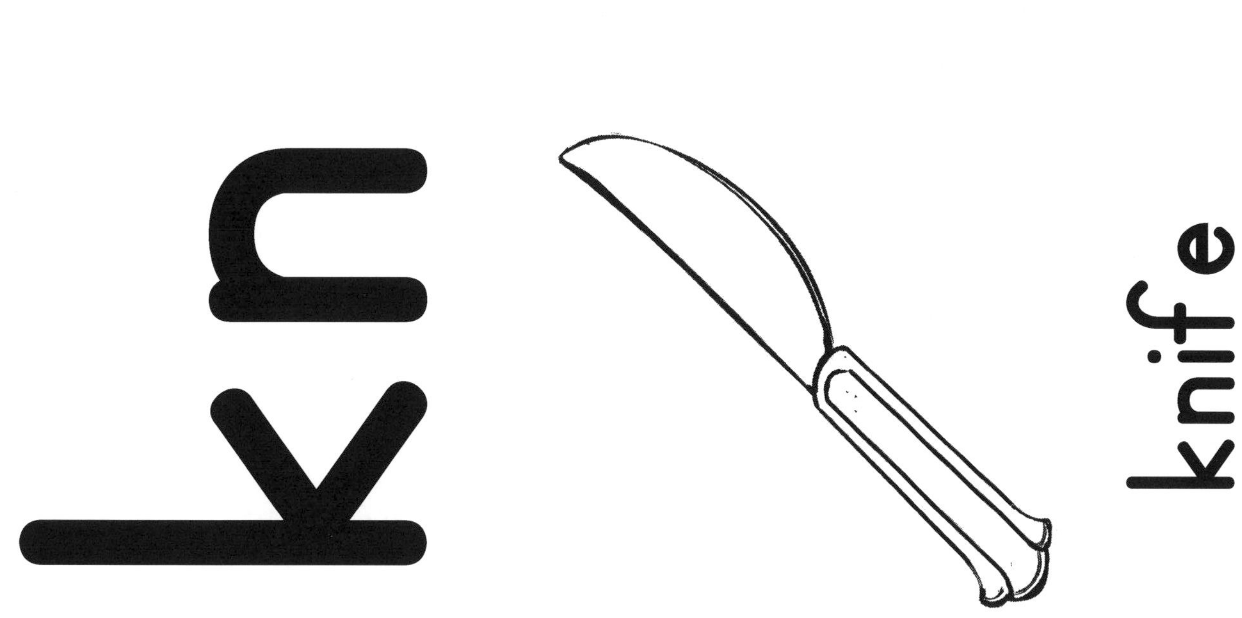

knife

gl

glasses

pl

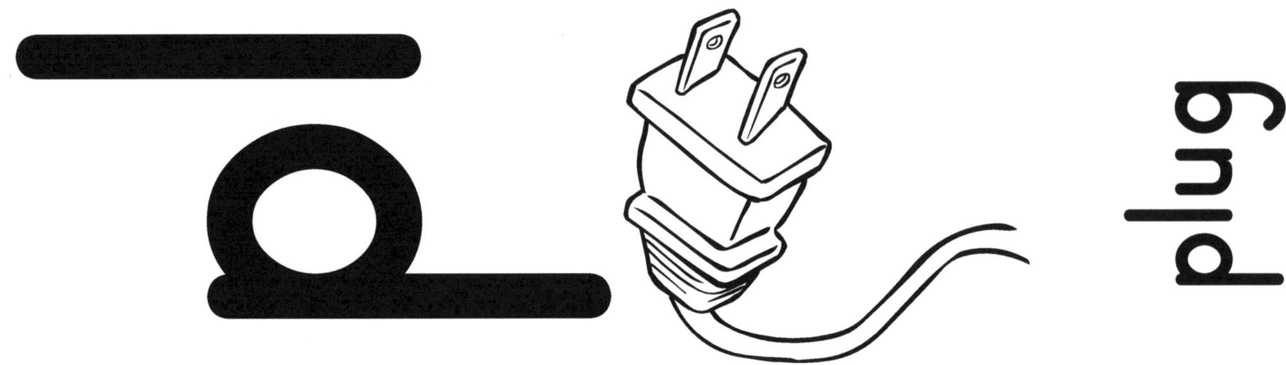

plug

ph

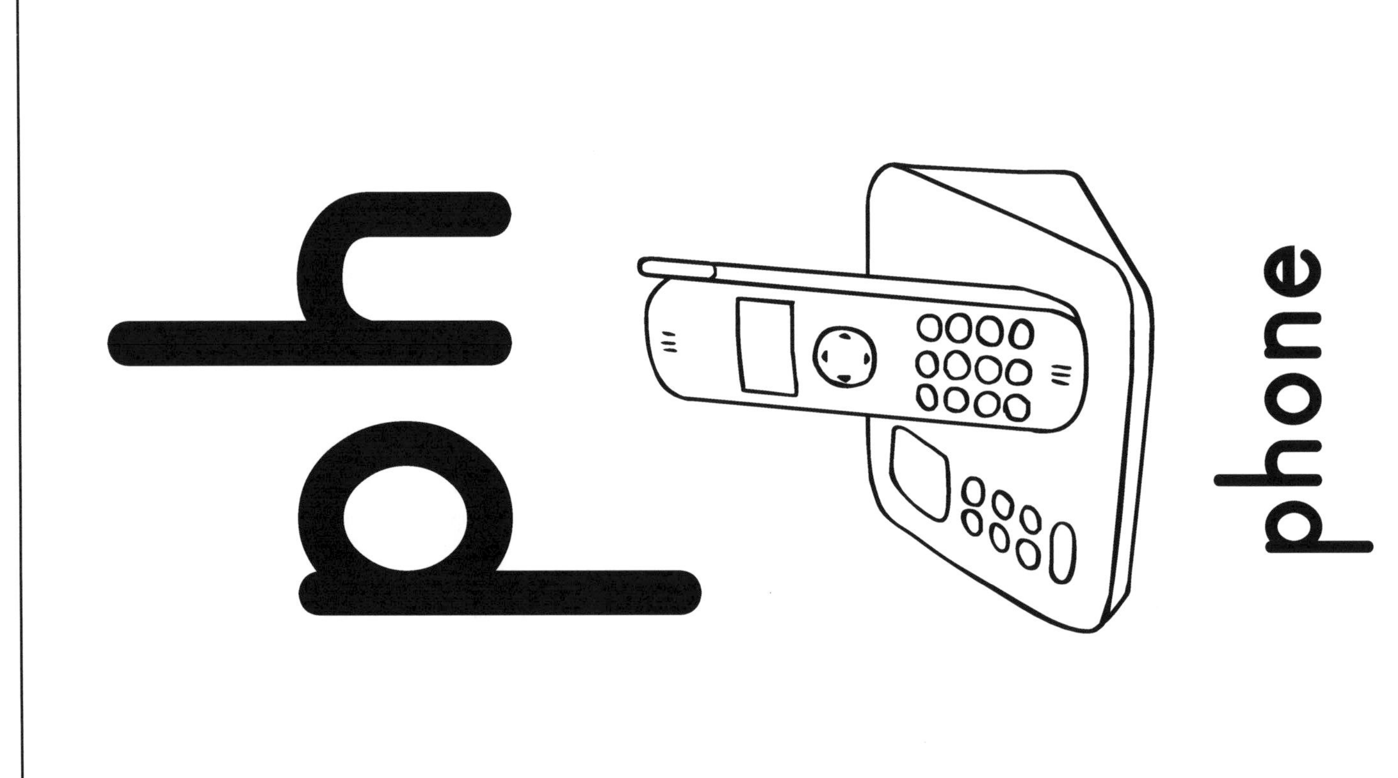

phone

sc

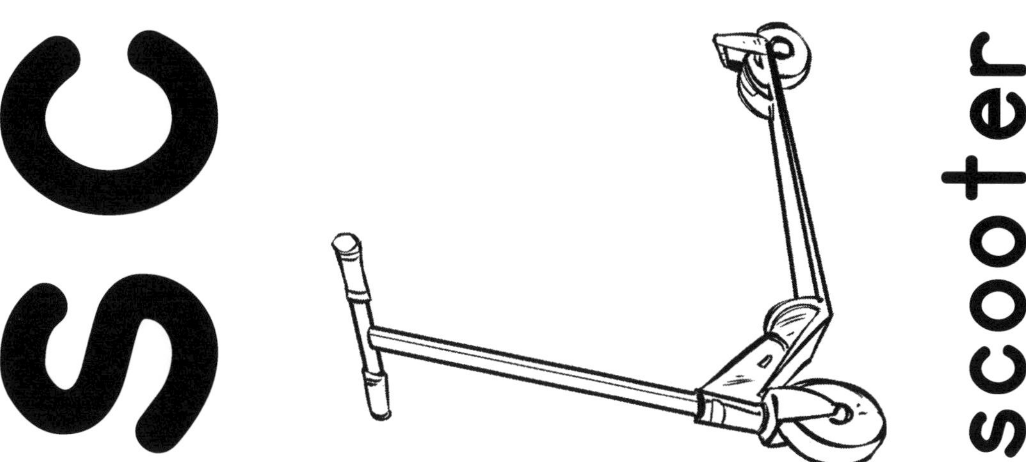

scooter

pr

present

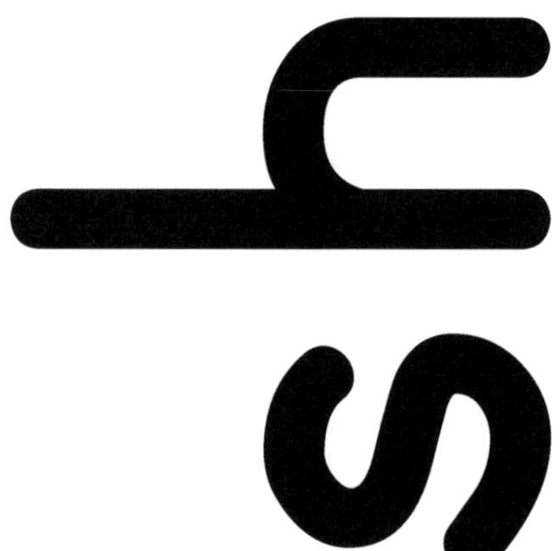

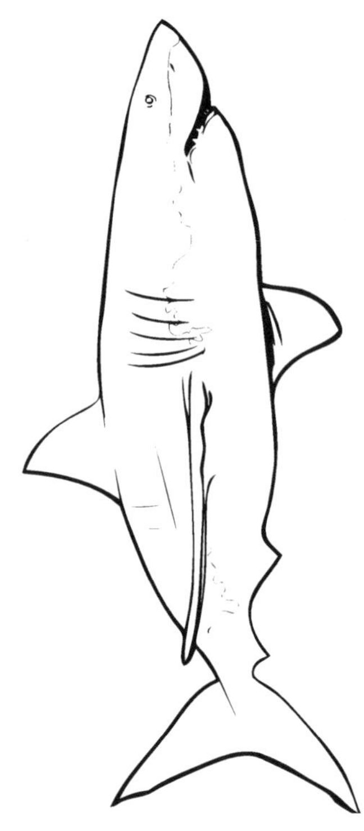

shark

scr

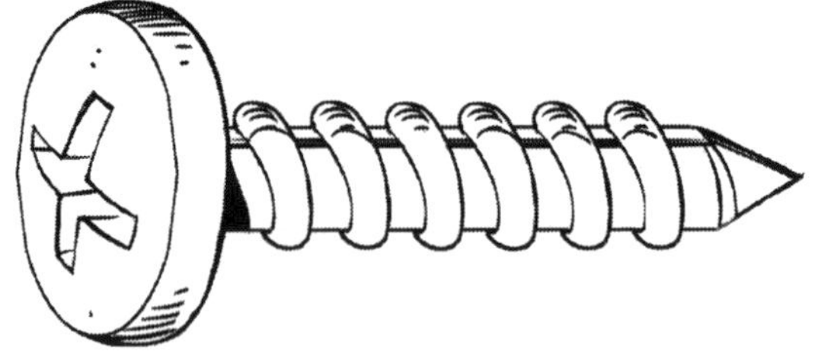

screw

slide

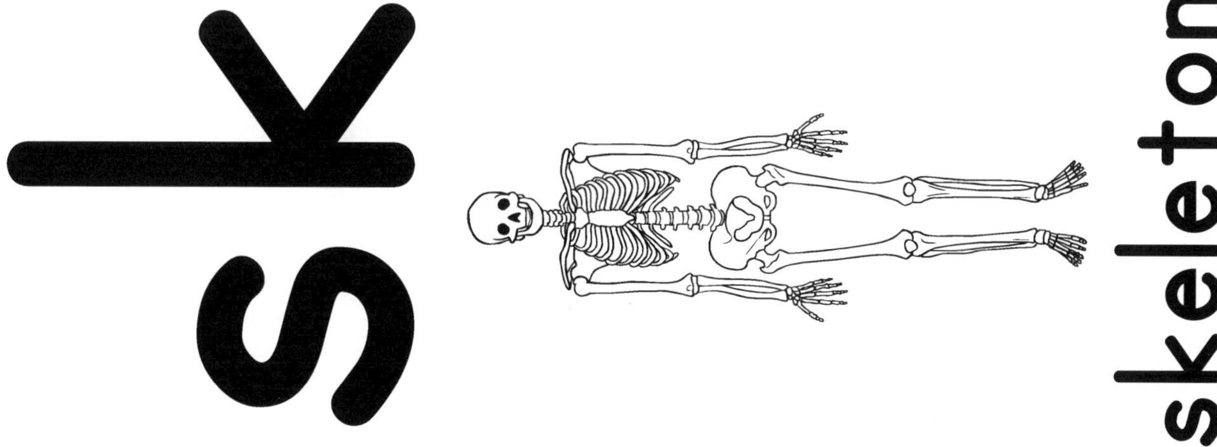

sn

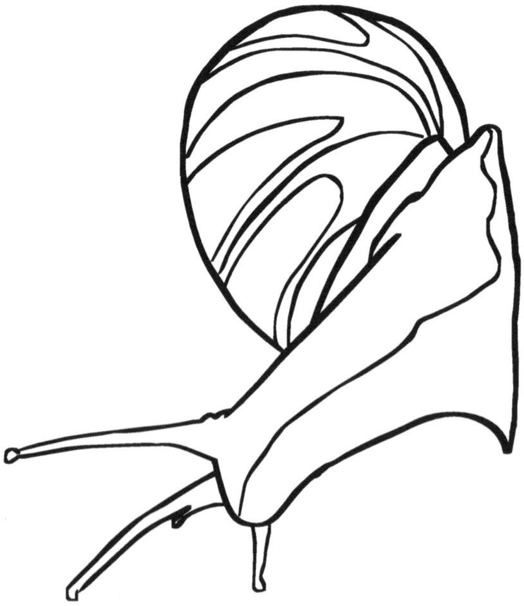

snail

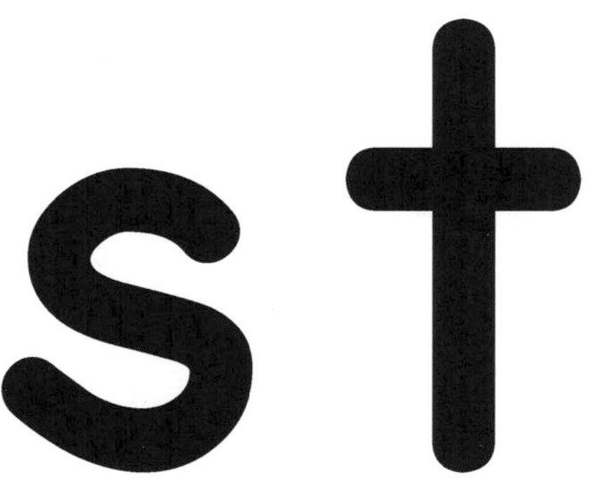

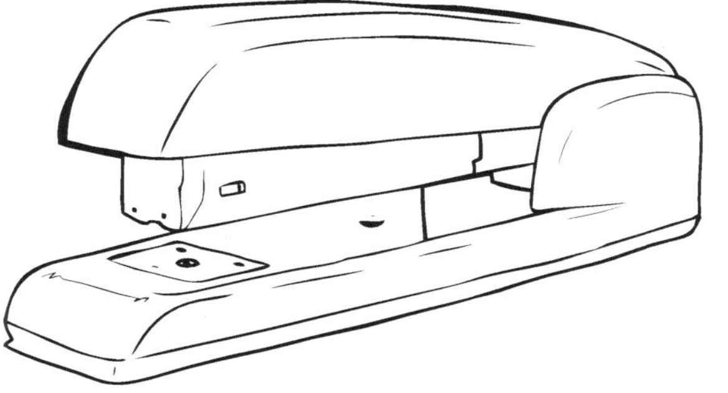

stapler

swan

tr

tree

th

thumb

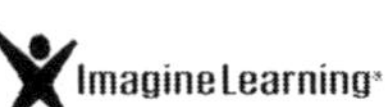

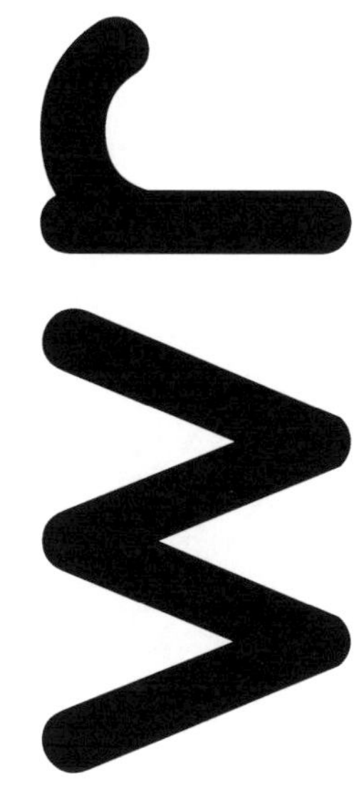

wrist

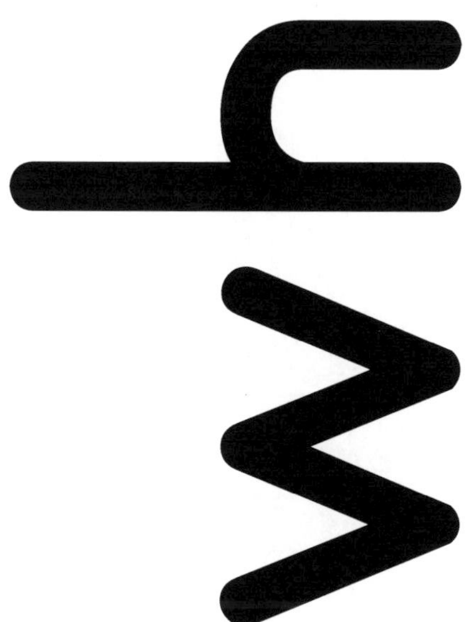

whale

LETTER SOUNDS

RETEACHING LESSONS

Developed with research-based methods for language learning and reading acquisition, these lessons use materials and strategies specifically designed for struggling learners. Each 10–20-minute lesson plan can be used for small group intervention or skill review.

Analyze data in the Imagine Learning Action Areas Tool to identify groups of students who struggle with particular letter-sound correspondences and use the Reteaching Lessons as a tool to support those students.

- Complete lesson plans that include guided instruction, independent practice, and assessment
- Sample lesson dialogue, examples, word banks, and extension ideas
- Print-ready picture cards for each letter sound

Progress Tracking Sheet

Date	Student Name	Lesson/Skill	Intervention Successful (Y/N)	Notes

Progress Tracking Sheet

Date	Student Name	Lesson/Skill	Intervention Successful (Y/N)	Notes

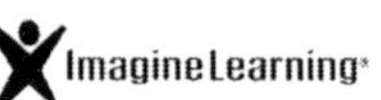

Notes

The Sound for A Is /ă/

LEARNING OBJECTIVE: Demonstrate letter-sound correspondence by producing the most common sound for the letter A.

LANGUAGE OBJECTIVE: Produce the sound for the letter A when shown a visual grapheme.

Lesson Overview

Introduce the letter sound, play a game to practice identifying the letter sound, and assess students' ability to associate a specific letter sound with a specific letter.

Materials	Preparation
• Letter and Picture Cards for *A* • Letter and Picture Cards for *M*	• Cut out all letter and picture cards.

Teach and Model

Show students the upper- and lowercase letter cards for *A*.

Say: ***This is* A. *The letter* A *stands for the sound /ă/. Make the sound with me: /ă/.*** Have students produce the sound with you.

Point to the letter card.

Say: ***Make the sound for this letter every time I put my finger on it.*** Have students produce the sound. Point to the card several times. Mix up the practice by asking individual students to say the sound.

Hold up a picture card.

Say: ***This word is* apple. *It begins with the letter sound /ă/. What is this?*** Have students repeat the name of the picture.

Say: ***What letter sound does* apple *begin with?*** Have students produce the */ă/* sound independently.

Repeat questions above with each picture card for */ă/*.

Picture cards for /ă/: ant, alligator, apple, astronaut, athlete, actor, alphabet, add

Connect Sound/Spelling: Thumbs Up, Thumbs Down for Beginning Sounds

Say: ***Show me thumbs up.*** Model what thumbs up looks like and help students show their thumbs up.

Explain: ***When you hear a word that begins with the letter sound /ă/, make a thumbs up and say the letter sound. If the word doesn't start with the letter sound /ă/, give me a thumbs down.*** Model thumbs down for students and help students show their thumbs down.

Say each word from the word bank below, alternating between words that begin with */ă/* and words that don't.

Words that begin with /ă/: ant, alligator, apple, astronaut, athlete, actor, alphabet, add

Words that don't begin with /ă/: lunch, horse, table, shoe

EXTENSION ACTIVITY: Ask students to think of other words that begin with */ă/*.

Connect Sound/Spelling: Letter Sound Sort

Shuffle picture cards for *A* and *M* together. Display letter cards for *A* on a table, allowing enough space for a column of picture cards below the letter cards. Display letter cards for *M* next to the letter cards for *A*.

Say: ***This is letter* M. M *stands for the sound /m/. Everyone say /m/.*** Have students produce the sound.

Show the stack of picture cards.

Explain: ***The pictures on these cards begin with the letter sound /ă/ or /m/. We are going to put them with their matching letter.***

Show the first picture card.

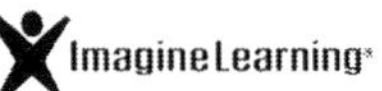

Demonstrate: **Ant. *This word begins with the letter sound /ă/: /ă/, /ă/,* ant. *Say /ă/, /ă/,* ant.** Have students repeat the sound and word.

Demonstrate: **Ant *goes with this card, /ă/.*** Place the picture card below the letter cards for *A*.

Have students draw the remaining picture cards from the stack and place them in a column under the matching letter card. As each card is added, direct students to say the letter sound twice and then name the picture: */ă/*, */ă/*, alphabet; */m/*, */m/*, mouse.

Picture cards for /m/: monkey, moth, moose, muffin, meat, milk, mountain, money

EXTENSION ACTIVITY: Randomly point to pictures in the two columns and instruct students to repeat the letter sound and name the picture.

Check Progress: Letter Flip

Observe each student during practice and use the following activity to check progress on the target skill. If student can correctly identify the letter sound twice, consider the intervention successful.

Point to the appropriate letter card as you say the sound.

Say: ***Repeat the letter sounds for these letters: /ă/, /m/.***

Put all the flash cards face down on the table and mix them up.

Say: ***Choose a card and tell me the letter sound.***

Have students choose a card and say the sound, mixing the cards between student turns. Give every student a turn, repeating until each student has had the opportunity to demonstrate knowledge on the target letter sound */ă/*.

Letter Sounds

The Sound for M Is /m/

Grade K

10 Min.

CCSS.RF.K.3a
TEKS 110.11.3.A

LEARNING OBJECTIVE: Demonstrate letter-sound correspondence by producing the most common sound for the letter *M*.

LANGUAGE OBJECTIVE: Produce the sound for the letter *M* when shown a visual grapheme.

Lesson Overview

Introduce the letter sound, play a game to practice identifying the letter sound, and assess students' ability to associate a specific letter sound with a specific letter.

Materials	Preparation
• Letter and Picture Cards for *M* • Letter and Picture Cards for *A*	• Cut out all letter and picture cards.

Teach and Model

Show students the upper- and lowercase letter cards for *M*.

Say: ***This is* M. *The letter* M *stands for the sound /m/. Make the sound with me: /m/.*** Have students produce the sound with you.

Point to the letter card.

Say: ***Make the sound for this letter every time I put my finger on it.*** Have students produce the sound. Point to the card several times. Mix up the practice by asking individual students to say the sound.

Hold up a picture card.

Say: ***This word is* monkey. *It begins with the letter sound /m/. What is this?*** Have students repeat the name of the picture.

Say: ***What letter sound does* monkey *begin with?*** Have students produce the */m/* sound independently.

Repeat questions above with each picture card for */m/*.

Picture cards for /m/: monkey, moth, moose, muffin, meat, milk, mountain, money

Connect Sound/Spelling: Letter Sound Lunch

Show letter card.

Explain: ***It's time for Letter Sound Lunch! For this lunch we can only order food that begins with the letter sound /m/.***

Model: ***I can order a* mango *because it begins with /m/.***

Have students think of things they can order that begin with the letter sound */m/*. Provide prompts (e.g., What do you pour on cereal?) to help them think of words from the word bank.

Word bank: mango, milk muffin, macadamia nut, mandarin orange, marshmallow, meat, milk, mint, mushroom, mustard, macaroni, melon, meat loaf, mayo(nnaise)

Connect Sound/Spelling: Animal Safari

Show the letter cards.

Explain: ***We are going on an animal safari. When you hear an animal name that starts with the letter sound /m/, stand up. Say the letter sound and the name of the animal. If the animal name doesn't start with /m/, sit down.***

Ask: ***How about* mouse?** Students should stand up.

Say: ***Yes!* Mouse *has /m/ at the beginning, so you stand up. Let's try another one:* seagull.** Students should sit down.

Say: ***Good!* Seagull *doesn't begin with the /m/ sound, so you sit down.***

Alternate between animal names that begin with */m/* and those that don't.

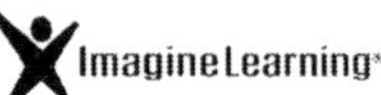

Words that begin with /m/: macaw, moose, mule, mosquito, moth, mole, mongoose, monkey

Words that don't begin with /m/: duck, buffalo, goat, peacock

EXTENSION ACTIVITY: Ask students to think of other words that begin with */m/*.

Check Progress: Letter Stack

Observe each student during practice and use the following activity to check progress on the target skill. If student can correctly identify the letter sound twice, consider the intervention successful.

Point to the appropriate letter card as you say the sound.

Say: ***Repeat the letter sounds for these letters:* /m/, /m/, /ă/, /ă/.**

Shuffle letter cards for *M* and *A* together in a stack.

Say: ***Choose a card and tell me the letter sound.***

Have students draw a card from the stack, say the sound, and put the card on the bottom of the stack. Repeat until every student has had several opportunities to demonstrate knowledge of the target letter sound */m/*.

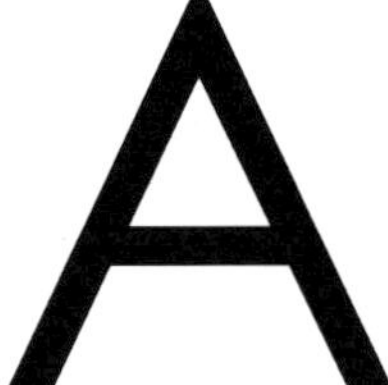

a

1+2=3

m

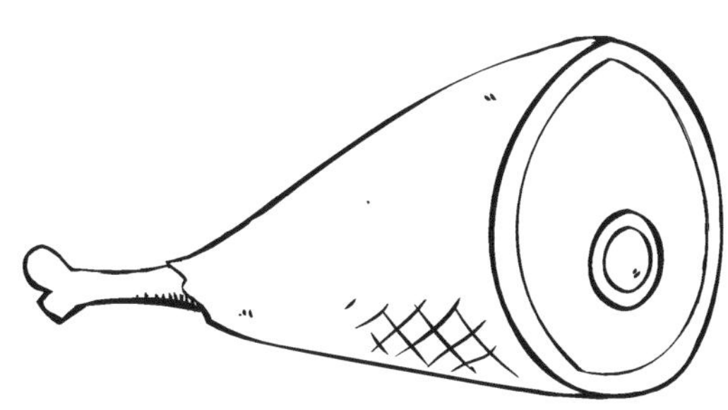

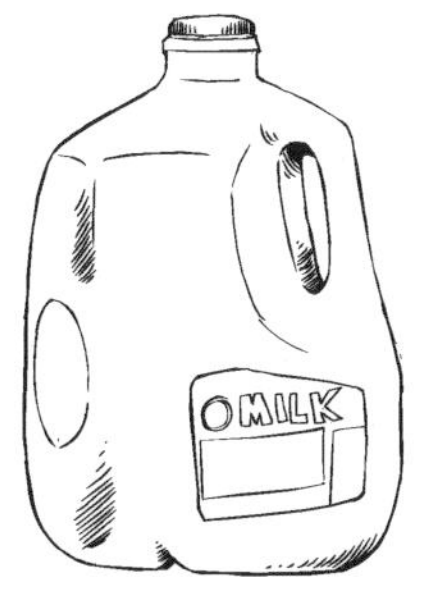

The Sound for D Is /d/

Grade K

10 Min.

CCSS.RF.K.3a
TEKS 110.11.3.A

LEARNING OBJECTIVE: Demonstrate letter-sound correspondence by producing the most common sound for the letter *D*.

LANGUAGE OBJECTIVE: Produce the sound for the letter *D* when shown a visual grapheme.

Lesson Overview

Introduce the letter sound, play a game to practice identifying the letter sound, and assess students' ability to associate a specific letter sound with a specific letter.

Materials	Preparation
• Letter and Picture Cards for *D* • Letter and Picture Cards for *S* • Paper bag	• Cut out all letter and picture cards.

Teach and Model

Show students the upper- and lowercase letter cards for *D*.

Say: ***This is* D. *The letter* D *stands for the sound /d/. Make the sound with me: /d/.*** Have students produce the sound with you.

Point to the letter card.

Say: ***Make the sound for this letter every time I put my finger on it.*** Have students produce the sound. Point to the card several times. Mix up the practice by asking individual students to say the sound.

Hold up a picture card.

Say: ***This word is* door. *It begins with the letter sound /d/. What is this?*** Have students repeat the name of the picture.

Say: ***What letter sound does* door *begin with?*** Have students produce the */d/* sound independently.

Repeat questions above with each picture card for */d/*.

Picture cards for /d/: door, doll, diamond, donut, dinosaur, dolphin, duck, dog

Connect Sound/Spelling: Letter Sound Bag

Put all letter and picture cards for *D* in the paper bag.

Explain: ***The pictures on these cards start with /d/. If you pull a letter card from the bag, tell me the letter sound. Then tell me a word that starts with that letter sound.***

Model: ***If I pull out* duck, *I say /d/, /d/, duck.***

Explain: ***If you pull a picture card, tell me the letter sound it starts with and what the picture is.***

Model: ***If I pull out a picture of a doll, I say /d/, /d/,* doll.**

Have students take turns drawing cards from the paper bag.

Word bank: dig, doctor, draw, drop, dust, dish, desk, dent

Connect Sound/Spelling: Animal Safari

Show the letter cards.

Explain: ***We are going on an animal safari. When you hear an animal name that starts with the letter sound /d/, stand up. Say the letter sound and the name of the animal. If the animal name doesn't start with /d/, sit down.***

Ask: ***How about dog?*** Students should stand up.

Say: ***Yes!* Dog *has /d/ at the beginning, so you stand up. Let's try another one:* starfish.** Students should sit down.

Say: ***Good!* Starfish *doesn't begin with the /d/ sound, so you sit down.***

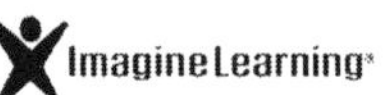

Alternate between animal names that begin with */d/* and those that don't.

Words that begin with /d/: deer, duck, dinosaur, dog, dolphin, donkey, dove, dragonfly

Words that don't begin with /d/: lamb, wolf, hen, sloth

EXTENSION ACTIVITY: Ask students to think of other words that begin with */d/*.

Check Progress: Letter Stack

Observe each student during practice and use the following activity to check progress on the target skill. If student can correctly identify the letter sound twice, consider the intervention successful.

Point to the appropriate letter card as you say the sound.

Say: ***Repeat the letter sounds for these letters: /d/, /d/, /s/, /s/.***

Shuffle letter cards for *D* and *S* together in a stack.

Say: ***Choose a card and tell me the letter sound.***

Have students draw a card from the stack, say the sound, and put the card on the bottom of the stack. Repeat until every student has had several opportunities to demonstrate knowledge of the target letter sound */d/*.

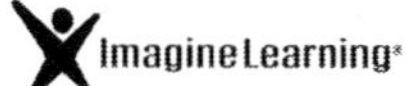

The Sound for S Is /s/

Grade K

10 Min.

CCSS.RF.K.3a
TEKS 110.11.3.A

LEARNING OBJECTIVE: Demonstrate letter-sound correspondence by producing the most common sound for the letter *S*.

LANGUAGE OBJECTIVE: Produce the sound for the letter *S* when shown a visual grapheme.

Lesson Overview

Introduce the letter sound, play a game to practice identifying the letter sound, and assess students' ability to associate a specific letter sound with a specific letter.

Materials	Preparation
• Letter and Picture Cards for *S* • Letter and Picture Cards for *D*	• Cut out all letter and picture cards.

Teach and Model

Show students the upper- and lowercase letter cards for *S*.

Say: ***This is* S. *The letter* S *stands for the sound /s/. Make the sound with me: /s/.*** Have students produce the sound with you.

Point to the letter card.

Say: ***Make the sound for this letter every time I put my finger on it.*** Have students produce the sound. Point to the card several times. Mix up the practice by asking individual students to say the sound.

Hold up a picture card.

Say: ***This word is* sun. *It begins with the letter sound /s/. What is this?*** Have students repeat the name of the picture.

Say: ***What letter sound does* sun *begin with?*** Have students produce the /s/ sound independently.

Repeat questions above with each picture card for /s/.

Picture cards for /s/: sun, snail, seal, spider, squirrel, sandwich, six, square

Connect Sound/Spelling: Letter Sound Lunch

Show letter card.

Explain: ***It's time for Letter Sound Lunch! For this lunch we can only order food that begins with the letter sound /s/.***

Model: ***I can order a* sandwich *because it begins with /s/.***

Have students think of things they can order that begin with the letter sound /s/. Provide prompts (e.g., What do you pour on pancakes?) to help them think of words from the word bank.

Word bank: sandwich, syrup, salad, salt, sauce, sausage, sugar, sushi, snack, soda, soup, spaghetti, spinach, squash, steak, stew, strawberry

Connect Sound/Spelling: Animal Safari

Show the letter cards.

Explain: ***We are going on an animal safari. When you hear an animal name that starts with the letter sound /s/, stand up. Say the letter sound and the name of the animal. If the animal name doesn't start with /s/, sit down.***

Ask: ***How about* seal?** Students should stand up.

Say: ***Yes!* Seal *has /s/ at the beginning, so you stand up. Let's try another one:* bear.** Students should sit down.

Say: ***Good!* Bear *doesn't begin with the /s/ sound, so you sit down.***

Alternate between animal names that begin with /s/ and those that don't.

Words that begin with /s/: salmon, skunk, scorpion, seagull, sea horse, spider, snake, sloth, slug, snail, stingray, swan, squirrel, starfish

Words that don't begin with /s/: moose, bear, camel, hawk

EXTENSION ACTIVITY: Ask students to think of other words that begin with /s/.

Check Progress: Letter Flip

Observe each student during practice and use the following activity to check progress on the target skill. If student can correctly identify the letter sound twice, consider the intervention successful.

Point to the appropriate letter card as you say the sound.

Say: ***Repeat the letter sounds for these letters: /s/, /d/.***

Put all the flash cards face down on the table and mix them up.

Say: ***Choose a card and tell me the letter sound.***

Have students choose a card and say the sound, mixing the cards between student turns. Give every student a turn, repeating until each student has had the opportunity to demonstrate knowledge on the target letter sound /s/.

D

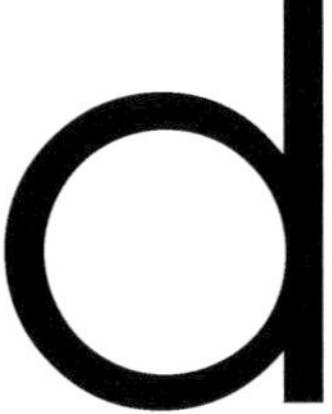

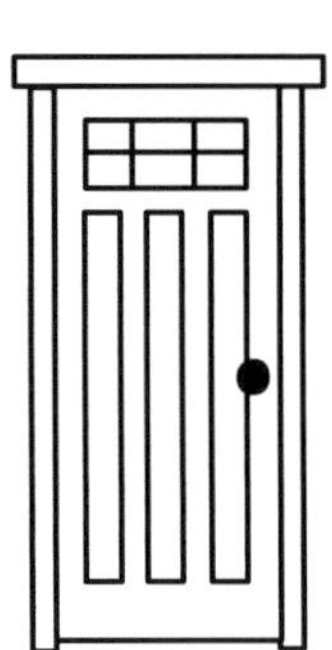

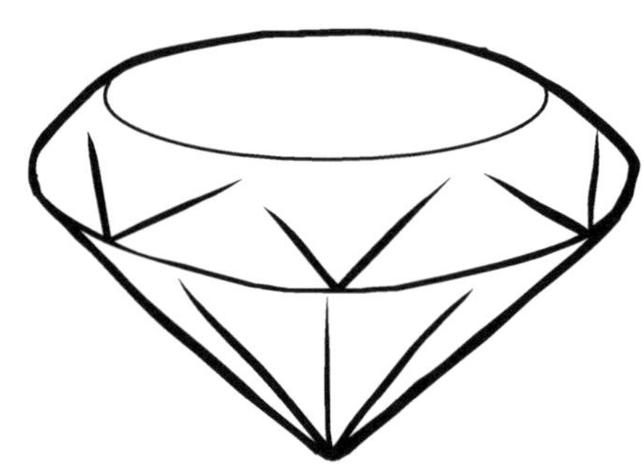

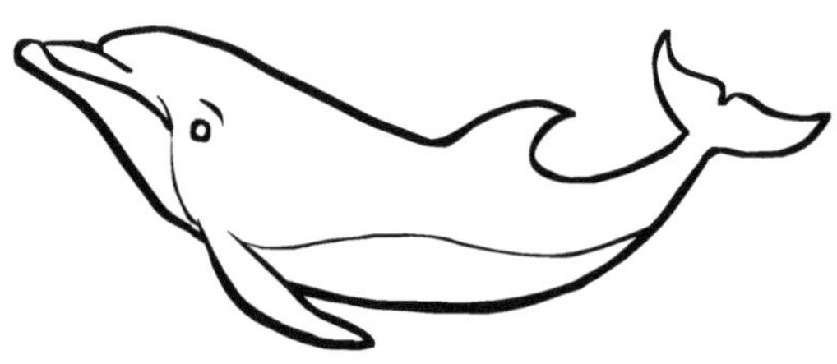

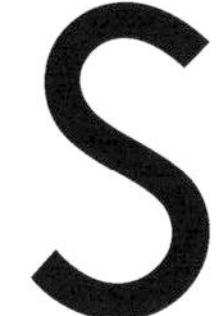

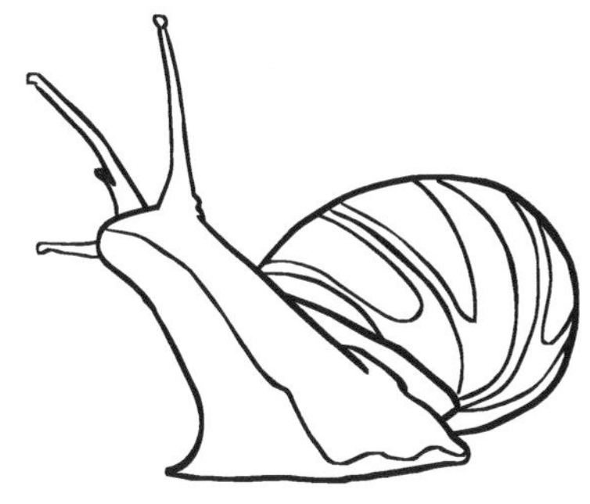

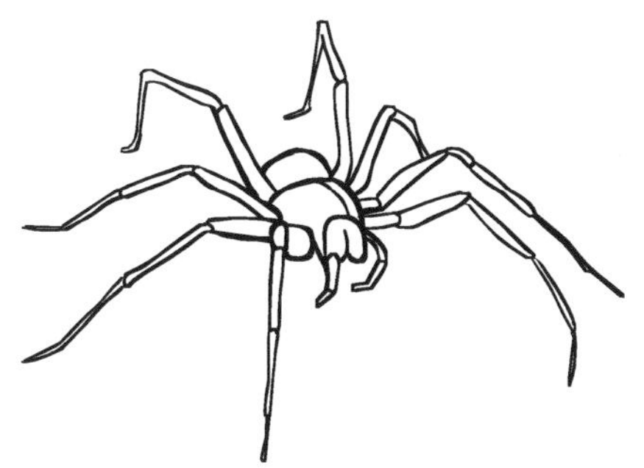

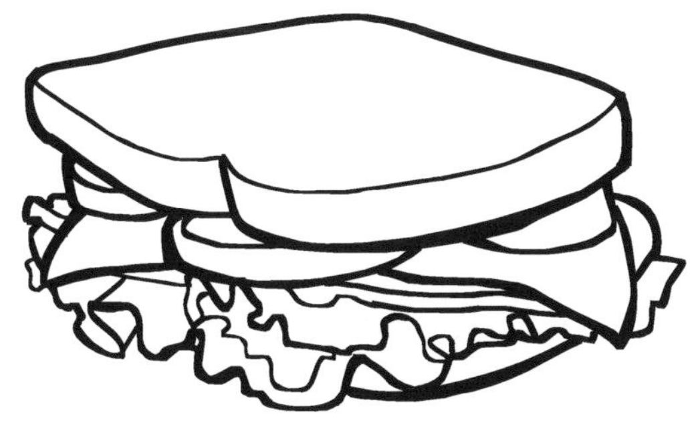

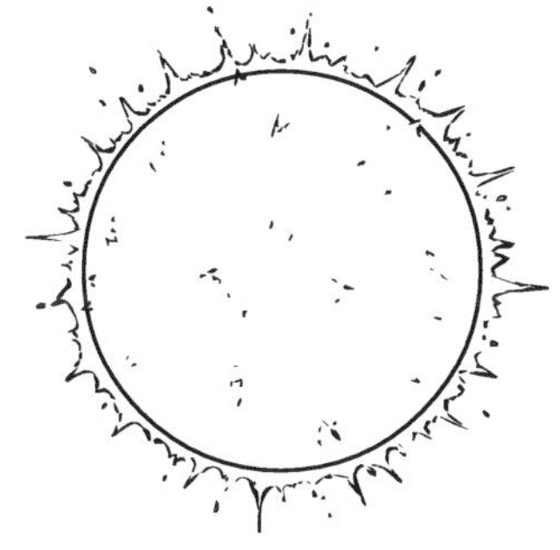

Letter Sounds

The Sound for T Is /t/

Grade K

10 Min.

CCSS.RF.K.3a
TEKS 110.11.3.A

LEARNING OBJECTIVE: Demonstrate letter-sound correspondence by producing the most common sound for the letter *T*.

LANGUAGE OBJECTIVE: Produce the sound for the letter *T* when shown a visual grapheme.

Lesson Overview

Introduce the letter sound, play a game to practice identifying the letter sound, and assess students' ability to associate a specific letter sound with a specific letter.

Materials	Preparation
• Letter and Picture Cards for *T* • Letter and Picture Cards for *P*	• Cut out all letter and picture cards.

Teach and Model

Show students the upper- and lowercase letter cards for *T*.

Say: ***This is* T. *The letter* T *stands for the sound /t/. Make the sound with me: /t/.*** Have students produce the sound with you.

Point to the letter card.

Say: ***Make the sound for this letter every time I put my finger on it.*** Have students produce the sound. Point to the card several times. Mix up the practice by asking individual students to say the sound.

Hold up a picture card.

Say: ***This word is* table. *It begins with the letter sound /t/. What is this?*** Have students repeat the name of the picture.

Say: ***What letter sound does* table *begin with?*** Have students produce the /t/ sound independently.

Repeat questions above with each picture card for /t/.

Picture cards for /t/: tiger, table, turtle, tomato, teacher, ten, triangle, train

Connect Sound/Spelling: Letter Sound Lunch

Show letter card.

Explain: ***It's time for Letter Sound Lunch! For this lunch we can only order food that begins with the letter sound /t/.***

Model: ***I can order a* taco *because it begins with /t/.***

Have students think of things they can order that begin with the letter sound /t/. Provide prompts (e.g., What do some people eat for breakfast that starts with /t/?) to help them think of words from the word bank.

Word bank: taco, toast, tangerine, tortilla, turkey, toffee, tomato, tuna, turnip

Connect Sound/Spelling: Animal Safari

Show the letter cards.

Explain: ***We are going on an animal safari. When you hear an animal name that starts with the letter sound /t/, stand up. Say the letter sound and the name of the animal. If the animal name doesn't start with /t/, sit down.***

Ask: ***How about* turtle?** Students should stand up.

Say: ***Yes!* Turtle *has /t/ at the beginning, so you stand up. Let's try another one:* shark.** Students should sit down.

Say: ***Good!* Shark *doesn't begin with the /t/ sound, so you sit down.***

Alternate between animal names that begin with /t/ and those that don't.

Words that begin with /t/: turtle, tarantula, tiger, toad, toucan, tuna, turkey, tadpole, tortoise

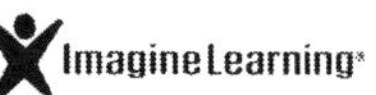

Words that don't begin with /t/: camel, raccoon, goat, lizard

EXTENSION ACTIVITY: Ask students to think of other words that begin with */t/*.

Check Progress: Letter Stack

Observe each student during practice and use the following activity to check progress on the target skill. If student can correctly identify the letter sound twice, consider the intervention successful.

Point to the appropriate letter card as you say the sound.

Say: ***Repeat the letter sounds for these letters: /t/, /t/, /p/, /p/.***

Shuffle letter cards for *T* and *P* together in a stack.

Say: ***Choose a card and tell me the letter sound.***

Have students draw a card from the stack, say the sound, and put the card on the bottom of the stack. Repeat until every student has had several opportunities to demonstrate knowledge of the target letter sound */t/*.

Reteaching Lessons

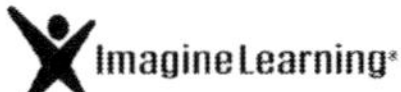

Letter Sounds

The Sound for P Is /p/

Grade K

10 Min.

CCSS.RF.K.3a
TEKS 110.11.3.A

LEARNING OBJECTIVE: Demonstrate letter-sound correspondence by producing the most common sound for the letter *P*.

LANGUAGE OBJECTIVE: Produce the sound for the letter *P* when shown a visual grapheme.

Lesson Overview

Introduce the letter sound, play a game to practice identifying the letter sound, and assess students' ability to associate a specific letter sound with a specific letter.

Materials	Preparation
• Letter and Picture Cards for *P* • Letter and Picture Cards for *T*	• Cut out all letter and picture cards.

Teach and Model

Show students the upper- and lowercase letter cards for *P*.

Say: ***This is* P. *The letter* P *stands for the sound /p/. Make the sound with me: /p/.*** Have students produce the sound with you.

Point to the letter card.

Say: ***Make the sound for this letter every time I put my finger on it.*** Have students produce the sound. Point to the card several times. Mix up the practice by asking individual students to say the sound.

Hold up a picture card.

Say: ***This word is* pillow. *It begins with the letter sound /p/. What is this?*** Have students repeat the name of the picture.

Say: ***What letter sound does* pillow *begin with?*** Have students produce the /p/ sound independently.

Repeat questions above with each picture card for /p/.

Picture cards for /p/: penguin, popcorn, pie, police, puzzle, piano, pan, pillow

Connect Sound/Spelling: Letter Sound Lunch

Show letter card.

Explain: ***It's time for Letter Sound Lunch! For this lunch we can only order food that begins with the letter sound /p/.***

Model: ***I can order a* pasta *because it begins with /p/.***

Have students think of things they can order that begin with the letter sound /p/. Provide prompts (e.g., Can you think of a fruit that starts with /p/?) to help them think of words from the word bank.

Word bank: popcorn, pineapple, peach, pear, plum, pancake, pickle, pie, pineapple, pasta, peas, peanut butter, pomegranate, potato, pretzel, pudding, pumpkin, pizza

Connect Sound/Spelling: Animal Safari

Show the letter cards.

Explain: ***We are going on an animal safari. When you hear an animal name that starts with the letter sound /p/, stand up. Say the letter sound and the name of the animal. If the animal name doesn't start with /p/, sit down.***

Ask: ***How about* panda?** Students should stand up.

Say: ***Yes! Panda has /p/ at the beginning, so you stand up. Let's try another one:* bear.** Students should sit down.

Say: ***Good!* Bear *doesn't begin with the /p/ sound, so you sit down.***

Alternate between animal names that begin with /p/ and those that don't.

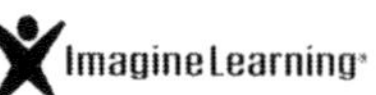

Words that begin with /p/: panda, puppy, parrot, peacock, pelican, penguin, pigeon, platypus, polar bear, panther, pony, poodle, porcupine, python

Words that don't begin with /p/: skunk, horse, wasp, turkey

EXTENSION ACTIVITY: Ask students to think of other words that begin with */p/*.

Check Progress: Letter Flip

Observe each student during practice and use the following activity to check progress on the target skill. If student can correctly identify the letter sound twice, consider the intervention successful.

Point to the appropriate letter card as you say the sound.

Say: ***Repeat the letter sounds for these letters: /p/, /t/.***

Put all the flash cards face down on the table and mix them up.

Say: ***Choose a card and tell me the letter sound.***

Have students choose a card and say the sound, mixing the cards between student turns. Give every student a turn, repeating until each student has had the opportunity to demonstrate knowledge on the target letter sound */p/*.

Reteaching Lessons ✓

T

t

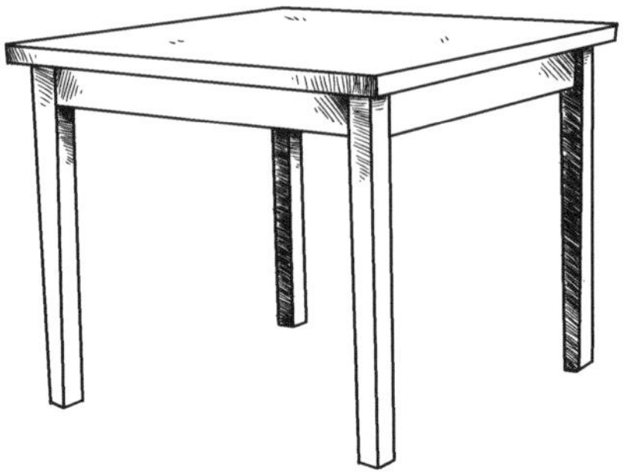

10

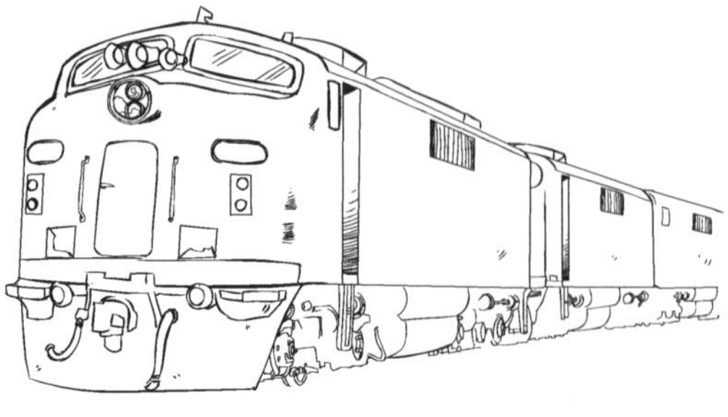

Letter and Picture Cards for T

P

p

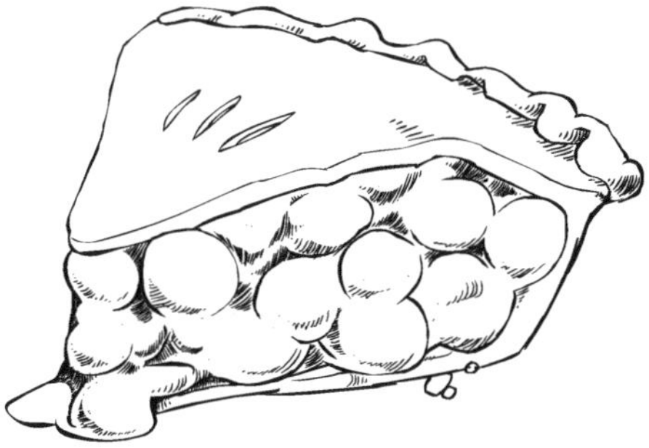

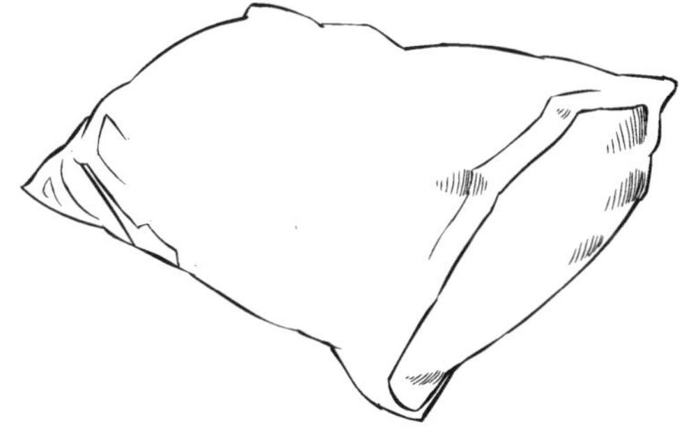

The Sound for B Is /b/

Grade K

10 Min.

CCSS.RF.K.3a
TEKS 110.11.3.A

LEARNING OBJECTIVE: Demonstrate letter-sound correspondence by producing the most common sound for the letter *B*.

LANGUAGE OBJECTIVE: Produce the sound for the letter *B* when shown a visual grapheme.

Lesson Overview

Introduce the letter sound, play a game to practice identifying the letter sound, and assess students' ability to associate a specific letter sound with a specific letter.

Materials	Preparation
• Letter and Picture Cards for *B* • Letter and Picture Cards for *O*	• Cut out all letter and picture cards.

Teach and Model

Show students the upper- and lowercase letter cards for *B*.

Say: ***This is* B. *The letter* B *stands for the sound /b/. Make the sound with me: /b/.*** Have students produce the sound with you.

Point to the letter card.

Say: ***Make the sound for this letter every time I put my finger on it.*** Have students produce the sound. Point to the card several times. Mix up the practice by asking individual students to say the sound.

Hold up a picture card.

Say: ***This word is* bird. *It begins with the letter sound /b/. What is this?*** Have students repeat the name of the picture.

Say: ***What letter sound does* bird *begin with?*** Have students produce the /*b*/ sound independently.

Repeat questions above with each picture card for /*b*/.

Picture cards for /b/: butterfly, bird, bear, bee, bread, banana, baby, bed

Connect Sound/Spelling: Letter Sound Lunch

Show letter card.

Explain: ***It's time for Letter Sound Lunch! For this lunch we can only order food that begins with the letter sound /b/.***

Model: ***I can order a* banana *because it begins with /b/.***

Have students think of things they can order that begin with the letter sound /*b*/. Provide prompts (e.g., What vegetable begins with /*b*/?) to help them think of words from the word bank.

Word bank: banana, broccoli, bacon, butter, beans, beef, beet, biscuit, blackberry, blueberry, bread, breakfast, broth, bun, bagel

Connect Sound/Spelling: Animal Safari

Show the letter cards.

Explain: ***We are going on an animal safari. When you hear an animal name that starts with the letter sound /b/, stand up. Say the letter sound and the name of the animal. If the animal name doesn't start with /b/, sit down.***

Ask: ***How about* bear?** Students should stand up.

Say: ***Yes!* Bear *has /b/ at the beginning, so you stand up. Let's try another one:* gorilla.** Students should sit down.

Say: ***Good!* Gorilla *doesn't begin with the /b/ sound, so you sit down.***

Alternate between animal names that begin with /*b*/ and those that don't.

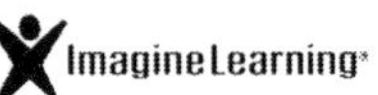

Words that begin with /b/: butterfly, bat, baboon, badger, beagle, bear, bull, beaver, bee, beetle, bird, bison, bobcat, buffalo, bulldog, bug

Words that don't begin with /b/: turtle, seagull, gorilla, lion, moth

EXTENSION ACTIVITY*:* Ask students to think of other words that begin with */b/*.

Check Progress: Letter Stack

Observe each student during practice and use the following activity to check progress on the target skill. If student can correctly identify the letter sound twice, consider the intervention successful.

Point to the appropriate letter card as you say the sound.

Say: ***Repeat the letter sounds for these letters: /b/, /b/, /ŏ/, /ŏ/.***

Shuffle letter cards for *B* and *O* together in a stack.

Say: ***Choose a card and tell me the letter sound.***

Have students draw a card from the stack, say the sound, and put the card on the bottom of the stack. Repeat until every student has had several opportunities to demonstrate knowledge of the target letter sound */b/*.

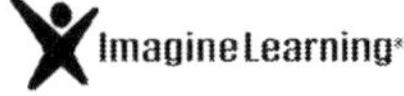

Letter Sounds

The Sound for O Is /ŏ/

Grade K

10 Min.

CCSS.RF.K.3a
TEKS 110.11.3.A

LEARNING OBJECTIVE: Demonstrate letter-sound correspondence by producing the most common sound for the letter *O*.

LANGUAGE OBJECTIVE: Produce the sound for the letter *O* when shown a visual grapheme.

Lesson Overview

Introduce the letter sound, play a game to practice identifying the letter sound, and assess students' ability to associate a specific letter sound with a specific letter.

Materials	Preparation
• Letter and Picture Cards for *O* • Letter and Picture Cards for *B* • Paper Bag	• Cut out all letter and picture cards.

Teach and Model

Show students the upper- and lowercase letter cards for *O*.

Say: ***This is* O. *The letter* O *stands for the sound /ŏ/. Make the sound with me: /ŏ/.*** Have students produce the sound with you.

Point to the letter card.

Say: ***Make the sound for this letter every time I put my finger on it.*** Have students produce the sound. Point to the card several times. Mix up the practice by asking individual students to say the sound.

Hold up a picture card.

Say: ***This word is* octopus. *It begins with the letter sound /ŏ/. What is this?*** Have students repeat the name of the picture.

Say: ***What letter sound does* octopus *begin with?*** Have students produce the /ŏ/ sound independently.

Repeat questions above with each picture card for /ŏ/.

Picture cards for /ŏ/: octopus, ostrich, otter, ox, olive, October, on, off

Connect Sound/Spelling: Letter Sound Bag

Put all letter and picture cards for *O* in the paper bag.

Explain: ***The pictures on these cards start with /ŏ/. If you pull a letter card from the bag, tell me the letter sound. Then tell me a word that starts with that letter sound.***

Model: ***If I pull out* often, *I say /ŏ/, /ŏ/,* often**

Explain: ***If you pull a picture card, tell me the letter sound it starts with and what the picture is.***

Model: ***If I pull out a picture of an octopus, I say /ŏ/, /ŏ/,* octopus.**

Have students take turns drawing cards from the paper bag.

Word bank: octopus, ostrich, otter, ox, olive, October, on, off

Connect Sound/Spelling: Thumbs Up, Thumbs Down for Beginning Sounds

Say: ***Show me thumbs up.*** Model what thumbs up looks like and help students show their thumbs up.

Explain: ***When you hear a word that begins with the letter sound /ŏ/, make a thumbs up and say the letter sound. If the word doesn't start with the letter sound /ŏ/, give me a thumbs down.*** Model thumbs down for students and help students show their thumbs down.

Say each word from the word bank below, alternating between words that begin with /ŏ/ and words that don't.

Words that begin with /ŏ/: odd, octagon, October, off, officer, observe, oxygen, opera, oxen

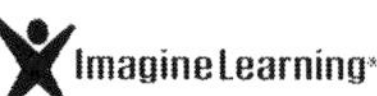

Words that don't begin with /ŏ/: igloo, ant, hot, doorbell

EXTENSION ACTIVITY: Ask students to think of other words that begin with /ŏ/.

Check Progress: Letter Flip

Observe each student during practice and use the following activity to check progress on the target skill. If student can correctly identify the letter sound twice, consider the intervention successful.

Point to the appropriate letter card as you say the sound.

Say: ***Repeat the letter sounds for these letters: /ŏ/, /b/.***

Put all the flash cards face down on the table and mix them up.

Say: ***Choose a card and tell me the letter sound.***

Have students choose a card and say the sound, mixing the cards between student turns. Give every student a turn, repeating until each student has had the opportunity to demonstrate knowledge on the target letter sound */ŏ/.*

B

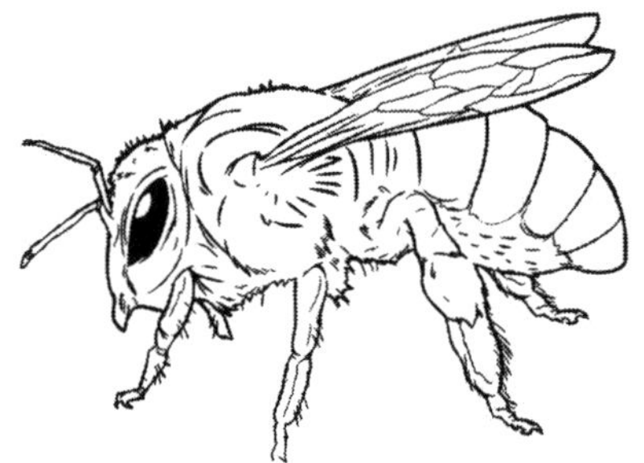

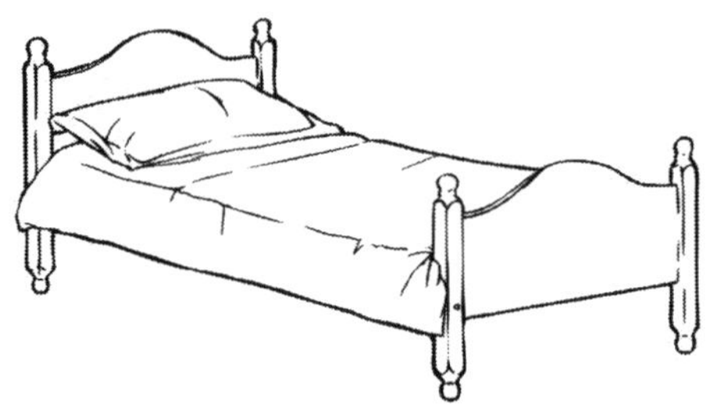

O

o

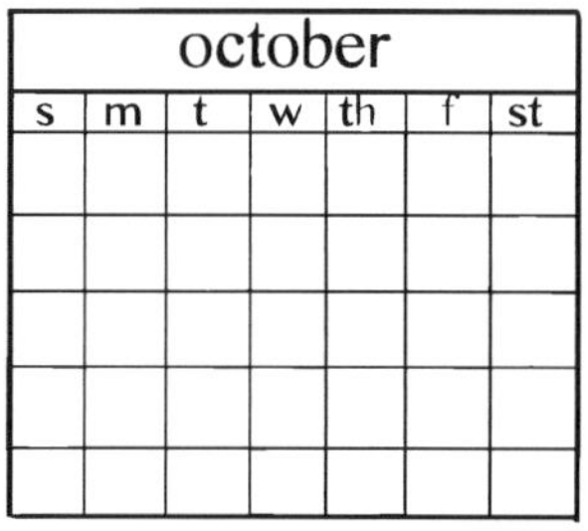

october

s	m	t	w	th	f	st

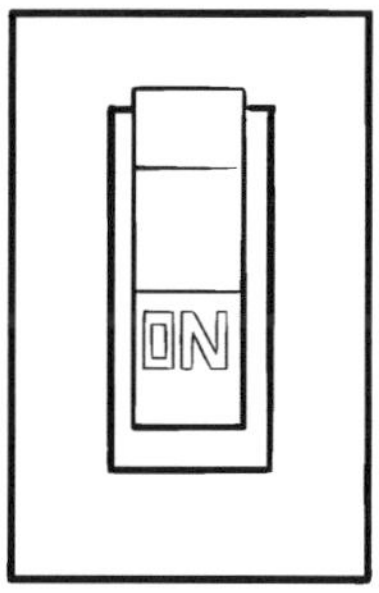

ON

OFF

Reteaching Lessons ✓

The Sound for N Is /n/

Grade K

10 Min.

CCSS.RF.K.3a
TEKS 110.11.3.A

LEARNING OBJECTIVE: Demonstrate letter-sound correspondence by producing the most common sound for the letter *N*.

LANGUAGE OBJECTIVE: Produce the sound for the letter *N* when shown a visual grapheme.

Lesson Overview

Introduce the letter sound, play a game to practice identifying the letter sound, and assess students' ability to associate a specific letter sound with a specific letter.

Materials	Preparation
• Letter and Picture Cards for *N* • Letter and Picture Cards for *H* • Paper bag	• Cut out all letter and picture cards.

Teach and Model

Show students the upper- and lowercase letter cards for *N*.

Say: ***This is* N. *The letter* N *stands for the sound /n/. Make the sound with me: /n/.*** Have students produce the sound with you.

Point to the letter card.

Say: ***Make the sound for this letter every time I put my finger on it.*** Have students produce the sound. Point to the card several times. Mix up the practice by asking individual students to say the sound.

Hold up a picture card.

Say: ***This word is* nest. *It begins with the letter sound /n/. What is this?*** Have students repeat the name of the picture.

Say: ***What letter sound does* nest *begin with?*** Have students produce the */n/* sound independently.

Repeat questions above with each picture card for */n/*.

Picture cards for /n/: nut, noodles, nurse, nine, nest, nose, net, necklace

Connect Sound/Spelling: Letter Sound Bag

Put all letter and picture cards for *N* in the paper bag.

Explain: ***The pictures on these cards start with /n/. If you pull a letter card from the bag, tell me the letter sound. Then tell me a word that starts with that letter sound.***

Model: ***If I pull out* new, *I say /n/, /n/, new***

Explain: ***If you pull a picture card, tell me the letter sound it starts with and what the picture is.***

Model: ***If I pull out a picture of a noodles, I say /n/, /n/,* noodles.**

Have students take turns drawing cards from the paper bag.

Word bank: new, night, now, name, neck, noon, noise, needle, nap

Connect Sound/Spelling: Thumbs Up, Thumbs Down for Beginning Sounds

Say: ***Show me thumbs up.*** Model what thumbs up looks like and help students show their thumbs up.

Explain: ***When you hear a word that begins with the letter sound /n/, make a thumbs up and say the letter sound. If the word doesn't start with the letter sound /n/, give me a thumbs down.*** Model thumbs down for students and help students show their thumbs down.

Say each word from the word bank below, alternating between words that begin with */n/* and words that don't.

Words that begin with /n/: net, noise, nail, neighbor, necklace, nine, nest, night, name, needle, north, nap, note, nature, napkin, news, notebook

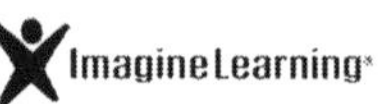

Words that don't begin with /n/: radio, water, laugh, mountain, library

EXTENSION ACTIVITY: Ask students to think of other words that begin with */n/*.

Check Progress: Letter Flip

Observe each student during practice and use the following activity to check progress on the target skill. If student can correctly identify the letter sound twice, consider the intervention successful.

Point to the appropriate letter card as you say the sound.

Say: ***Repeat the letter sounds for these letters: /n/, /h/.***

Put all the flash cards face down on the table and mix them up.

Say: ***Choose a card and tell me the letter sound.***

Have students choose a card and say the sound, mixing the cards between student turns. Give every student a turn, repeating until each student has had the opportunity to demonstrate knowledge on the target letter sound */n/*.

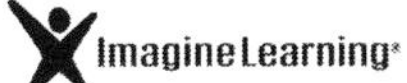

The Sound for H Is /h/

Grade K

10 Min.

CCSS.RF.K.3a
TEKS 110.11.3.A

LEARNING OBJECTIVE: Demonstrate letter-sound correspondence by producing the most common sound for the letter *H*.

LANGUAGE OBJECTIVE: Produce the sound for the letter *H* when shown a visual grapheme.

Lesson Overview

Introduce the letter sound, play a game to practice identifying the letter sound, and assess students' ability to associate a specific letter sound with a specific letter.

Materials	Preparation
• Letter and Picture Cards for *H* • Letter and Picture Cards for *N* • Paper bag	• Cut out all letter and picture cards.

Teach and Model

Show students the upper- and lowercase letter cards for *H*.

Say: ***This is* H. *The letter* H *stands for the sound /h/. Make the sound with me: /h/.*** Have students produce the sound with you.

Point to the letter card.

Say: ***Make the sound for this letter every time I put my finger on it.*** Have students produce the sound. Point to the card several times. Mix up the practice by asking individual students to say the sound.

Hold up a picture card.

Say: ***This word is* hand. *It begins with the letter sound /h/. What is this?*** Have students repeat the name of the picture.

Say: ***What letter sound does* hand *begin with?*** Have students produce the */h/* sound independently.

Repeat questions above with each picture card for */h/*.

Picture cards for /h/: horse, hen, hamburger, hot dog, hat, heart, hammer, hand

Connect Sound/Spelling: Letter Sound Bag

Put all letter and picture cards for *H* in the paper bag.

Explain: ***The pictures on these cards start with /h/. If you pull a letter card from the bag, tell me the letter sound. Then tell me a word that starts with that letter sound.***

Model: ***If I pull out* hair, *I say /h/, /h/, hair***

Explain: ***If you pull a picture card, tell me the letter sound it starts with and what the picture is.***

Model: ***If I pull out a picture of a hat, I say /h/, /h/, hat.***

Have students take turns drawing cards from the paper bag.

Word bank: hair, her, him, hug, hello, hose, home, horn, help, hide, heavy

Connect Sound/Spelling: Animal Safari

Show the letter cards.

Explain: ***We are going on an animal safari. When you hear an animal name that starts with the letter sound /h/, stand up. Say the letter sound and the name of the animal. If the animal name doesn't start with /h/, sit down.***

Ask: ***How about* horse?** Students should stand up.

Say: ***Yes!* Horse *has /h/ at the beginning, so you stand up. Let's try another one:* lizard.** Students should sit down.

Say: ***Good!* Lizard *doesn't begin with the /h/ sound, so you sit down.***

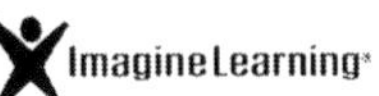

Alternate between animal names that begin with */h/* and those that don't.

Words that begin with /h/*:* horse, hamster, hippo(potamus), hawk, hedgehog, hen, hyena, hog, hornet, hummingbird

Words that don't begin with /h/*:* snake, beaver, goose, caterpillar

EXTENSION ACTIVITY: Ask students to think of other words that begin with */h/*.

Check Progress: Letter Stack

Observe each student during practice and use the following activity to check progress on the target skill. If student can correctly identify the letter sound twice, consider the intervention successful.

Point to the appropriate letter card as you say the sound.

Say: ***Repeat the letter sounds for these letters:* /h/, /h/, /n/, /n/.**

Shuffle letter cards for *H* and *N* together in a stack.

Say: ***Choose a card and tell me the letter sound.***

Have students draw a card from the stack, say the sound, and put the card on the bottom of the stack. Repeat until every student has had several opportunities to demonstrate knowledge of the target letter sound */h/*.

Reteaching Lessons

N	n
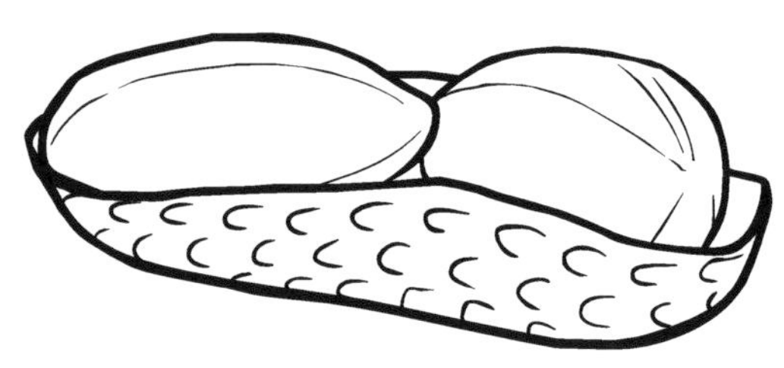	

	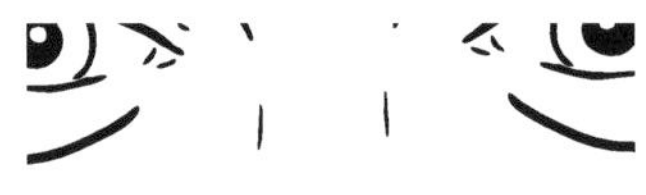 

Letter and Picture Cards for N

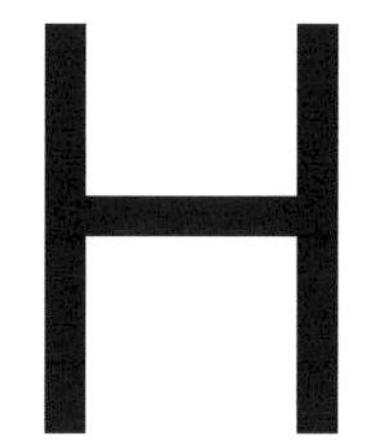

h

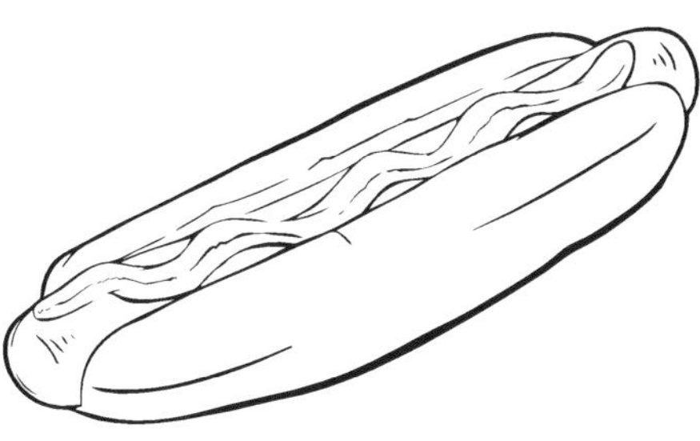

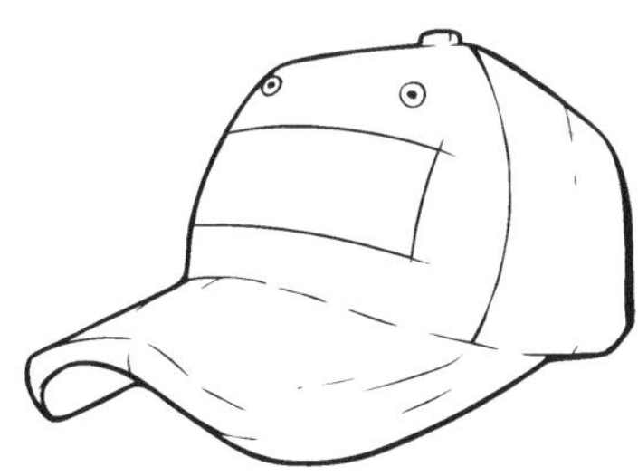

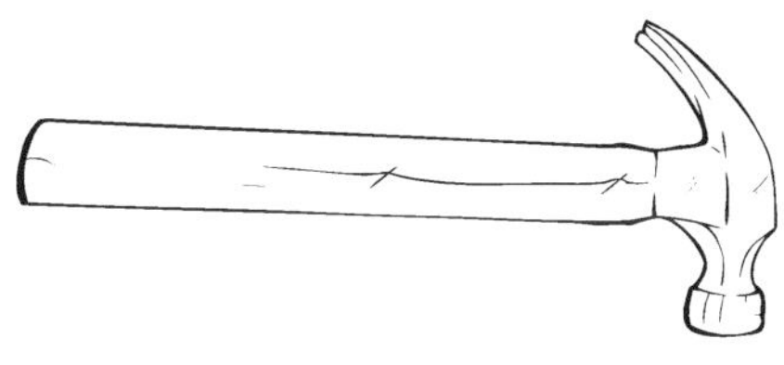

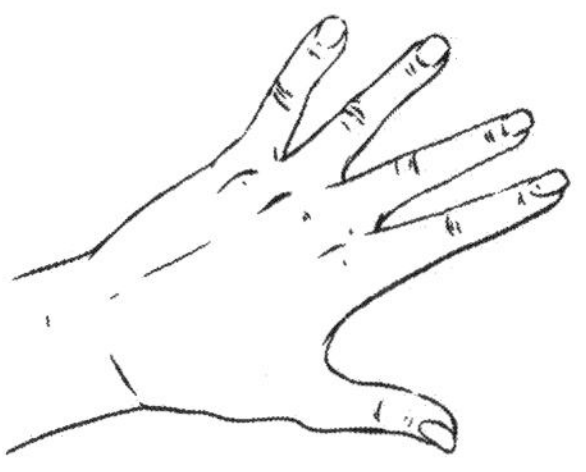

Letter Sounds

The Sound for C Is /k/

Grade K

10 Min.

CCSS.RF.K.3a
TEKS 110.11.3.A

LEARNING OBJECTIVE: Demonstrate letter-sound correspondence by producing the most common sound for the letter *C*.

LANGUAGE OBJECTIVE: Produce the sound for the letter *C* when shown a visual grapheme.

Lesson Overview

Introduce the letter sound, play a game to practice identifying the letter sound, and assess students' ability to associate a specific letter sound with a specific letter.

Materials	Preparation
• Letter and Picture Cards for *C* • Letter and Picture Cards for *F*	• Cut out all letter and picture cards.

Teach and Model

Show students the upper- and lowercase letter cards for *C*.

Say: ***This is* C. *The letter* C *stands for the sound /k/. Make the sound with me: /k/.*** Have students produce the sound with you.

Point to the letter card.

Say: ***Make the sound for this letter every time I put my finger on it.*** Have students produce the sound. Point to the card several times. Mix up the practice by asking individual students to say the sound.

Hold up a picture card.

Say: ***This word is* cat. *It begins with the letter sound /k/. What is this?*** Have students repeat the name of the picture.

Say: ***What letter sound does* cat *begin with?*** Have students produce the /*k*/ sound independently.

Repeat questions above with each picture card for /*k*/.

Picture cards for /k/: cat, cow, caterpillar, cake, car, castle, cactus, computer

Connect Sound/Spelling: Letter Sound Lunch

Show letter card.

Explain: ***It's time for Letter Sound Lunch! For this lunch we can only order food that begins with the letter sound /k/.***

Model: ***I can order a* cake *because it begins with /k/.***

Have students think of things they can order that begin with the letter sound /*k*/. Provide prompts (e.g., What do rabbits like to eat that is orange and starts with /*k*/?) to help them think of words from the word bank.

Word bank: cake, corn, cabbage, carrot, cantaloupe, caramel, cucumber, cashew, cauliflower, coconut, cookie, cotton candy, cracker, cranberry, cream

Connect Sound/Spelling: Animal Safari

Show the letter cards.

Explain: ***We are going on an animal safari. When you hear an animal name that starts with the letter sound /k/, stand up. Say the letter sound and the name of the animal. If the animal name doesn't start with /k/, sit down.***

Ask: ***How about camel?*** Students should stand up.

Say: ***Yes!* Camel *has /k/ at the beginning, so you stand up. Let's try another one:* snake.** Students should sit down.

Say: ***Good!* Snake *doesn't begin with the /k/ sound, so you sit down.***

Alternate between animal names that begin with /*k*/ and those that don't.

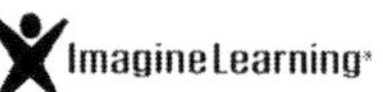

Words that begin with /k/: cat, condor, camel, canary, caribou, crocodile, caterpillar, cow, cobra, cockroach, cricket, crab, cougar

Words that don't begin with /k/: dragonfly, pony, gecko, moth

Check Progress: Letter Flip

Observe each student during practice and use the following activity to check progress on the target skill. If student can correctly identify the letter sound twice, consider the intervention successful.

Point to the appropriate letter card as you say the sound.

Say: ***Repeat the letter sounds for these letters: /k/, /f/.***

Put all the flash cards face down on the table and mix them up.

Say: ***Choose a card and tell me the letter sound.***

Have students choose a card and say the sound, mixing the cards between student turns. Give every student a turn, repeating until each student has had the opportunity to demonstrate knowledge on the target letter sound */k/*.

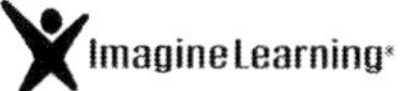

The Sound for F Is /f/

Grade K

10 Min.

CCSS.RF.K.3a
TEKS 110.11.3.A

LEARNING OBJECTIVE: Demonstrate letter-sound correspondence by producing the most common sound for the letter *F*.

LANGUAGE OBJECTIVE: Produce the sound for the letter *F* when shown a visual grapheme.

Lesson Overview

Introduce the letter sound, play a game to practice identifying the letter sound, and assess students' ability to associate a specific letter sound with a specific letter.

Materials	Preparation
• Letter and Picture Cards for *F* • Letter and Picture Cards for *K* • Small, soft ball or toy	• Cut out all letter and picture cards.

Teach and Model

Show students the upper- and lowercase letter cards for *F*.

Say: ***This is* F. *The letter* F *stands for the sound /f/. Make the sound with me: /f/.*** Have students produce the sound with you.

Point to the letter card.

Say: ***Make the sound for this letter every time I put my finger on it.*** Have students produce the sound. Point to the card several times. Mix up the practice by asking individual students to say the sound.

Hold up a picture card.

Say: ***This word is* fish. *It begins with the letter sound /f/. What is this?*** Have students repeat the name of the picture.

Say: ***What letter sound does* fish *begin with?*** Have students produce the /*f*/ sound independently.

Repeat questions above with each picture card for /*f*/.

Picture cards for /f/: fish, fox, frog, fruit, farmer, firefighter, flag, fork

Connect Sound/Spelling: Letter Sound Toss

Show the ball and the letter cards.

Explain: ***When I toss this ball to you, say the letter sound /f/ twice. Then say a word that begins with that letter sound and toss the ball to a classmate.***

Model: **/f/, /f/, fish.** Demonstrate the sequence with a volunteer.

Toss the ball to a student. Provide prompts as needed (e.g., What do you use to eat spaghetti?). Continue until all students have had several turns.

Prompt as needed using words from the word bank.

Word bank: fish, fork, fox, frog, fruit, farmer, firefighter flag, frozen, farm, fossil, fabric, fire fly, food

Connect Sound/Spelling: Thumbs Up, Thumbs Down for Beginning Sounds

Say: ***Show me thumbs up.*** Model what thumbs up looks like and help students show their thumbs up.

Explain: ***When you hear a word that begins with the letter sound /f/, make a thumbs up and say the letter sound. If the word doesn't start with the letter sound /f/, give me a thumbs down.*** Model thumbs down for students and help students show their thumbs down.

Say each word from the word bank below, alternating between words that begin with /*f*/ and words that don't.

Words that begin with /f/: fork, fan, fairy, factory, farm, field, faucet, floss, frame, friend, farmer, fire fighter, float, flag, fire, forest, flood, fog, frost, frozen

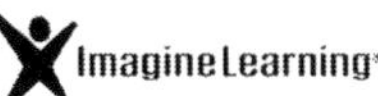

Words that don't begin with /f/: teacher, hand, running, pencil, glass, orange

EXTENSION ACTIVITY: Ask students to think of other words that begin with */f/*.

Check Progress: Letter Flip

Observe each student during practice and use the following activity to check progress on the target skill. If student can correctly identify the letter sound twice, consider the intervention successful.

Point to the appropriate letter card as you say the sound.

Say: ***Repeat the letter sounds for these letters: /f/, /k/.***

Put all the flash cards face down on the table and mix them up.

Say: ***Choose a card and tell me the letter sound.***

Have students choose a card and say the sound, mixing the cards between student turns. Give every student a turn, repeating until each student has had the opportunity to demonstrate knowledge on the target letter sound */f/*.

Reteaching Lessons

Letter and Picture Cards for C

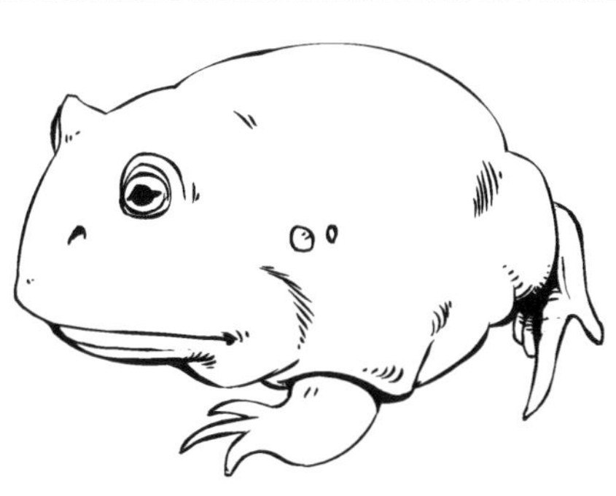

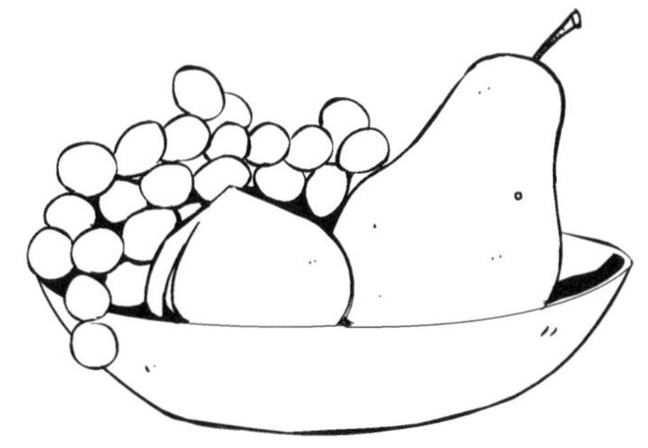

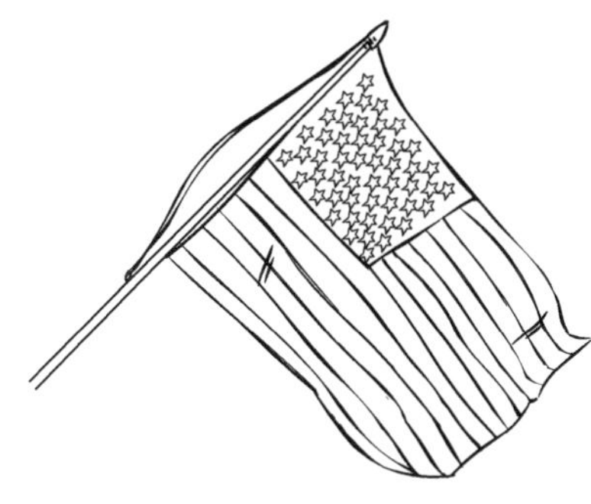

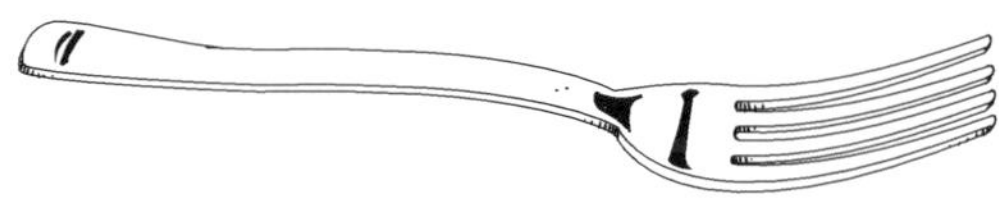

The Sound for V Is /v/

Grade K

10 Min.

CCSS.RF.K.3a
TEKS 110.11.3.A

LEARNING OBJECTIVE: Demonstrate letter-sound correspondence by producing the most common sound for the letter *V*.

LANGUAGE OBJECTIVE: Produce the sound for the letter *V* when shown a visual grapheme.

Lesson Overview

Introduce the letter sound, play a game to practice identifying the letter sound, and assess students' ability to associate a specific letter sound with a specific letter.

Materials	Preparation
• Letter and Picture Cards for *V* • Letter and Picture Cards for *I*	• Cut out all letter and picture cards.

Teach and Model

Show students the upper- and lowercase letter cards for *V*.

Say: ***This is* V*. The letter* V *stands for the sound /v/. Make the sound with me: /v/.*** Have students produce the sound with you.

Point to the letter card.

Say: ***Make the sound for this letter every time I put my finger on it.*** Have students produce the sound. Point to the card several times. Mix up the practice by asking individual students to say the sound.

Hold up a picture card.

Say: ***This word is* violin*. It begins with the letter sound /v/. What is this?*** Have students repeat the name of the picture.

Say: ***What letter sound does* violin *begin with?*** Have students produce the /v/ sound independently.

Repeat questions above with each picture card for /v/.

Picture cards for /v/: van, violin, vegetables, vet, vest, volcano, valley, vitamins

Connect Sound/Spelling: Letter Sound Sort

Shuffle picture cards for *V* and *I* together. Display letter cards for *V* on a table, allowing enough space for a column of picture cards below the letter cards. Display letter cards for *I* next to the letter cards for *V*.

Say: ***This is letter* I*.* I *stands for the sound /ĭ/. Everyone say /ĭ/.*** Have students produce the sound.

Show the stack of picture cards.

Explain: ***The pictures on these cards begin with the letter sound /v/ or /ĭ/. We are going to put them with their matching letter.***

Show the first picture card.

Demonstrate: ***Vest. This picture begins with the letter sound /v/: /v/, /v/, vest. Say /v/, /v/, vest.*** Have students repeat the sound and word.

Demonstrate: ***Vest goes with this card, /v/.*** Place the picture card below the letter cards for *V*.

Have students draw the remaining picture cards from the stack and place them in a column under the matching letter card. As each card is added, direct students to say the letter sound twice and then name the picture: /v/, /v/, van; /ĭ/, /ĭ/, igloo.

Picture cards for /ĭ/: insect, iguana, igloo, inch, ill, inside, India, itch

EXTENSION ACTIVITY: Randomly point to pictures in the two columns and instruct students to repeat the letter sound and name the picture.

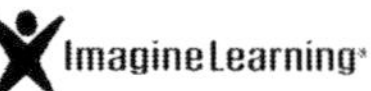

Connect Sound/Spelling: Thumbs Up, Thumbs Down for Beginning Sounds

Say: ***Show me thumbs up.*** Model what thumbs up looks like and help students show their thumbs up.

Explain: ***When you hear a word that begins with the letter sound /v/, make a thumbs up and say the letter sound. If the word doesn't start with the letter sound /v/, give me a thumbs down.*** Model thumbs down for students and help students show their thumbs down.

Say each word from the word bank below, alternating between words that begin with /v/ and words that don't.

Words that begin with /v/: vase. van. violin. vet. visitor, vest, valley, volcano

Words that don't begin with /v/: sky, dress, trade, friend

EXTENSION ACTIVITY: Ask students to think of other words that begin with /v/.

Check Progress: Letter Flip

Observe each student during practice and use the following activity to check progress on the target skill. If student can correctly identify the letter sound twice, consider the intervention successful.

Point to the appropriate letter card as you say the sound.

Say: ***Repeat the letter sounds for these letters: /v/, /ĭ/.***

Put all the flash cards face down on the table and mix them up.

Say: ***Choose a card and tell me the letter sound.***

Have students choose a card and say the sound, mixing the cards between student turns. Give every student a turn, repeating until each student has had the opportunity to demonstrate knowledge on the target letter sound /v/.

The Sound for I Is /ĭ/

Grade K

10 Min.

CCSS.RF.K.3a
TEKS 110.11.3.A

LEARNING OBJECTIVE: Demonstrate letter-sound correspondence by producing the most common sound for the letter *I*.

LANGUAGE OBJECTIVE: Produce the sound for the letter *I* when shown a visual grapheme.

Lesson Overview

Introduce the letter sound, play a game to practice identifying the letter sound, and assess students' ability to associate a specific letter sound with a specific letter.

Materials	Preparation
• Letter and Picture Cards for *I* • Letter and Picture Cards for *V*	• Cut out all letter and picture cards.

Teach and Model

Show students the upper- and lowercase letter cards for *I*.

Say: ***This is* I. *The letter* I *stands for the sound /ĭ/. Make the sound with me: /ĭ/.*** Have students produce the sound with you.

Point to the letter card.

Say: ***Make the sound for this letter every time I put my finger on it.*** Have students produce the sound. Point to the card several times. Mix up the practice by asking individual students to say the sound.

Hold up a picture card.

Say: ***This word is* igloo. *It begins with the letter sound /ĭ/. What is this?*** Have students repeat the name of the picture.

Say: ***What letter sound does* igloo *begin with?*** Have students produce the /ĭ/ sound independently.

Repeat questions above with each picture card for /ĭ/.

Picture cards for /ĭ/: insect, iguana, igloo, inch, ill, inside, India, itch

Connect Sound/Spelling: Letter Sound Sort

Shuffle picture cards for *I* and *V* together. Display letter cards for *I* on a table, allowing enough space for a column of picture cards below the letter cards. Display letter cards for *V* next to the letter cards for *I*.

Say: ***This is letter* V. V *stands for the sound /v/. Everyone say /v/.*** Have students produce the sound.

Show the stack of picture cards.

Explain: ***The pictures on these cards begin with the letter sound /ĭ/ or /v/. We are going to put them with their matching letter.***

Show the first picture card.

Demonstrate: **Igloo*. This picture begins with the letter sound /ĭ/: /ĭ/, /ĭ/,* igloo. *Say /ĭ/, /ĭ/,* igloo.** Have students repeat the sound and word.

Demonstrate: **Igloo *goes with this card, /ĭ/.*** Place the picture card below the letter cards for *I*.

Have students draw the remaining picture cards from the stack and place them in a column under the matching letter card. As each card is added, direct students to say the letter sound twice and then name the picture: /ĭ/, /ĭ/, itch; /v/, /v/, van.

Picture cards for /v/: van, violin, vegetables, vet, vest, volcano, valley, vitamins

EXTENSION ACTIVITY: Randomly point to pictures in the two columns and instruct students to repeat the letter sound and name the picture.

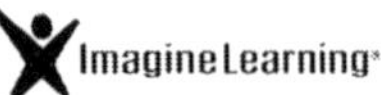

Connect Sound/Spelling: Thumbs Up, Thumbs Down for Beginning Sounds

Say: ***Show me thumbs up.*** Model what thumbs up looks like and help students show their thumbs up.

Explain: ***When you hear a word that begins with the letter sound /ĭ/, make a thumbs up and say the letter sound. If the word doesn't start with the letter sound /ĭ/, give me a thumbs down.*** Model thumbs down for students and help students show their thumbs down.

Say each word from the word bank below, alternating between words that begin with /ĭ/ and words that don't.

Words that begin with /ĭ/: inch, inside, ill, injury, igloo, initial, invent, itch, inhale

Words that don't begin with /ĭ/: bed, fork, piano, ouch

EXTENSION ACTIVITY: Ask students to think of other words that begin with /ĭ/.

Check Progress: Letter Stack

Observe each student during practice and use the following activity to check progress on the target skill. If student can correctly identify the letter sound twice, consider the intervention successful.

Point to the appropriate letter card as you say the sound.

Say: ***Repeat the letter sounds for these letters: /ĭ/, /ĭ/, /v/, /v/.***

Shuffle letter cards for *I* and *V* together in a stack.

Say: ***Choose a card and tell me the letter sound.***

Have students draw a card from the stack, say the sound, and put the card on the bottom of the stack. Repeat until every student has had several opportunities to demonstrate knowledge of the target letter sound /ĭ/.

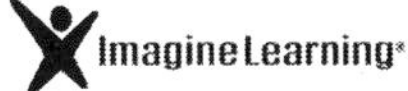

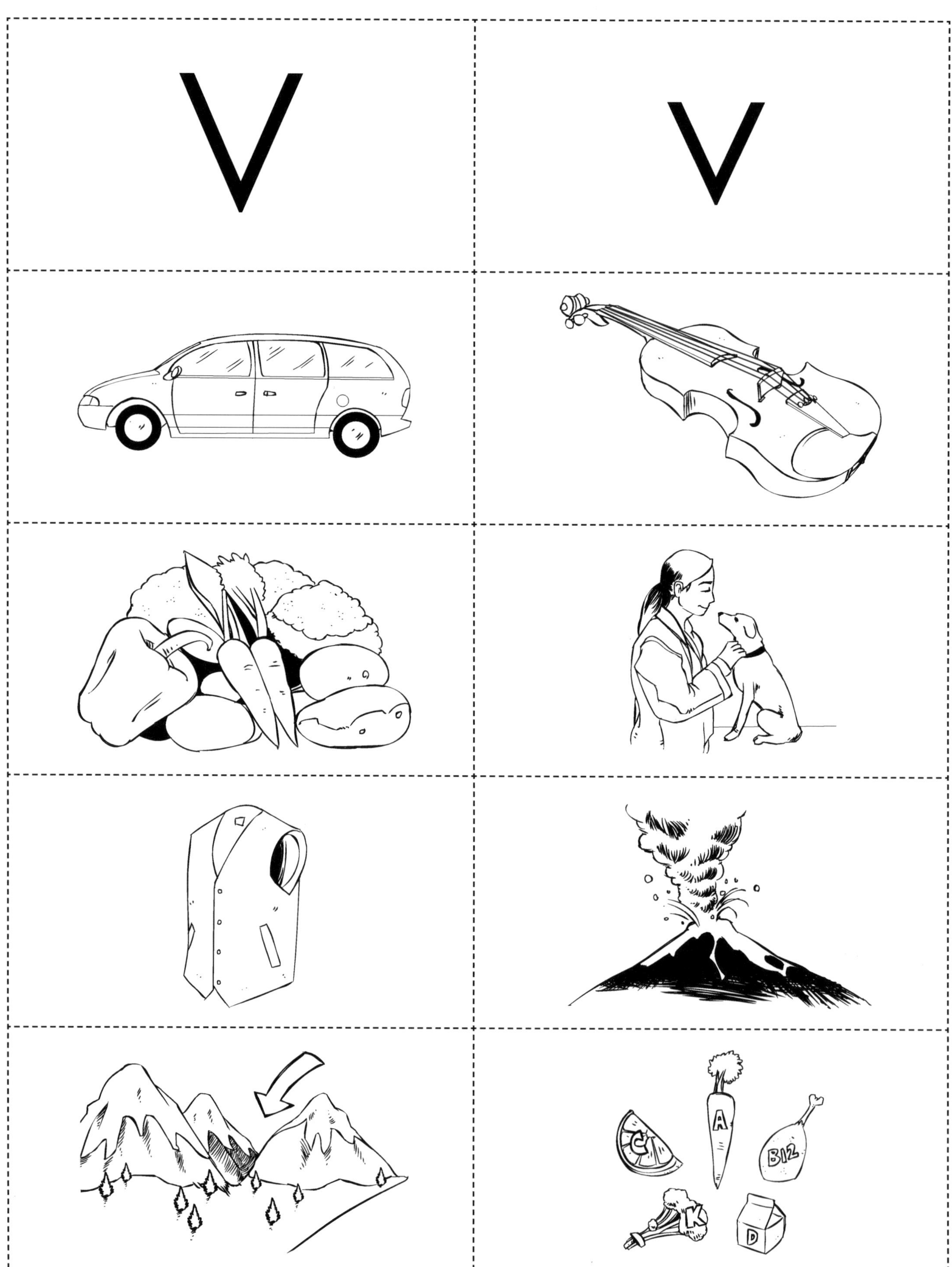

Letter and Picture Cards for V

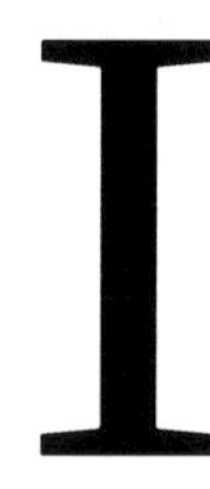

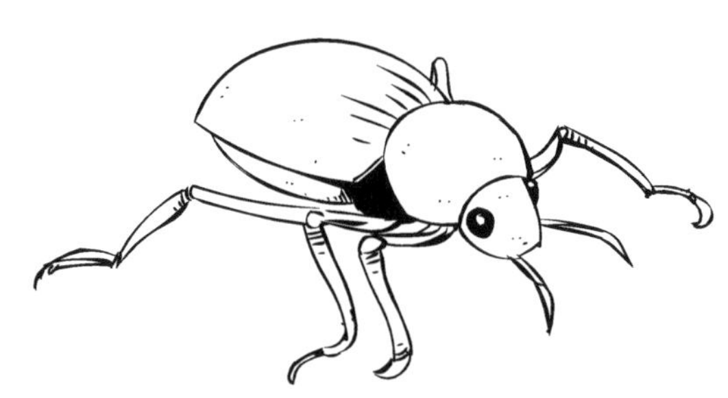

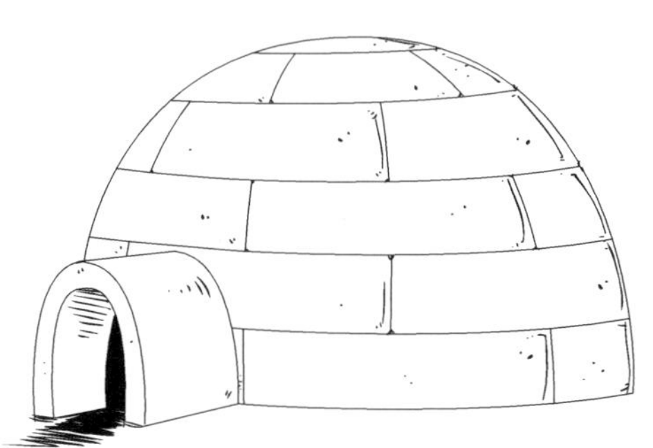

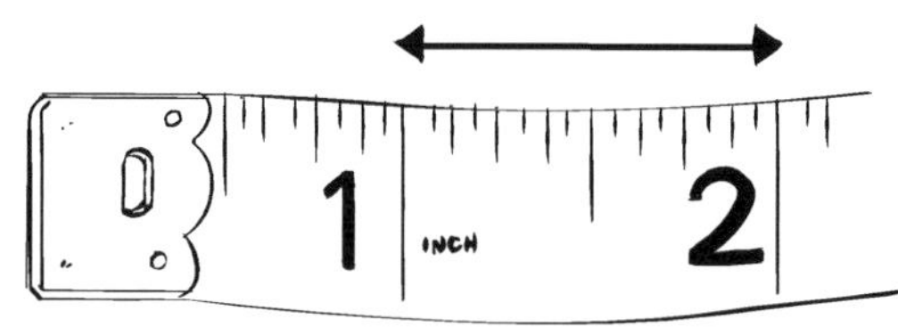

Reteaching Lessons ✓

The Sound for U Is /ŭ/

Grade K

10 Min.

CCSS.RF.K.3a
TEKS 110.11.3.A

LEARNING OBJECTIVE: Demonstrate letter-sound correspondence by producing the most common sound for the letter *U*.

LANGUAGE OBJECTIVE: Produce the sound for the letter *U* when shown a visual grapheme.

Lesson Overview

Introduce the letter sound, play a game to practice identifying the letter sound, and assess students' ability to associate a specific letter sound with a specific letter.

Materials	Preparation
• **Letter and Picture Cards for** ***U*** • **Letter and Picture Cards for** ***R***	• Cut out all letter and picture cards.

Teach and Model

Show students the upper- and lowercase letter cards for *U*.

Say: ***This is* U. *The letter* U *stands for the sound /ŭ/. Make the sound with me: /ŭ/.*** Have students produce the sound with you.

Point to the letter card.

Say: ***Make the sound for this letter every time I put my finger on it.*** Have students produce the sound. Point to the card several times. Mix up the practice by asking individual students to say the sound.

Hold up a picture card.

Say: ***This word is* umbrella. *It begins with the letter sound /ŭ/. What is this?*** Have students repeat the name of the picture.

Say: ***What letter sound does* umbrella *begin with?*** Have students produce the /ŭ/ sound independently.

Repeat questions above with each picture card for /ŭ/.

Picture cards for /ŭ/: umbrella, umpire, up, under, unhappy, uncle, unzip, untie

Connect Sound/Spelling: Thumbs Up, Thumbs Down for Beginning Sounds

Say: ***Show me thumbs up.*** Model what thumbs up looks like and help students show their thumbs up.

Explain: ***When you hear a word that begins with the letter sound /ŭ/, make a thumbs up and say the letter sound. If the word doesn't start with the letter sound /ŭ/, give me a thumbs down.*** Model thumbs down for students and help students show their thumbs down.

Say each word from the word bank below, alternating between words that begin with /ŭ/ and words that don't.

Words that begin with /ŭ/: up, under, unhappy, uppercase, ugly, unsafe, umpire, uncle, umbrella, untie

Words that don't begin with /ŭ/: alligator, train, pan, butter

EXTENSION ACTIVITY: Ask students to think of other words that begin with /ŭ/.

Connect Sound/Spelling: Letter Sound Sort

Shuffle picture cards for *U* and *R* together. Display letter cards for *U* on a table, allowing enough space for a column of picture cards below the letter cards. Display letter cards for *R* next to the letter cards for *U*.

Say: ***This is letter* R. R *stands for the sound /r/. Everyone say /r/.*** Have students produce the sound.

Show the stack of picture cards.

Explain: ***The pictures on these cards begin with the letter sound /ŭ/ or /r/. We are going to put them with their matching letter.***

Show the first picture card.

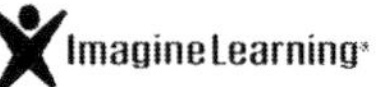

Demonstrate: **Umbrella*. This picture begins with the letter sound /ŭ/: /ŭ/, /ŭ/,* umbrella*. Say /ŭ/, /ŭ/,* umbrella.** Have students repeat the sound and word.

Demonstrate: **Umbrella *goes with this card, /ŭ/.*** Place the picture card below the letter cards for *U*.

Have students draw the remaining picture cards from the stack and place them in a column under the matching letter card. As each card is added, direct students to say the letter sound twice and then name the picture: */ŭ/, /ŭ/, under; /r/, /r/, ring*.

Picture cards for /r/: rabbit, raccoon, rug, rectangle, rope, rainbow, rock, ring

EXTENSION ACTIVITY: Randomly point to pictures in the two columns and instruct students to repeat the letter sound and name the picture.

Check Progress: Letter Flip

Observe each student during practice and use the following activity to check progress on the target skill. If student can correctly identify the letter sound twice, consider the intervention successful.

Point to the appropriate letter card as you say the sound.

Say: ***Repeat the letter sounds for these letters: /ŭ/, /r/.***

Put all the flash cards face down on the table and mix them up.

Say: ***Choose a card and tell me the letter sound.***

Have students choose a card and say the sound, mixing the cards between student turns. Give every student a turn, repeating until each student has had the opportunity to demonstrate knowledge on the target letter sound */ŭ/*.

Reteaching Lessons

The Sound for R Is /r/

Grade K

10 Min.

CCSS.RF.K.3a
TEKS 110.11.3.A

LEARNING OBJECTIVE: Demonstrate letter-sound correspondence by producing the most common sound for the letter *R*.

LANGUAGE OBJECTIVE: Produce the sound for the letter *R* when shown a visual grapheme.

Lesson Overview

Introduce the letter sound, play a game to practice identifying the letter sound, and assess students' ability to associate a specific letter sound with a specific letter.

Materials	Preparation
• Letter and Picture Cards for *R* • Letter and Picture Cards for *U* • Paper bag	• Cut out all letter and picture cards.

Teach and Model

Show students the upper- and lowercase letter cards for *R*.

Say: ***This is* R. *The letter* R *stands for the sound /r/. Make the sound with me: /r/.*** Have students produce the sound with you.

Point to the letter card.

Say: ***Make the sound for this letter every time I put my finger on it.*** Have students produce the sound. Point to the card several times. Mix up the practice by asking individual students to say the sound.

Hold up a picture card.

Say: ***This word is* ring. *It begins with the letter sound /r/. What is this?*** Have students repeat the name of the picture.

Say: ***What letter sound does* ring *begin with?*** Have students produce the /r/ sound independently.

Repeat questions above with each picture card for /r/.

Picture cards for /r/: rabbit, raccoon, rug, rectangle, rope, rainbow, rock, ring

Connect Sound/Spelling: Letter Sound Bag

Put all letter and picture cards for *R* in the paper bag.

Explain: ***The pictures on these cards start with /r/. If you pull a letter card from the bag, tell me the letter sound. Then tell me a word that starts with that letter sound.***

Model: ***If I pull out* red, *I say /r/, /r/,* red.**

Explain: ***If you pull a picture card, tell me the letter sound it starts with and what the picture is.***

Model: ***If I pull out a picture of a* rock, *I say /r/, /r/,* rock.**

Have students take turns drawing cards from the paper bag.

Word bank: red, rim, ride, road, raft, reef, room, root, rush, rest

Connect Sound/Spelling: Animal Safari

Show the letter cards.

Explain: ***We are going on an animal safari. When you hear an animal name that starts with the letter sound /r/, stand up. Say the letter sound and the name of the animal. If the animal name doesn't start with /r/, sit down.***

Ask: ***How about* rabbit?** Students should stand up.

Say: ***Yes!* Rabbit *has /r/ at the beginning, so you stand up. Let's try another one:* chicken.** Students should sit down.

Say: ***Good!* Chicken *doesn't begin with the /r/ sound, so you sit down.***

Alternate between animal names that begin with /r/ and those that don't.

Words that begin with /r/: rooster, raccoon, rabbit, ram, rat, rattlesnake, raven, reindeer, rhino(ceros), robin

Words that don't begin with /r/: bee, walrus, hamster, deer

EXTENSION ACTIVITY: Ask students to think of other words that begin with /r/.

Check Progress: Letter Stack

Observe each student during practice and use the following activity to check progress on the target skill. If student can correctly identify the letter sound twice, consider the intervention successful.

Point to the appropriate letter card as you say the sound.

Say: ***Repeat the letter sounds for these letters: /r/, /r/, /ŭ/, /ŭ/.***

Shuffle letter cards for *R* and *U* together in a stack.

Say: ***Choose a card and tell me the letter sound.***

Have students draw a card from the stack, say the sound, and put the card on the bottom of the stack. Repeat until every student has had several opportunities to demonstrate knowledge of the target letter sound /r/.

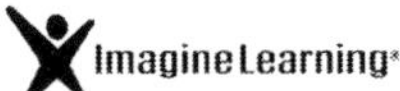

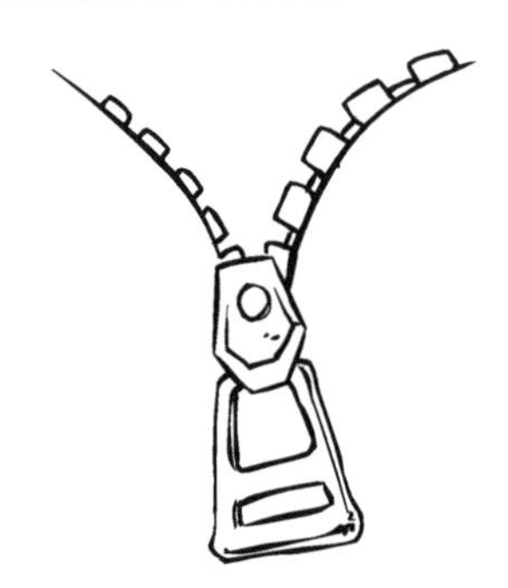
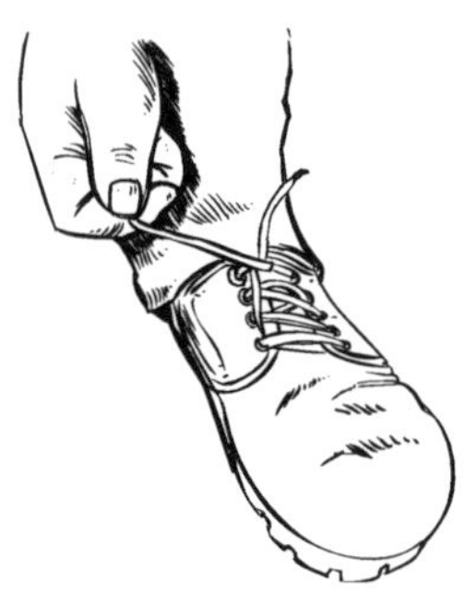

Letter and Picture Cards for U

Letter and Picture Cards for R

The Sound for G Is /g/

Grade K

10 Min.

CCSS.RF.K.3a
TEKS 110.11.3.A

LEARNING OBJECTIVE: Demonstrate letter-sound correspondence by producing the most common sound for the letter *G*.

LANGUAGE OBJECTIVE: Produce the sound for the letter *G* when shown a visual grapheme.

Lesson Overview

Introduce the letter sound, play a game to practice identifying the letter sound, and assess students' ability to associate a specific letter sound with a specific letter.

Materials	Preparation
• Letter and Picture Cards for *G* • Letter and Picture Cards for *K* • Small, soft ball or toy	• Cut out all letter and picture cards.

Teach and Model

Show students the upper- and lowercase letter cards for *G*.

Say: ***This is* G. *The letter* G *stands for the sound /g/. Make the sound with me: /g/.*** Have students produce the sound with you.

Point to the letter card.

Say: ***Make the sound for this letter every time I put my finger on it.*** Have students produce the sound. Point to the card several times. Mix up the practice by asking individual students to say the sound.

Hold up a picture card.

Say: ***This word is* gorilla. *It begins with the letter sound /g/. What is this?*** Have students repeat the name of the picture.

Say: ***What letter sound does* gorilla *begin with?*** Have students produce the /*g*/ sound independently.

Repeat questions above with each picture card for /*g*/.

Picture cards for /g/: gorilla, gecko, goat, grapes, gloves, glasses, glue, guitar

Connect Sound/Spelling: Letter Sound Toss

Show the ball and the letter cards.

Explain: ***When I toss this ball to you, say the letter sound /g/ twice. Then say a word that begins with that letter sound and toss the ball to a classmate.***

Model: **/g/, /g/, glue.** Demonstrate the sequence with a volunteer.

Toss the ball to a student. Provide prompts as needed (e.g., What do you wear that helps you to see?). Continue until all students have had several turns.

Prompt as needed using words from the word bank.

Word bank: glue, glasses, golf, game, guitar, gold, garden, galaxy, gravel, glacier, ground, gloves, garbage can, gift

Connect Sound/Spelling: Animal Safari

Show the letter cards.

Explain: ***We are going on an animal safari. When you hear an animal name that starts with the letter sound /g/, stand up. Say the letter sound and the name of the animal. If the animal name doesn't start with /g/, sit down.***

Ask: ***How about* gorilla?** Students should stand up.

Say: ***Yes!* Gorilla *has /g/ at the beginning, so you stand up. Let's try another one:* rabbit.** Students should sit down.

Say: ***Good!* Rabbit *doesn't begin with the /g/ sound, so you sit down.***

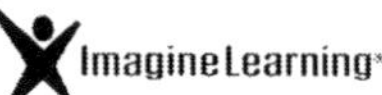

Alternate between animal names that begin with /g/ and those that don't.

Words that begin with /g/: gorilla, gazelle, gecko, goat, goldfish, goose, gopher, grasshopper, guinea pig

Words that don't begin with /g/: alligator, zebra, elephant, beaver

EXTENSION ACTIVITY*:* Ask students to think of other words that begin with /g/.

Check Progress: Letter Flip

Observe each student during practice and use the following activity to check progress on the target skill. If student can correctly identify the letter sound twice, consider the intervention successful.

Point to the appropriate letter card as you say the sound.

Say: ***Repeat the letter sounds for these letters: /g/, /k/.***

Put all the flash cards face down on the table and mix them up.

Say: ***Choose a card and tell me the letter sound.***

Have students choose a card and say the sound, mixing the cards between student turns. Give every student a turn, repeating until each student has had the opportunity to demonstrate knowledge on the target letter sound /g/.

The Sound for K Is /k/

Grade K

10 Min.

CCSS.RF.K.3a
TEKS 110.11.3.A

LEARNING OBJECTIVE: Demonstrate letter-sound correspondence by producing the most common sound for the letter *K*.

LANGUAGE OBJECTIVE: Produce the sound for the letter *K* when shown a visual grapheme.

Lesson Overview

Introduce the letter sound, play a game to practice identifying the letter sound, and assess students' ability to associate a specific letter sound with a specific letter.

Materials	Preparation
• Letter and Picture Cards for *K* • Letter and Picture Cards for *G* • Paper Bag	• Cut out all letter and picture cards.

Teach and Model

Show students the upper- and lowercase letter cards for *K*.

Say: ***This is* K. *The letter* K *stands for the sound /k/. Make the sound with me: /k/.*** Have students produce the sound with you.

Point to the letter card.

Say: ***Make the sound for this letter every time I put my finger on it.*** Have students produce the sound. Point to the card several times. Mix up the practice by asking individual students to say the sound.

Hold up a picture card.

Say: ***This word is* kite. *It begins with the letter sound /k/. What is this?*** Have students repeat the name of the picture.

Say: ***What letter sound does* kite *begin with?*** Have students produce the /*k*/ sound independently.

Repeat questions above with each picture card for /*k*/.

Picture cards for /k/: kite, kangaroo, key, kettle, kick, kid, kitten, kit

Connect Sound/Spelling: Letter Sound Bag

Put all letter and picture cards for *K* in the paper bag.

Explain: ***The pictures on these cards start with /k/. If you pull a letter card from the bag, tell me the letter sound. Then tell me a word that starts with that letter sound.***

Model: ***If I pull out* kangaroo, *I say /k/, /k/,* kangaroo.**

Explain: ***If you pull a picture card, tell me the letter sound it starts with and what the picture is.***

Model: ***If I pull out a picture of a* kite, *I say /k/, /k/,* kite.**

Have students take turns drawing cards from the paper bag.

Word bank: kite, kangaroo, key, kettle, kick, kid, kitten, kit

Connect Sound/Spelling: Thumbs Up, Thumbs Down for Beginning Sounds

Say: ***Show me thumbs up.*** Model what thumbs up looks like and help students show their thumbs up.

Explain: ***When you hear a word that begins with the letter sound /k/, make a thumbs up and say the letter sound. If the word doesn't start with the letter sound /k/, give me a thumbs down.*** Model thumbs down for students and help students show their thumbs down.

Say each word from the word bank below, alternating between words that begin with /*k*/ and words that don't.

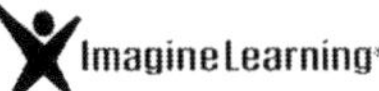

Words that begin with /k/: kite, key, kitchen, kit, kiss, kettle, kick, king, kid

Words that don't begin with /k/: ten, soup, pony, first

Check Progress: Letter Stack

Observe each student during practice and use the following activity to check progress on the target skill. If student can correctly identify the letter sound twice, consider the intervention successful.

Point to the appropriate letter card as you say the sound.

Say: ***Repeat the letter sounds for these letters: /k/, /k/, /g/, /g/.***

Shuffle letter cards for *K* and *G* together in a stack.

Say: ***Choose a card and tell me the letter sound.***

Have students draw a card from the stack, say the sound, and put the card on the bottom of the stack. Repeat until every student has had several opportunities to demonstrate knowledge of the target letter sound */k/*.

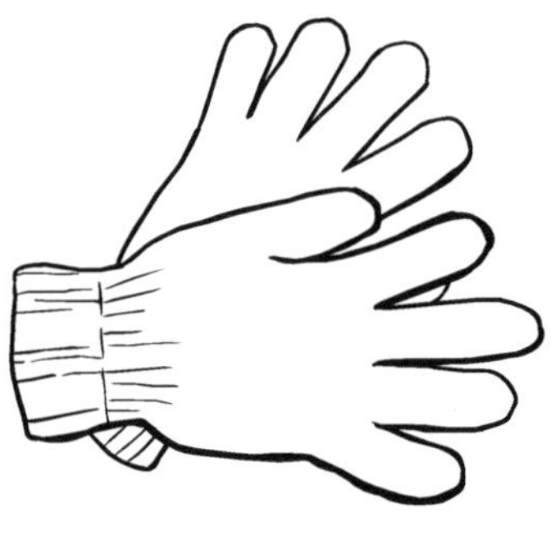

Reteaching Lessons

Letter and Picture Cards for G

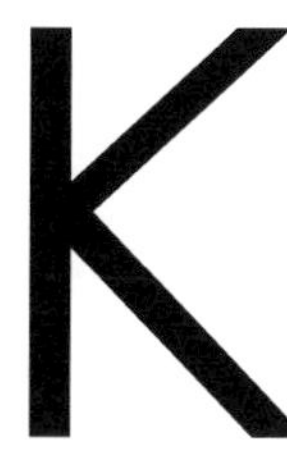

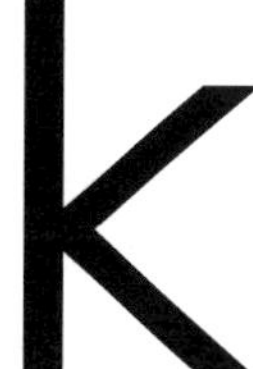

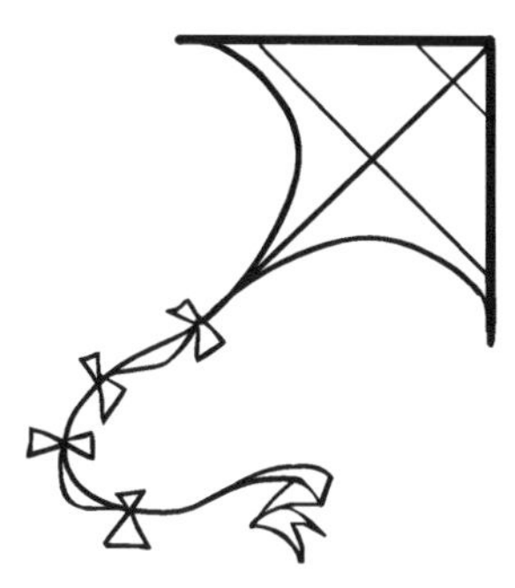

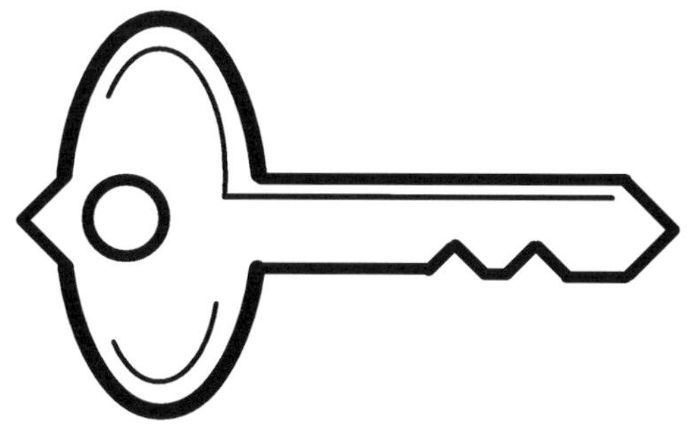

Reteaching Lessons ✓

Letter Sounds

The Sound for E Is /ĕ/

Grade K | 10 Min. | CCSS.RF.K.3a TEKS 110.11.3.A

LEARNING OBJECTIVE: Demonstrate letter-sound correspondence by producing the most common sound for the letter *E*.

LANGUAGE OBJECTIVE: Produce the sound for the letter *E* when shown a visual grapheme.

Lesson Overview

Introduce the letter sound, play a game to practice identifying the letter sound, and assess students' ability to associate a specific letter sound with a specific letter.

Materials	Preparation
• Letter and Picture Cards for *E* • Letter and Picture Cards for *L*	• Cut out all letter and picture cards.

Teach and Model

Show students the upper- and lowercase letter cards for *E*.

Say: ***This is* E*. The letter* E *stands for the sound /ĕ/. Make the sound with me: /ĕ/.*** Have students produce the sound with you.

Point to the letter card.

Say: ***Make the sound for this letter every time I put my finger on it.*** Have students produce the sound. Point to the card several times. Mix up the practice by asking individual students to say the sound.

Hold up a picture card.

Say: ***This word is* echo. *It begins with the letter sound /ĕ/. What is this?*** Have students repeat the name of the picture.

Say: ***What letter sound does* echo *begin with?*** Have students produce the /ĕ/ sound independently.

Repeat questions above with each picture card for /ĕ/.

Picture cards for /ĕ/: echo, egg, elephant, elk, explorers, envelope, exit, engine

Connect Sound/Spelling: Letter Sound Sort

Shuffle picture cards for *E* and *L* together. Display letter cards for *E* on a table, allowing enough space for a column of picture cards below the letter cards. Display letter cards for *L* next to the letter cards for *E*.

Say: ***This is letter* L. L *stands for the sound /l/. Everyone say /l/.*** Have students produce the sound.

Show the stack of picture cards.

Explain: ***The pictures on these cards begin with the letter sound /ĕ/ or /l/. We are going to put them with their matching letter.***

Show the first picture card.

Demonstrate: **Exit.** ***This picture begins with the letter sound /ĕ/: /ĕ/, /ĕ/,* exit. *Say /ĕ/, /ĕ/,* exit.** Have students repeat the sound and word.

Demonstrate: **Exit *goes with this card, /ĕ/.*** Place the picture card below the letter cards for *E*.

Have students draw the remaining picture cards from the stack and place them in a column under the matching letter card. As each card is added, direct students to say the letter sound twice and then name the picture: */ĕ/, /ĕ/, explorer; /l/, /l/, lemon.*

Picture cards for /l/: lamp, lion, leaf, ladybug, llama, log, leg, ladder

EXTENSION ACTIVITY: Randomly point to pictures in the two columns and instruct students to repeat the letter sound and name the picture.

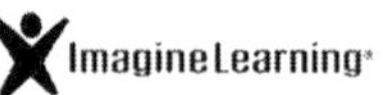

Connect Sound/Spelling: Thumbs Up, Thumbs Down for Beginning Sounds

Say: ***Show me thumbs up.*** Model what thumbs up looks like and help students show their thumbs up.

Explain: ***When you hear a word that begins with the letter sound /ĕ/, make a thumbs up and say the letter sound. If the word doesn't start with the letter sound /ĕ/, give me a thumbs down.*** Model thumbs down for students and help students show their thumbs down.

Say each word from the word bank below, alternating between words that begin with /ĕ/ and words that don't.

Words that begin with /ĕ/: envelope, exit, enter, extra, engine, explorers, echo, exam

Words that don't begin with /ĕ/: hat, desk, necklace, violin

EXTENSION ACTIVITY: Ask students to think of other words that begin with /ĕ/.

Check Progress: Letter Flip

Observe each student during practice and use the following activity to check progress on the target skill. If student can correctly identify the letter sound twice, consider the intervention successful.

Point to the appropriate letter card as you say the sound.

Say: ***Repeat the letter sounds for these letters: /ĕ/, /l/.***

Put all the flash cards face down on the table and mix them up.

Say: ***Choose a card and tell me the letter sound.***

Have students choose a card and say the sound, mixing the cards between student turns. Give every student a turn, repeating until each student has had the opportunity to demonstrate knowledge on the target letter sound /ĕ/.

Reteaching Lessons

The Sound for L Is /l/

Grade K

10 Min.

CCSS.RF.K.3a
TEKS 110.11.3.A

LEARNING OBJECTIVE: Demonstrate letter-sound correspondence by producing the most common sound for the letter *L*.

LANGUAGE OBJECTIVE: Produce the sound for the letter *L* when shown a visual grapheme.

Lesson Overview

Introduce the letter sound, play a game to practice identifying the letter sound, and assess students' ability to associate a specific letter sound with a specific letter.

Materials	Preparation
• Letter and Picture Cards for *L* • Letter and Picture Cards for *E*	• Cut out all letter and picture cards.

Teach and Model

Show students the upper- and lowercase letter cards for *L*.

Say: ***This is* L. *The letter* L *stands for the sound /l/. Make the sound with me: /l/.*** Have students produce the sound with you.

Point to the letter card.

Say: ***Make the sound for this letter every time I put my finger on it.*** Have students produce the sound. Point to the card several times. Mix up the practice by asking individual students to say the sound.

Hold up a picture card.

Say: ***This word is* lemon. *It begins with the letter sound /l/. What is this?*** Have students repeat the name of the picture.

Say: ***What letter sound does* lemon *begin with?*** Have students produce the /l/ sound independently.

Repeat questions above with each picture card for /l/.

Picture cards for /l/: lamp, lion, leaf, ladybug, llama, log, leg, ladder

Connect Sound/Spelling: Letter Sound Lunch

Show letter card.

Explain: ***It's time for Letter Sound Lunch! For this lunch we can only order food that begins with the letter sound /l/.***

Model: ***I can order a* lemon *because it begins with /l/.***

Have students think of things they can order that begin with the letter sound /l/. Provide prompts (e.g., What can you put on a hamburger that starts with /l/?) to help them think of words from the word bank.

Word bank: lemon, lettuce, lasagna, leek, lemonade, lentil, lime, licorice, lunch meat

Connect Sound/Spelling: Animal Safari

Show the letter cards.

Explain: ***We are going on an animal safari. When you hear an animal name that starts with the letter sound /l/, stand up. Say the letter sound and the name of the animal. If the animal name doesn't start with /l/, sit down.***

Ask: ***How about* lion?** Students should stand up.

Say: ***Yes!* Lion *has /l/ at the beginning, so you stand up. Let's try another one:* hawk.** Students should sit down.

Say: ***Good!* Hawk *doesn't begin with the /l/ sound, so you sit down.***

Alternate between animal names that begin with /l/ and those that don't.

Words that begin with /l/: ladybug, lamb, lark, lemur, leopard, lion, lizard, llama, lobster

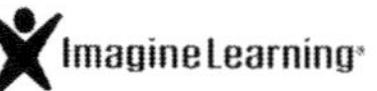

Words that don't begin with /l/: swan, pig, zebra, buffalo

EXTENSION ACTIVITY: Ask students to think of other words that begins with /l/.

Check Progress: Letter Stack

Observe each student during practice and use the following activity to check progress on the target skill. If student can correctly identify the letter sound twice, consider the intervention successful.

Point to the appropriate letter card as you say the sound.

Say: ***Repeat the letter sounds for these letters: /l/, /l/, /ĕ/, /ĕ/.***

Shuffle letter cards for *L* and *E* together in a stack.

Say: ***Choose a card and tell me the letter sound.***

Have students draw a card from the stack, say the sound, and put the card on the bottom of the stack. Repeat until every student has had several opportunities to demonstrate knowledge of the target letter sound /l/.

Reteaching Lessons

E

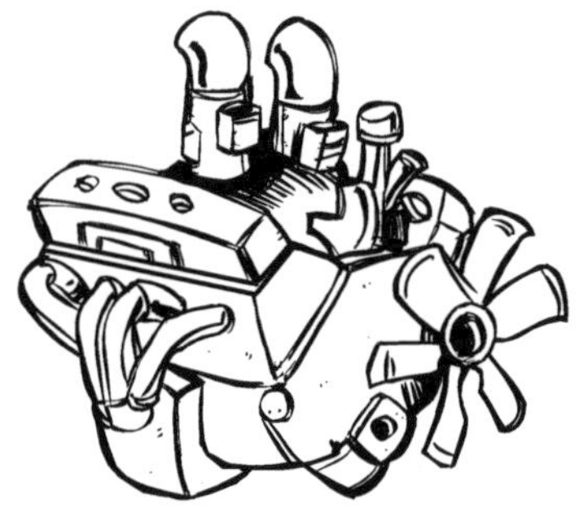

L	l

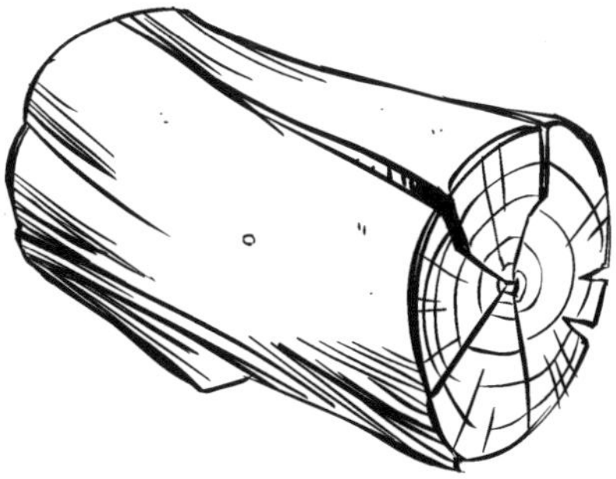

The Sound for J Is /j/

Grade K

10 Min.

CCSS.RF.K.3a
TEKS 110.11.3.A

LEARNING OBJECTIVE: Demonstrate letter-sound correspondence by producing the most common sound for the letter *J*.

LANGUAGE OBJECTIVE: Produce the sound for the letter *J* when shown a visual grapheme.

Lesson Overview

Introduce the letter sound, play a game to practice identifying the letter sound, and assess students' ability to associate a specific letter sound with a specific letter.

Materials	Preparation
• Letter and Picture Cards for *J* • Letter and Picture Cards for *Y* • Paper bag	• Cut out all letter and picture cards.

Teach and Model

Show students the upper- and lowercase letter cards for *J*.

Say: ***This is J. The letter J stands for the sound /j/. Make the sound with me: /j/.*** Have students produce the sound with you.

Point to the letter card.

Say: ***Make the sound for this letter every time I put my finger on it.*** Have students produce the sound. Point to the card several times. Mix up the practice by asking individual students to say the sound.

Hold up a picture card.

Say: ***This word is* jet. *It begins with the letter sound /j/. What is this?*** Have students repeat the name of the picture.

Say: ***What letter sound does* jet *begin with?*** Have students produce the */j/* sound independently.

Repeat questions above with each picture card for */j/*.

Picture cards for /j/: jellyfish, jam, juice, jungle, juggle, jet, jump rope, jacket

Connect Sound/Spelling: Letter Sound Luggage

Show the letter cards.

Say: ***Let's pretend we are packing for a trip. Everything we take on the trip will start with the letter sound /j/.***

Model: ***I'm going on a trip and I'm going to pack* a jump rope, a jacket, and juice..**

Ask: ***What else can we pack that starts with the letter sound /j/?*** Have students respond. Show flash cards or provide prompts as necessary (e.g., What do you wear that starts with */j/*?).

Word bank: jar, jacket, jump rope, jerky, jewels, joke book, jeans, journal, juice, jelly beans, jet

Connect Sound/Spelling: Letter Sound Bag

Put all letter and picture cards for *J* in the paper bag.

Explain: ***The pictures on these cards start with /j/. If you pull a letter card from the bag, tell me the letter sound. Then tell me a word that starts with that letter sound.***

Model: ***If I pull out* jar, *I say /j/, /j/,* jar.**

Explain: ***If you pull a picture card, tell me the letter sound it starts with and what the picture is.***

Model: ***If I pull out a picture of a jacket, I say /j/, /j/,* jacket.**

Have students take turns drawing cards from the paper bag.

Word bank: jar, job, jeans, joke, joystick, jump, junk

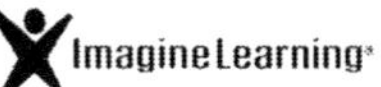

Check Progress: Letter Flip

Observe each student during practice and use the following activity to check progress on the target skill. If student can correctly identify the letter sound twice, consider the intervention successful.

Point to the appropriate letter card as you say the sound.

Say: ***Repeat the letter sounds for these letters: /j/, /y/.***

Put all the flash cards face down on the table and mix them up.

Say: ***Choose a card and tell me the letter sound.***

Have students choose a card and say the sound, mixing the cards between student turns. Give every student a turn, repeating until each student has had the opportunity to demonstrate knowledge on the target letter sound */j/*.

Reteaching Lessons

The Sound for Y Is /y/

LEARNING OBJECTIVE: Demonstrate letter-sound correspondence by producing the most common sound for the letter *Y*.

LANGUAGE OBJECTIVE: Produce the sound for the letter *Y* when shown a visual grapheme.

Lesson Overview

Introduce the letter sound, play a game to practice identifying the letter sound, and assess students' ability to associate a specific letter sound with a specific letter.

Materials	Preparation
• Letter and Picture Cards for *Y* • Letter and Picture Cards for *J* • Small, soft ball or toy	• Cut out all letter and picture cards.

Teach and Model

Show students the upper- and lowercase letter cards for *Y*.

Say: ***This is* Y. *The letter* Y *stands for the sound /y/. Make the sound with me: /y/.*** Have students produce the sound with you.

Point to the letter card.

Say: ***Make the sound for this letter every time I put my finger on it.*** Have students produce the sound. Point to the card several times. Mix up the practice by asking individual students to say the sound.

Hold up a picture card.

Say: ***This word is* yarn. *It begins with the letter sound /y/. What is this?*** Have students repeat the name of the picture.

Say: ***What letter sound does* yarn *begin with?*** Have students produce the */y/* sound independently.

Repeat questions above with each picture card for */y/*.

Picture cards for /y/: yarn, yolk, yam, yo-yo, yawn, yak, year, yogurt

Connect Sound/Spelling: Thumbs Up, Thumbs Down for Beginning Sounds

Say: ***Show me thumbs up.*** Model what thumbs up looks like and help students show their thumbs up.

Explain: ***When you hear a word that begins with the letter sound /y/, make a thumbs up and say the letter sound. If the word doesn't start with the letter sound /y/, give me a thumbs down.*** Model thumbs down for students and help students show their thumbs down.

Say each word from the word bank below, alternating between words that begin with */y/* and words that don't.

Words that begin with /y/: yodel, yardstick, young, yellow, yacht, yearbook, yummy, yard, yell, yield, yoga, you

Words that don't begin with /y/: six, next, label, twist

EXTENSION ACTIVITY: Ask students to think of other words that begin with */y/*.

Connect Sound/Spelling: Letter Sound Toss

Show the ball and the letter cards.

Explain: ***When I toss this ball to you, say the letter sound /y/ twice. Then say a word that begins with that letter sound and toss the ball to a classmate.***

Model: **/y/, /y/, yarn.** Demonstrate the sequence with a volunteer.

Toss the ball to a student. Provide prompts as needed (e.g., What is the yellow part of the egg that starts with */y/*?). Continue until all students have had several turns.

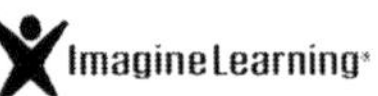

Prompt as needed using words from the word bank.

Word bank: yarn, yolk, yam, yo-yo, yawn, yak, year, yogurt, yard, yellow, young, you, yo-yo

Check Progress: Letter Stack

Observe each student during practice and use the following activity to check progress on the target skill. If student can correctly identify the letter sound twice, consider the intervention successful.

Point to the appropriate letter card as you say the sound.

Say: ***Repeat the letter sounds for these letters: /y/, /y/, /j/, /j/.***

Shuffle letter cards for *Y* and *J* together in a stack.

Say: ***Choose a card and tell me the letter sound.***

Have students draw a card from the stack, say the sound, and put the card on the bottom of the stack. Repeat until every student has had several opportunities to demonstrate knowledge of the target letter sound */y/*.

Reteaching Lessons

J
j
S

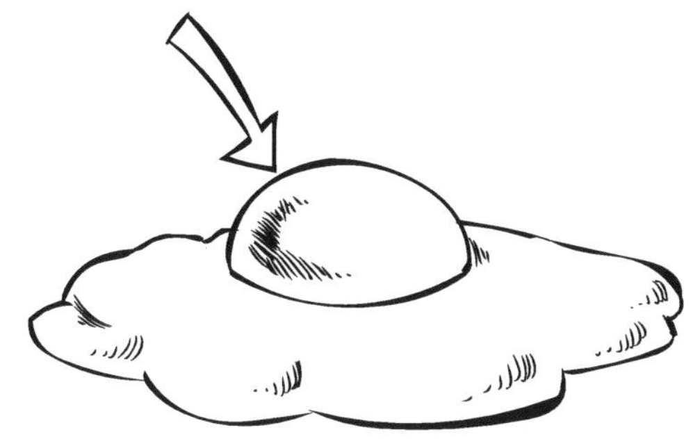
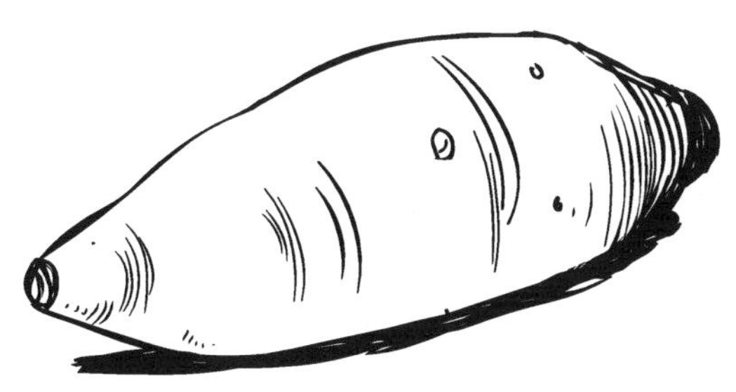

Reteaching Lessons ✓

Letter Sounds

The Sound for W Is /w/

Grade K

10 Min.

CCSS.RF.K.3a
TEKS 110.11.3.A

LEARNING OBJECTIVE: Demonstrate letter-sound correspondence by producing the most common sound for the letter *W*.

LANGUAGE OBJECTIVE: Produce the sound for the letter *W* when shown a visual grapheme.

Lesson Overview

Introduce the letter sound, play a game to practice identifying the letter sound, and assess students' ability to associate a specific letter sound with a specific letter.

Materials	Preparation
• Letter and Picture Cards for *W* • Letter and Picture Cards for *Z* • Paper bag	• Cut out all letter and picture cards.

Teach and Model

Show students the upper- and lowercase letter cards for *W*.

Say: ***This is* W. *The letter* W *stands for the sound /w/. Make the sound with me: /w/.*** Have students produce the sound with you.

Point to the letter card.

Say: ***Make the sound for this letter every time I put my finger on it.*** Have students produce the sound. Point to the card several times. Mix up the practice by asking individual students to say the sound.

Hold up a picture card.

Say: ***This word is* wig. *It begins with the letter sound /w/. What is this?*** Have students repeat the name of the picture.

Say: ***What letter sound does* wig *begin with?*** Have students produce the /*w*/ sound independently.

Repeat questions above with each picture card for /*w*/.

Picture cards for /w/: wig, window, wolf, worm, walrus, watermelon, web, wagon

Connect Sound/Spelling: Letter Sound Bag

Put all letter and picture cards for *W* in the paper bag.

Explain: ***The pictures on these cards start with /w/. If you pull a letter card from the bag, tell me the letter sound. Then tell me a word that starts with that letter sound.***

Model: ***If I pull out* water, *I say /w/, /w/,* water.**

Explain: ***If you pull a picture card, tell me the letter sound it starts with and what the picture is.***

Model: ***If I pull out a picture of a* worm, *I say /w/, /w/,* worm.**

Have students take turns drawing cards from the paper bag.

Word bank: water, walnut, warm, watch, wave, weather, wet, work, wash, win, word, want

Connect Sound/Spelling: Animal Safari

Show the letter cards.

Explain: ***We are going on an animal safari. When you hear an animal name that starts with the letter sound /w/, stand up. Say the letter sound and the name of the animal. If the animal name doesn't start with /w/, sit down.***

Ask: ***How about* walrus?** Students should stand up.

Say: ***Yes!* Walrus *has /w/ at the beginning, so you stand up. Let's try another one:* eagle.** Students should sit down.

Say: ***Good!* Eagle *doesn't begin with the /w/ sound, so you sit down.***

Alternate between animal names that begin with */w/* and those that don't.

Words that begin with /w/: walrus, warthog, wasp, weasel, wolf, woodpecker, worm

Words that don't begin with /w/: dog, camel, horse, alligator

EXTENSION ACTIVITY: Ask students to think of other words that begin with */w/*.

Check Progress: Letter Flip

Observe each student during practice and use the following activity to check progress on the target skill. If student can correctly identify the letter sound twice, consider the intervention successful.

Point to the appropriate letter card as you say the sound.

Say: ***Repeat the letter sounds for these letters: /w/, /z/.***

Put all the flash cards face down on the table and mix them up.

Say: ***Choose a card and tell me the letter sound.***

Have students choose a card and say the sound, mixing the cards between student turns. Give every student a turn, repeating until each student has had the opportunity to demonstrate knowledge on the target letter sound */w/.*

Reteaching Lessons

The Sound for Z Is /z/

Grade K | 10 Min. | CCSS.RF.K.3a TEKS 110.11.3.A

LEARNING OBJECTIVE: Demonstrate letter-sound correspondence by producing the most common sound for the letter *Z*.

LANGUAGE OBJECTIVE: Produce the sound for the letter *Z* when shown a visual grapheme.

Lesson Overview

Introduce the letter sound, play a game to practice identifying the letter sound, and assess students' ability to associate a specific letter sound with a specific letter.

Materials	Preparation
• Letter and Picture Cards for *Z* • Letter and Picture Cards for *W*	• Cut out all letter and picture cards.

Teach and Model

Show students the upper- and lowercase letter cards for *Z*.

Say: ***This is* Z*. The letter* Z *stands for the sound /z/. Make the sound with me: /z/.*** Have students produce the sound with you.

Point to the letter card.

Say: ***Make the sound for this letter every time I put my finger on it.*** Have students produce the sound. Point to the card several times. Mix up the practice by asking individual students to say the sound.

Hold up a picture card.

Say: ***This word is* zebra*. It begins with the letter sound /z/. What is this?*** Have students repeat the name of the picture.

Say: ***What letter sound does* zebra *begin with?*** Have students produce the /z/ sound independently.

Repeat questions above with each picture card for /z/.

Picture cards for /z/: zebra, zipper, zoo, zero, zucchini, zig-zag, zone, zeppelin

Connect Sound/Spelling: Letter Sound Sort

Shuffle picture cards for *Z* and *W* together. Display letter cards for *Z* on a table, allowing enough space for a column of picture cards below the letter cards. Display letter cards for *W* next to the letter cards for *Z*.

Say: ***This is letter* W*.* W *stands for the sound /w/. Everyone say /w/.*** Have students produce the sound.

Show the stack of picture cards.

Explain: ***The pictures on these cards begin with the letter sound /z/ or /w/. We are going to put them with their matching letter.***

Show the first picture card.

Demonstrate: **Zebra*. This picture begins with the letter sound /z/: /z/, /z/,* zebra*. Say /z/, /z/,* zebra.** Have students repeat the sound and word.

Demonstrate: **Zebra *goes with this card, /z/.*** Place the picture card below the letter cards for *Z*.

Have students draw the remaining picture cards from the stack and place them in a column under the matching letter card. As each card is added, direct students to say the letter sound twice and then name the picture: /z/, /z/, zipper; /w/, /w/, wig.

Picture cards for /w/: window. wolf, worm, walrus, watermelon, web, wagon, wig

EXTENSION ACTIVITY: Randomly point to pictures in the two columns and instruct students to repeat the letter sound and name the picture.

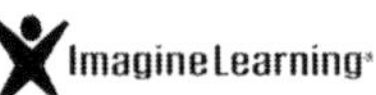

Connect Sound/Spelling: Thumbs Up, Thumbs Down for Ending Sounds

Say: ***Show me thumbs up.*** Model what thumbs up looks like and help students show their thumbs up.

Explain: ***When you hear a word that ends with the letter sound /z/, use your thumbs up sign. If the word doesn't end with the /z/ sound, give me the thumbs down sign.*** Model thumbs down for students and help students show their thumbs down.

Say each word from the word bank below, alternating between words that end in /z/ and words that don't.

Words that end with /z/: jazz, buzz, fuzz, quiz, whiz, fizz, waltz, frizz, razz, fez

Words that don't end with /z/: moth, flip, car, kit, swan, rope

Check Progress: Letter Stack

Observe each student during practice and use the following activity to check progress on the target skill. If student can correctly identify the letter sound twice, consider the intervention successful.

Point to the appropriate letter card as you say the sound.

Say: ***Repeat the letter sounds for these letters: /z/, /z/, /w/, /w/.***

Shuffle letter cards for *Z* and *W* together in a stack.

Say: ***Choose a card and tell me the letter sound.***

Have students draw a card from the stack, say the sound, and put the card on the bottom of the stack. Repeat until every student has had several opportunities to demonstrate knowledge of the target letter sound /z/.

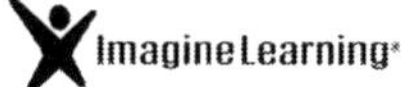

W

w

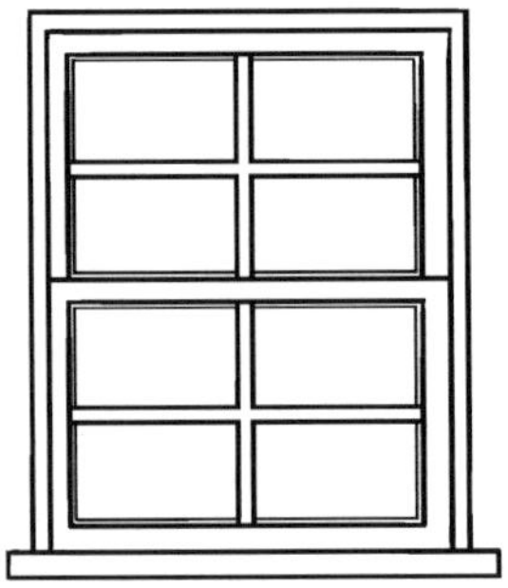

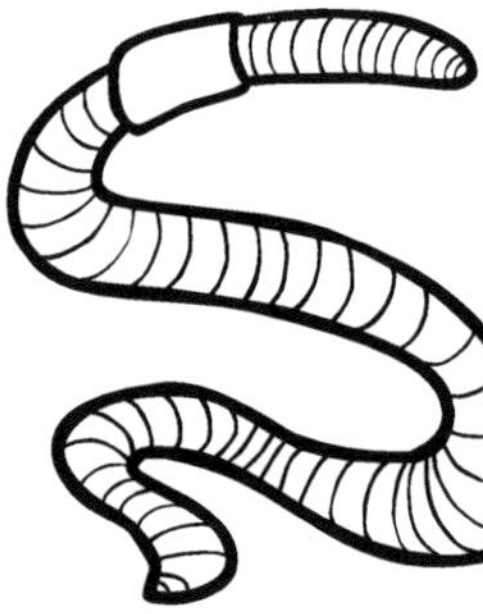

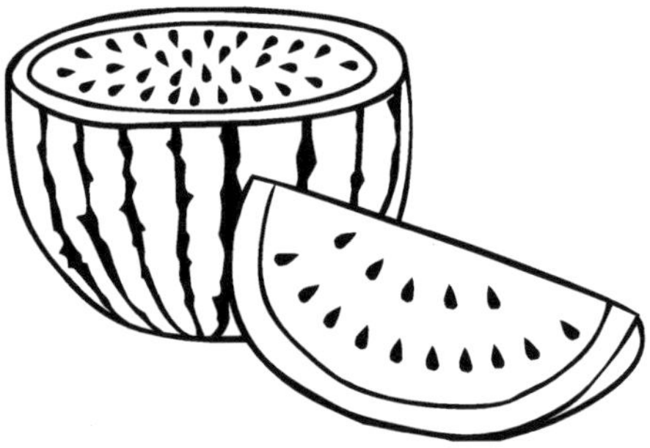

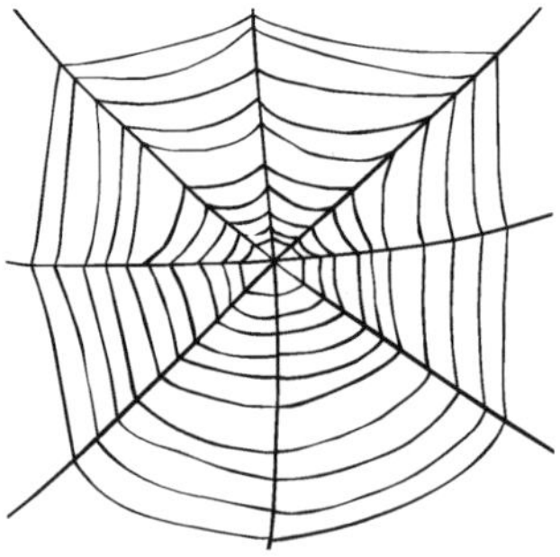

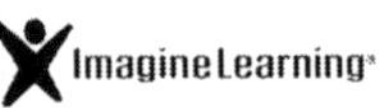

Z

z

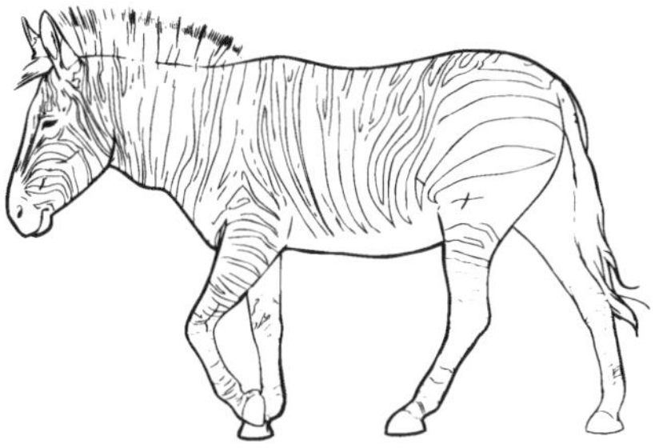

0

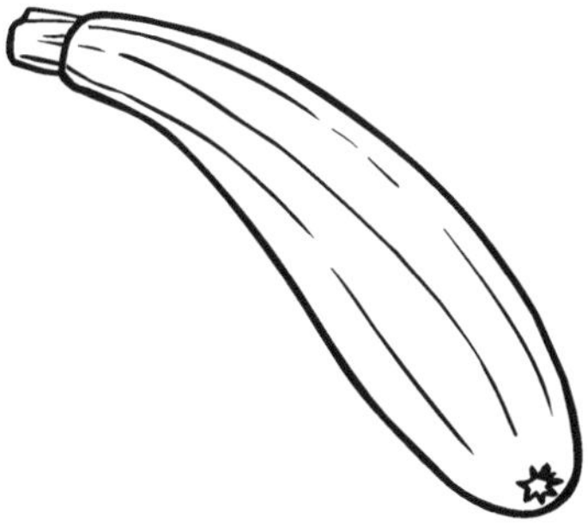

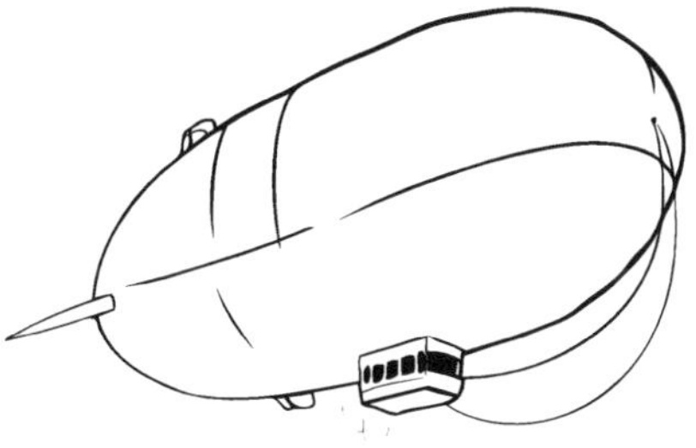

zone

The Sound for Q Is /kw/

Grade K

10 Min.

CCSS.RF.K.3a
TEKS 110.11.3.A

LEARNING OBJECTIVE: Demonstrate letter-sound correspondence by producing the most common sound for the letter Q.

LANGUAGE OBJECTIVE: Produce the sound for the letter Q when shown a visual grapheme.

Lesson Overview

Introduce the letter sound, play a game to practice identifying the letter sound, and assess students' ability to associate a specific letter sound with a specific letter.

Materials	Preparation
• Letter and Picture Cards for *Q* • Letter and Picture Cards for *X* • Small, soft ball or toy	• Cut out all letter and picture cards.

Teach and Model

Show students the upper- and lowercase letter cards for Q.

Say: ***This is Q. The letter Q stands for the sound /kw/. Make the sound with me: /kw/.*** Have students produce the sound with you.

Point to the letter card.

Say: ***Make the sound for this letter every time I put my finger on it.*** Have students produce the sound. Point to the card several times. Mix up the practice by asking individual students to say the sound.

Hold up a picture card.

Say: ***This word is* quilt. *It begins with the letter sound /kw/. What is this?*** Have students repeat the name of the picture.

Say: ***What letter sound does* quilt *begin with?*** Have students produce the */kw/* sound independently.

Repeat questions above with each picture card for */kw/*.

Picture cards for /kw/: quilt, queen, quarter, question, quail, quiet, quiz, quack

Connect Sound/Spelling: Thumbs Up, Thumbs Down for Beginning Sounds

Say: ***Show me thumbs up.*** Model what thumbs up looks like and help students show their thumbs up.

Explain: ***When you hear a word that begins with the letter sound /kw/, make a thumbs up and say the letter sound. If the word doesn't start with the letter sound /kw/, give me a thumbs down.*** Model thumbs down for students and help students show their thumbs down.

Say each word from the word bank below, alternating between words that begin with */kw/* and words that don't.

Words that begin with /kw/: quicksand, quality, quick, quit, queen, quarter, question

Words that don't begin with /kw/: kite, seal, rain, crunch

EXTENSION ACTIVITY: Ask students to think of other words that begin with */kw/*.

Connect Sound/Spelling: Letter Sound Toss

Show the ball and the letter cards.

Explain: ***When I toss this ball to you, say the letter sound /kw/ twice. Then say a word that begins with that letter sound and toss the ball to a classmate.***

Model: **/kw/, /kw/, quack.** Demonstrate the sequence with a volunteer.

Toss the ball to a student. Provide prompts as needed (e.g., What sound does a duck make?). Continue until all students have had several turns.

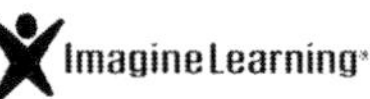

Prompt as needed using words from the word bank.

Word bank: queen, quack, quick, quite, quart, quiet, quail, quote, quiz, quarter, question

Check Progress: Letter Flip

Observe each student during practice and use the following activity to check progress on the target skill. If student can correctly identify the letter sound twice, consider the intervention successful.

Point to the appropriate letter card as you say the sound.

Say: ***Repeat the letter sounds for these letters: /kw/, /ks/.***

Put all the flash cards face down on the table and mix them up.

Say: ***Choose a card and tell me the letter sound.***

Have students choose a card and say the sound, mixing the cards between student turns. Give every student a turn, repeating until each student has had the opportunity to demonstrate knowledge on the target letter sound */kw/*.

The Sound for X Is /ks/

LEARNING OBJECTIVE: Demonstrate letter-sound correspondence by producing the most common sound for the letter *X*.

LANGUAGE OBJECTIVE: Produce the sound for the letter *X* when shown a visual grapheme.

Lesson Overview

Introduce the letter sound, play a game to practice identifying the letter sound, and assess students' ability to associate a specific letter sound with a specific letter.

Materials	Preparation
• Letter and Picture Cards for *X* • Letter and Picture Cards for *Q* • Paper bag	• Cut out all letter and picture cards.

Teach and Model

Show students the upper- and lowercase letter cards for *X*.

Say: ***This is* X. *The letter* X *stands for the sound /ks/. Make the sound with me: /ks/.*** Have students produce the sound with you.

Point to the letter card.

Say: ***Make the sound for this letter every time I put my finger on it.*** Have students produce the sound. Point to the card several times. Mix up the practice by asking individual students to say the sound.

Hold up a picture card.

Say: ***This word is* box. *It begins with the letter sound /ks/. What is this?*** Have students repeat the name of the picture.

Say: ***What letter sound does* box *begin with?*** Have students produce the */ks/* sound independently.

Repeat questions above with each picture card for */ks/*.

Picture cards for /ks/: box, fox, six, wax, fix, mix, axe, tux

Connect Sound/Spelling: Letter Sound Bag

Put all letter and picture cards for *X* in the paper bag.

Explain: ***The pictures on these cards end with /ks/. If you pull a letter card from the bag, tell me the letter sound. Then tell me a word that ends with that letter sound.***

Model: ***If I pull out* box*, I say /ks/, /ks/,* box.**

Explain: ***If you pull a picture card, tell me the letter sound it ends with and what the picture is.***

Model: ***If I pull out a picture of a fox, I say /ks/, /ks/,* fox.**

Have students take turns drawing cards from the paper bag.

Word bank: box, fox, six, wax, fix, mix, axe, tux

Connect Sound/Spelling: Thumbs Up, Thumbs Down for Ending Sounds

Say: ***Show me thumbs up.*** Model what thumbs up looks like and help students show their thumbs up.

Explain: ***When you hear a word that ends with the letter sound /ks/, use your thumbs up sign. If the word doesn't end with the /ks/ sound, give me the thumbs down sign.*** Model thumbs down for students and help students show their thumbs down.

Say each word from the word bank below, alternating between words that end in */ks/* and words that don't.

Words that end with /ks/: box, mix, wax, six, tux, sandbox, reflex, tax, relax, toolbox, lunchbox, duplex

Words that don't end with /ks/: car, goat, desk, finish, radio

Check Progress: Letter Stack

Observe each student during practice and use the following activity to check progress on the target skill. If student can correctly identify the letter sound twice, consider the intervention successful.

Point to the appropriate letter card as you say the sound.

Say: ***Repeat the letter sounds for these letters: /ks/, /ks/, /kw/, /kw/.***

Shuffle letter cards for *X* and Q together in a stack.

Say: ***Choose a card and tell me the letter sound.***

Have students draw a card from the stack, say the sound, and put the card on the bottom of the stack. Repeat until every student has had several opportunities to demonstrate knowledge of the target letter sound */ks/*.

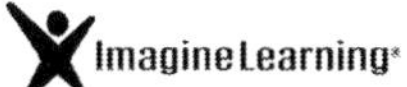

Q	q

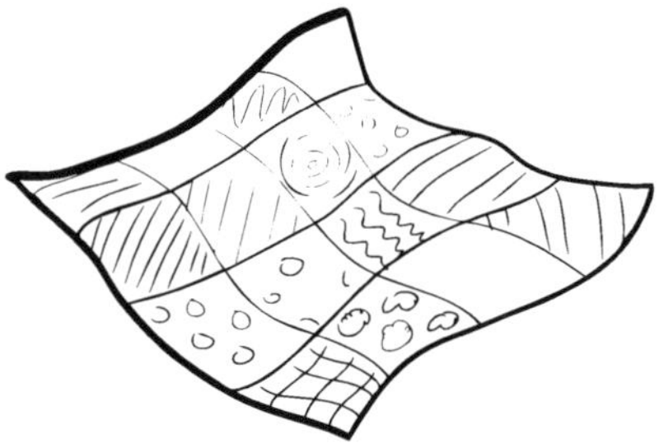

Reteaching Lessons

Letter and Picture Cards for Q

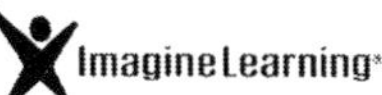

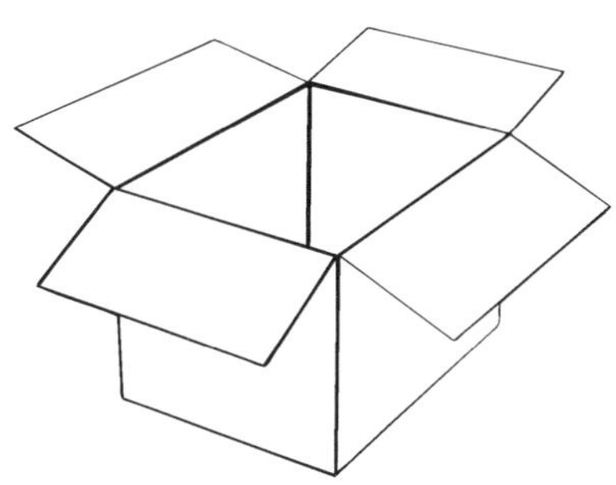

6

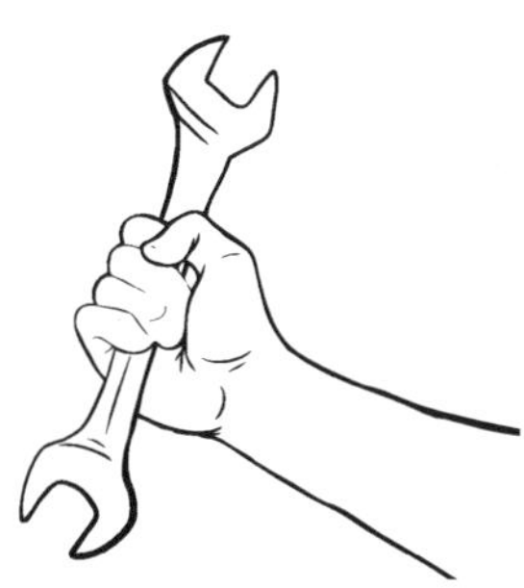

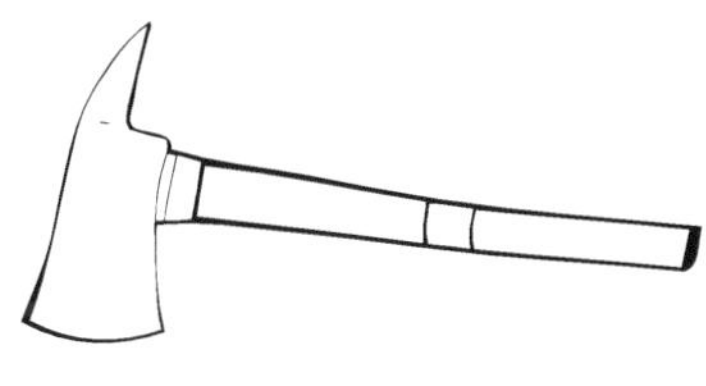

Reteaching Lessons

The Sound for br Is /br/

LEARNING OBJECTIVE: Demonstrate letter-sound correspondence by blending two consonant sounds.

LANGUAGE OBJECTIVE: Produce the sounds in a consonant blend when shown a visual grapheme.

Lesson Overview

Introduce the consonant blend, play a game to practice identifying the consonant blend, and assess students' ability to associate a consonant blend with a specific letter combination.

Materials	Preparation
• Letter and Picture Cards for *br* • Letter and Picture Cards for *sl*	• Cut out all letter and picture cards

Teach and Model

Show students the upper- and lowercase letter cards for *br*.

Say: ***This is /br/. The letters* b *and* r *blend together to stand for the sound /br/. Make the blend with me: /br/***. Have students produce the sound with you.

Point to the letter card.

Say: ***Make the blend /br/ every time I put my finger on it.*** Have students produce the sound. Point to the card several times. Mix up the practice by asking individual students to say the sound.

Hold up a picture card.

Say: ***This word is* broom*. It begins with the blend /br/. What is this?*** Have students repeat the name of the picture.

Say: ***What sound does* broom *begin with?*** Have students produce the */br/* sound independently.

Repeat questions above with each picture card for */br/*.

Picture cards for /br/: bread, broccoli, bridge, brush, broom, brain, broken, bride

Connect Sound/Spelling: Letter Sound Sort

Shuffle picture cards for *br* and *sl* together. Display letter cards for *br* on a table, allowing enough space for a column of picture cards below the letter cards. Display letter cards for *sl* next to the letter cards for *br*.

Say: ***This is letter* sl*.* Sl *stands for the sound /sl/. Everyone say /sl/.*** Have students produce the sound.

Show the stack of picture cards.

Explain: ***The pictures on these cards begin with the letter sound /br/ or /sl/. We are going to put them with their matching letter.***

Show the first picture card.

Demonstrate: **Brain.** ***This picture begins with the letter sound /br/: /br/, /br/,* brain*. Say /br/, /br/,* brain.** Have students repeat the sound and word.

Demonstrate: **Brain *goes with this card, /br/.*** Place the picture card below the letter cards for *br*.

Have students draw the remaining picture cards from the stack and place them in a column under the matching letter card. As each card is added, direct students to say the letter sound twice and then name the picture: */br/*, */br/*, bread; */sl/*, */sl/*, sled.

Picture cards for /sl/: sled, sleep, slide, slippers, sleet, slow, sloth, slug

EXTENSION ACTIVITY: Randomly point to pictures in the two columns and instruct students to repeat the letter sound and name the picture.

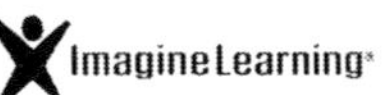

Connect Sound/Spelling: Thumbs Up, Thumbs Down for Beginning Sounds

Say: ***Show me thumbs up.*** Model what thumbs up looks like and help students show their thumbs up.

Explain: ***When you hear a word that begins with the blend /br/, make a thumbs up and say the blend. If the word doesn't start with the blend /br/, give me a thumbs down.*** Model thumbs down for students and help students show their thumbs down.

Say each word from the word bank below, alternating between words that begin with */br/* and words that don't.

Words that begin with /br/: brush, broom, blanket, braces, breath, breeze, bright, broken, brown, brain, brick, bridge, bride, brother

Words that don't begin with /br/: spider, guitar, banana, kitten

EXTENSION ACTIVITY: Ask students to think of other words that start with */br/*.

Check Progress: Letter Stack

Observe each student during practice and use the following activity to check progress on the target skill. If student can correctly identify the blend twice, consider the intervention successful.

Point to the appropriate letter card as you say the sound.

Say: ***Repeat the blends for these letters: /br/, /br/, /sl/, /sl/.***

Shuffle letter cards for *br* and *sl* together in a stack.

Say: ***Choose a card and tell me the blend.***

Have students draw a card from the stack, say the sound, and put the card on the bottom of the stack. Repeat until every student has had several opportunities to demonstrate knowledge of the target blend */br/*.

The Sound for sl Is /sl/

Grade K

10 Min.

CCSS.RF.K.3a
TEKS 110.11.3.A

LEARNING OBJECTIVE: Demonstrate letter-sound correspondence by blending two consonant sounds.

LANGUAGE OBJECTIVE: Produce the sounds in a consonant blend when shown a visual grapheme.

Lesson Overview

Introduce the consonant blend, play a game to practice identifying the consonant blend, and assess students' ability to associate a consonant blend with a specific letter combination.

Materials	Preparation
• Letter and Picture Cards for *sl* • Letter and Picture Cards for *br*	• Cut out all letter and picture cards.

Teach and Model

Show students the upper- and lowercase letter cards for *sl*.

Say: ***This is /sl/. The letters* s *and* l *blend together to stand for the sound /sl/. Make the blend with me: /sl/*.** Have students produce the sound with you.

Point to the letter card.

Say: ***Make the blend /sl/ every time I put my finger on it.*** Have students produce the sound. Point to the card several times. Mix up the practice by asking individual students to say the sound.

Hold up a picture card.

Say: ***This word is* sled*. It begins with the blend /sl/. What is this?*** Have students repeat the name of the picture.

Say: ***What sound does* sled *begin with?*** Have students produce the */sl/* sound independently.

Repeat questions above with each picture card for */sl/*.

Picture cards for /sl/: sled, sleep, slide, slippers, slip, slow, sloth, slug

Connect Sound/Spelling: Letter Sound Sort

Shuffle picture cards for *sl* and *br* together. Display letter cards for *sl* on a table, allowing enough space for a column of picture cards below the letter cards. Display letter cards for *br* next to the letter cards for *sl*.

Say: ***These are the letters* b *and* r*.* Br *stands for the sound /br/. Everyone say /br/.*** Have students produce the sound.

Show the stack of picture cards.

Explain: ***The pictures on these cards begin with the letter sound /sl/ or /br/. We are going to put them with their matching letter.***

Show the first picture card.

Demonstrate: **Sloth*. This picture begins with the letter sound /sl/: /sl/, /sl/,* sloth*. Say /sl/, /sl/,* sloth*.*** Have students repeat the sound and word.

Demonstrate: **Sloth *goes with this card, /sl/.*** Place the picture card below the letter cards for *sl*.

Have students draw the remaining picture cards from the stack and place them in a column under the matching letter card. As each card is added, direct students to say the letter sound twice and then name the picture: */sl/*, */sl/*, sled; */br/*, */br/*, bread.

Picture cards for /br/: bread, broccoli, bridge, brush, broom, briefcase, broken, bride

EXTENSION ACTIVITY: Randomly point to pictures in the two columns and instruct students to repeat the letter sound and name the picture.

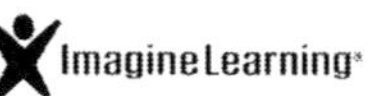

Connect Sound/Spelling: Thumbs Up, Thumbs Down for Beginning Sounds

Say: ***Show me thumbs up.*** Model what thumbs up looks like and help students show their thumbs up.

Explain: ***When you hear a word that begins with the blend /sl/, make a thumbs up and say the blend. If the word doesn't start with the blend /sl/, give me a thumbs down.*** Model thumbs down for students and help students show their thumbs down.

Say each word from the word bank below, alternating between words that begin with */sl/* and words that don't.

Words that begin with /sl/: sled, sleep, slime, slow, slush, slop, slide, slippers, slip

Words that don't begin with /sl/: puzzle, rug, six, bear

EXTENSION ACTIVITY: Ask students to think of other words that begin with /sl/.

Check Progress: Letter Stack

Observe each student during practice and use the following activity to check progress on the target skill. If student can correctly identify the blend twice, consider the intervention successful.

Point to the appropriate letter card as you say the sound.

Say: ***Repeat the blends for these letters: /sl/, /sl/, /br/, /br/.***

Shuffle letter cards for *sl* and *br* together in a stack.

Say: ***Choose a card and tell me the blend.***

Have students draw a card from the stack, say the sound, and put the card on the bottom of the stack. Repeat until every student has had several opportunities to demonstrate knowledge of the target blend */sl/*.

Reteaching Lessons

Br	br
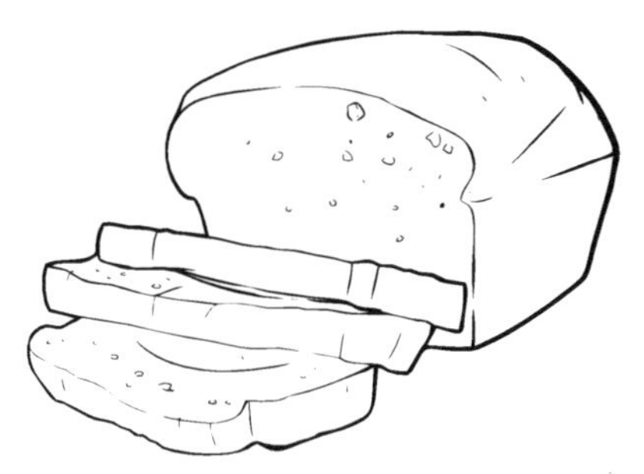	
	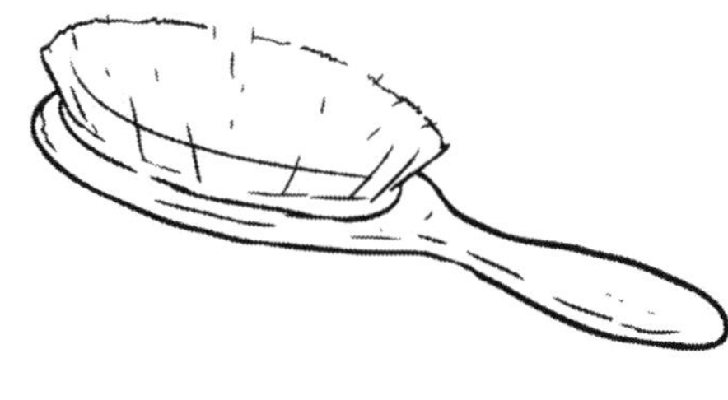
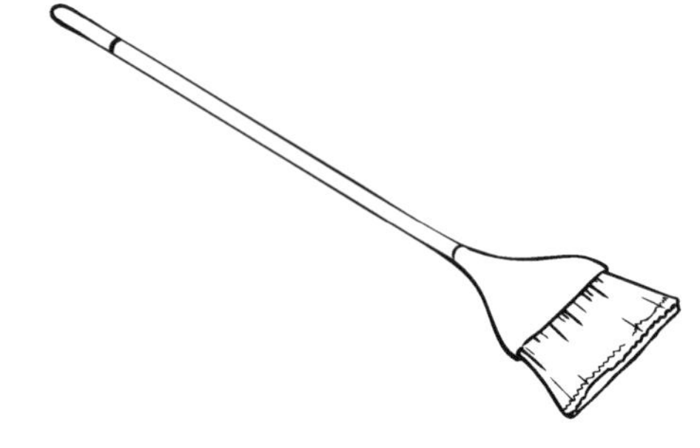	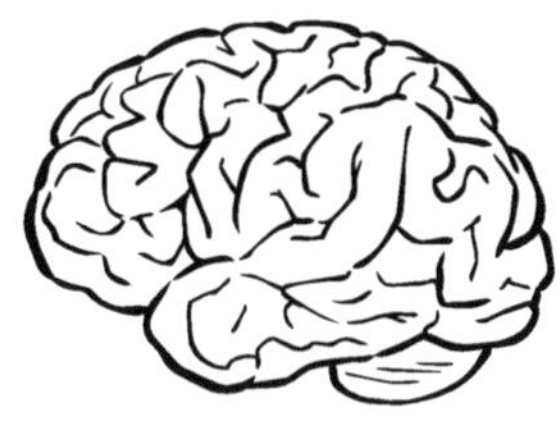
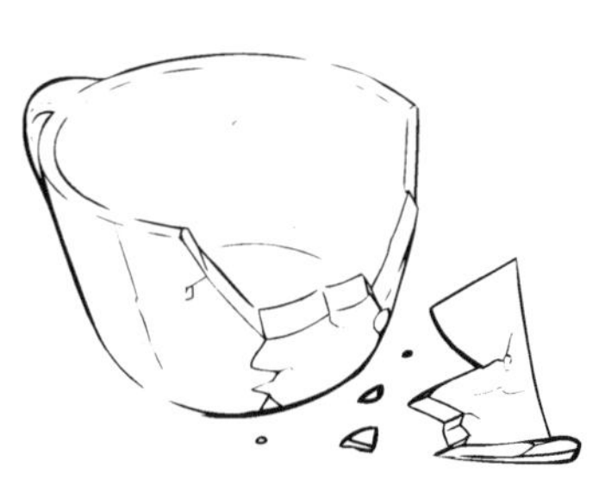	

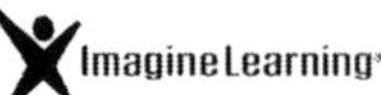

Sl	sl
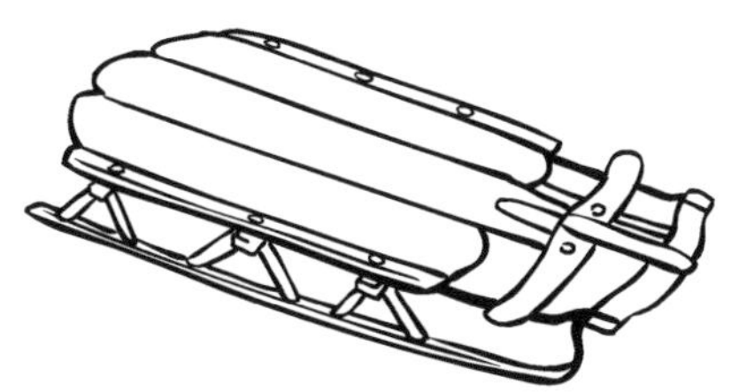	
	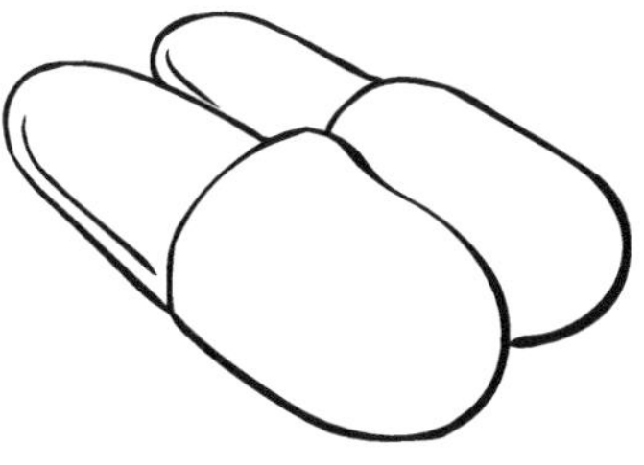

Reteaching Lessons

The Sound for bl Is /bl/

Grade K

10 Min.

CCSS.RF.K.3a
TEKS 110.11.3.A

LEARNING OBJECTIVE: Demonstrate letter-sound correspondence by blending two consonant sounds.

LANGUAGE OBJECTIVE: Produce the sounds in a consonant blend when shown a visual grapheme.

Lesson Overview

Introduce the consonant blend, play a game to practice identifying the consonant blend, and assess students' ability to associate a consonant blend with a specific letter combination.

Materials	Preparation
• Letter and Picture Cards for *bl* • Letter and Picture Cards for *dr* • Paper bag	• Cut out all letter and picture cards.

Teach and Model

Show students the upper- and lowercase letter cards for *bl*.

Say: ***This is /bl/. The letters* b *and* l *blend together to stand for the sound /bl/. Make the blend with me: /bl/.*** Have students produce the sound with you.

Point to the letter card.

Say: ***Make the blend /bl/ every time I put my finger on it.*** Have students produce the sound. Point to the card several times. Mix up the practice by asking individual students to say the sound.

Hold up a picture card.

Say: ***This word is* blimp. *It begins with the blend /bl/. What is this?*** Have students repeat the name of the picture.

Say: ***What sound does* blimp *begin with?*** Have students produce the */bl/* sound independently.

Repeat questions above with each picture card for */bl/*.

Picture cards for /bl/: block, bleach, blow-dryer, blimp, blanket, blueberry, blueprint, blind

Connect Sound/Spelling: Thumbs Up, Thumbs Down for Beginning Sounds

Say: ***Show me thumbs up.*** Model what thumbs up looks like and help students show their thumbs up.

Explain: ***When you hear a word that begins with the blend /bl/, make a thumbs up and say the blend. If the word doesn't start with the blend /bl/, give me a thumbs down.*** Model thumbs down for students and help students show their thumbs down.

Say each word from the word bank below, alternating between words that begin with */bl/* and words that don't.

Words that begin with /bl/: bleach, blow-dryer, blimp, block, blade, blanket, blind, blister, blood, black, blue

Words that don't begin with /bl/: muffin, duck, ring, bird, rocket

EXTENSION ACTIVITY: Ask students to think of other words that start with */bl/*.

Connect Sound/Spelling: Letter Sound Bag

Put all letter and picture cards for *bl* in the paper bag.

Explain: ***The pictures on these cards start with /bl/. If you pull a letter card from the bag, tell me the blend. Then tell me a word that starts with that blend.***

Model: ***If I pull out* blue, *I say /bl/, /bl/, blue.***

Explain: ***If you pull a picture card, tell me the blend it starts with and what the picture is.***

Model: ***If I pull out a picture of a blimp, I say /bl/, /bl/, blimp.***

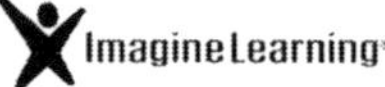

Have students take turns drawing cards from the paper bag.

Word bank: blue, black, bloom, blond, blinds, blood, blink, blubber

Check Progress: Letter Flip

Observe each student during practice and use the following activity to check progress on the target skill. If student can correctly identify the blend twice, consider the intervention successful.

Point to the appropriate letter card as you say the sound.

Say: ***Repeat the blends for these letters: /bl/, /sl/.***

Put all the flash cards face down on the table and mix them up.

Say: ***Choose a card and tell me the blend.***

Have students choose a card and say the sound, mixing the cards between student turns. Give every student a turn, repeating until each student has had the opportunity to demonstrate knowledge on the target blend */bl/*.

Letter Sounds

The Sound for dr Is /dr/

Grade K

10 Min.

CCSS.RF.K.3a
TEKS 110.11.3.A

LEARNING OBJECTIVE: Demonstrate letter-sound correspondence by blending two consonant sounds.

LANGUAGE OBJECTIVE: Produce the sounds in a consonant blend when shown a visual grapheme.

Lesson Overview

Introduce the consonant blend, play a game to practice identifying the consonant blend, and assess students' ability to associate a consonant blend with a specific letter combination.

Materials	Preparation
• Letter and Picture Cards for *dr* • Letter and Picture Cards for *bl*	• Cut out all letter and picture cards.

Teach and Model

Show students the upper- and lowercase letter cards for *dr*.

Say: ***This is /dr/. The letters* d *and* r *blend together to stand for the sound /dr/. Make the blend with me: /dr/***. Have students produce the sound with you.

Point to the letter card.

Say: ***Make the blend /dr/ every time I put my finger on it.*** Have students produce the sound. Point to the card several times. Mix up the practice by asking individual students to say the sound.

Hold up a picture card.

Say: ***This word is* drum. *It begins with the blend /dr/. What is this?*** Have students repeat the name of the picture.

Say: ***What sound does* drum *begin with?*** Have students produce the */dr/* sound independently.

Repeat questions above with each picture card for */dr/*.

Picture cards for /dr/: dragonfly, dress, drum, drink, dresser, dream, drawer, drill

Connect Sound/Spelling: Letter Sound Sort

Shuffle picture cards for *dr* and */bl/* together. Display letter cards for *dr* on a table, allowing enough space for a column of picture cards below the letter cards. Display letter cards for *bl* next to the letter cards for *dr*.

Say: ***These are the letters* b and l. */bl/ stands for the sound /bl/. Everyone say /bl/.*** Have students produce the sound.

Show the stack of picture cards.

Explain: ***The pictures on these cards begin with the letter sound /dr/ or /bl/. We are going to put them with their matching letter.***

Show the first picture card.

Demonstrate: **Drum*. This picture begins with the letter sound /dr/: /dr/, /dr/,* drum*. Say /dr/, /dr/,* drum.** Have students repeat the sound and word.

Demonstrate: **Drum *goes with this card, /dr/.*** Place the picture card below the letter cards for *dr*.

Have students draw the remaining picture cards from the stack and place them in a column under the matching letter card. As each card is added, direct students to say the letter sound twice and then name the picture: */dr/*, */dr/*, drink; */bl/*, */bl/*, block.

Picture cards for /bl/: block, bleach, blow-dryer, blimp, blanket, blueberry, blueprint, blush

EXTENSION ACTIVITY: Randomly point to pictures in the two columns and instruct students to repeat the letter sound and name the picture.

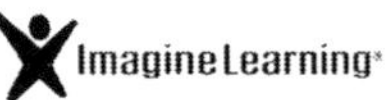

Connect Sound/Spelling: Letter Sound Luggage

Show the letter cards.

Say: ***Let's pretend we are packing for a trip. Everything we take on the trip will start with the blend /dr/.***

Model: ***I'm going on a trip and I'm going to pack* a dress and a drink.**

Ask: ***What else can we pack that starts with the blend /dr/?*** Have students respond. Show flash cards or provide prompts as necessary (e.g., What do you put your clothes in that starts with /dr/?).

Word bank: dresser, drawer, drumstick, drill, drum, dragon, drapes, dream, dragonfly, drink, dryer, drawing

Check Progress: Letter Flip

Observe each student during practice and use the following activity to check progress on the target skill. If student can correctly identify the blend twice, consider the intervention successful.

Point to the appropriate letter card as you say the sound.

Say: ***Repeat the blends for these letters: /dr/, /bl/.***

Put all the flash cards face down on the table and mix them up.

Say: ***Choose a card and tell me the blend.***

Have students choose a card and say the sound, mixing the cards between student turns. Give every student a turn, repeating until each student has had the opportunity to demonstrate knowledge on the target blend */dr/*.

Reteaching Lessons

Bl	bl

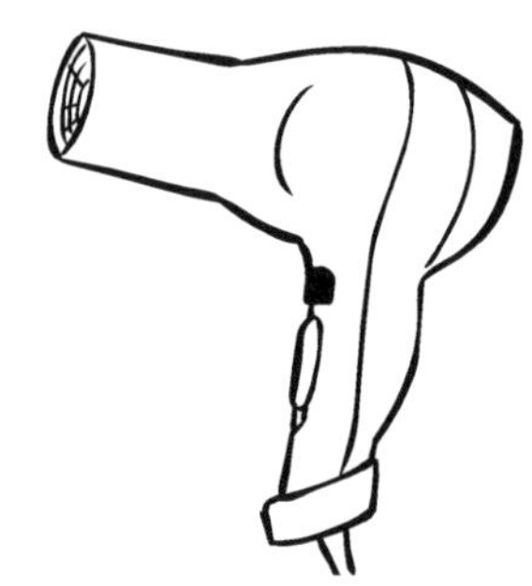	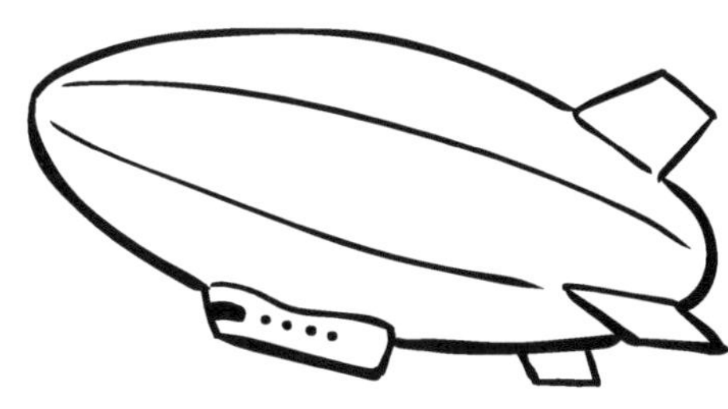
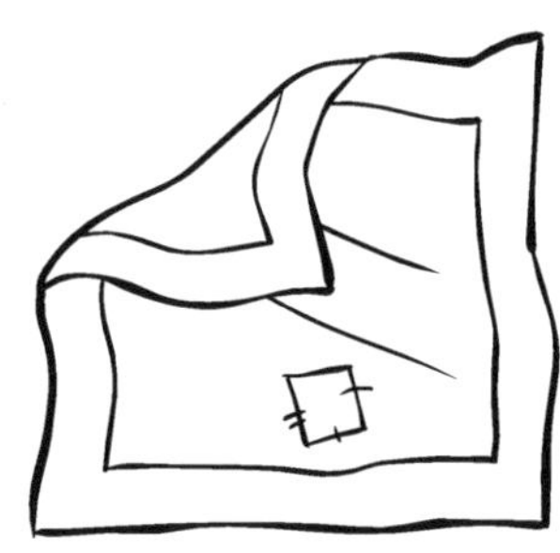	
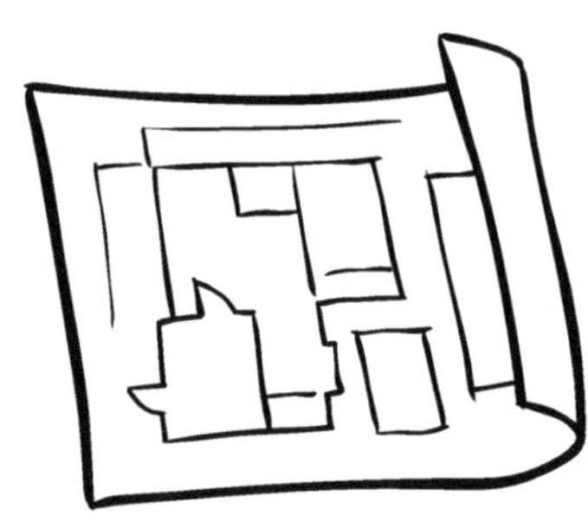	

Letter and Picture Cards for bl

Dr	dr
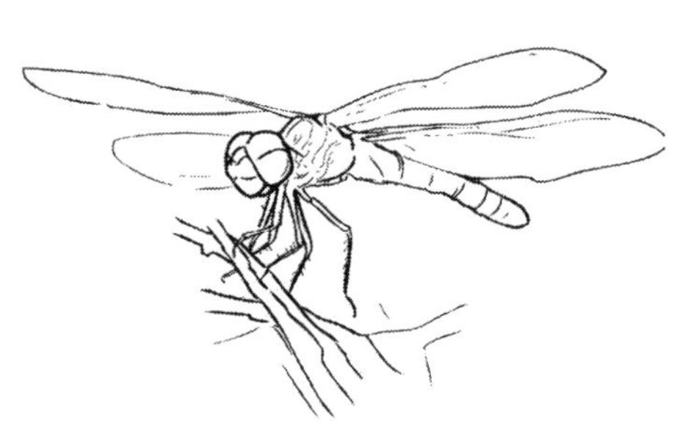	
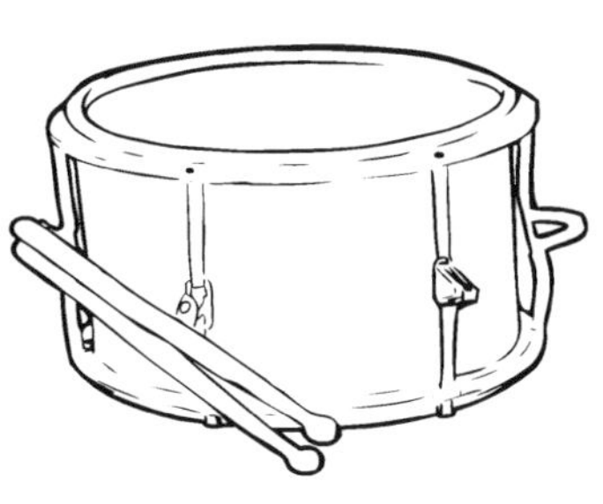	

	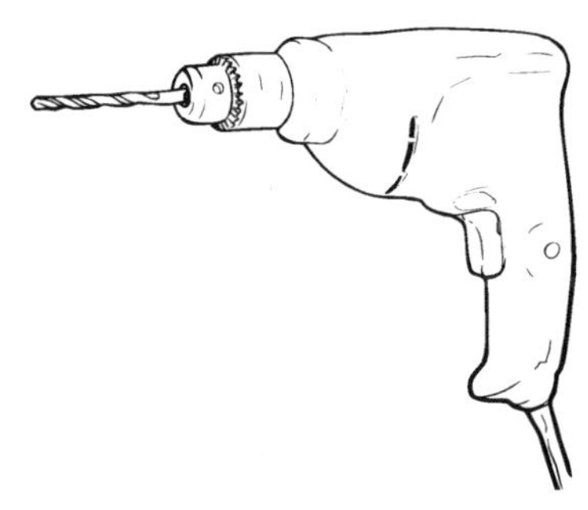

Reteaching Lessons

The Sound for cl Is /cl/

LEARNING OBJECTIVE: Demonstrate letter-sound correspondence by blending two consonant sounds.

LANGUAGE OBJECTIVE: Produce the sounds in a consonant blend when shown a visual grapheme.

Lesson Overview

Introduce the consonant blend, play a game to practice identifying the consonant blend, and assess students' ability to associate a consonant blend with a specific letter combination.

Materials	Preparation
• Letter and Picture Cards for *cl* • Letter and Picture Cards for *sc* • Small, soft ball or toy	• Cut out all letter and picture cards.

Teach and Model

Show students the upper- and lowercase letter cards for *cl*.

Say: ***This is /cl/. The letters* c *and* l *blend together to stand for the sound /cl/. Make the blend with me: /cl/***. Have students produce the sound with you.

Point to the letter card.

Say: ***Make the blend /cl/ every time I put my finger on it.*** Have students produce the sound. Point to the card several times. Mix up the practice by asking individual students to say the sound.

Hold up a picture card.

Say: ***This word is* cloud. *It begins with the blend /cl/. What is this?*** Have students repeat the name of the picture.

Say: ***What sound does* cloud *begin with?*** Have students produce the */cl/* sound independently.

Repeat questions above with each picture card for */cl/*.

Picture cards for /cl/: clam, clown, clothes, cliff, cloud, clock, claw, clay

Connect Sound/Spelling: Letter Sound Sort

Shuffle picture cards for *cl* and *sc* together. Display letter cards for *cl* on a table, allowing enough space for a column of picture cards below the letter cards. Display letter cards for *sc* next to the letter cards for *cl*.

Say: ***This is letter* sc. Sc *stands for the sound /sc/. Everyone say /sc/.*** Have students produce the sound.

Show the stack of picture cards.

Explain: ***The pictures on these cards begin with the letter sound /cl/ or /sc/. We are going to put them with their matching letter.***

Show the first picture card.

Demonstrate: **Cloud*. This picture begins with the letter sound /cl/: /cl/, /cl/,* cloud. *Say /cl/, /cl/,* cloud.** Have students repeat the sound and word.

Demonstrate: **Cloud *goes with this card, /cl/.*** Place the picture card below the letter cards for *cl*.

Have students draw the remaining picture cards from the stack and place them in a column under the matching letter card. As each card is added, direct students to say the letter sound twice and then name the picture: */cl/*, */cl/*, clam; */sc/*, */sc/*, scarf.

Picture cards for /sc/: scooter, scale, scorpion, scarecrow, scuba diver, scared, scout, scarf

EXTENSION ACTIVITY: Randomly point to pictures in the two columns and instruct students to repeat the letter sound and name the picture.

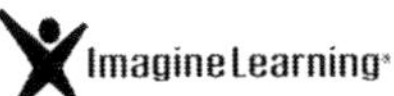

Connect Sound/Spelling: Letter Sound Toss

Show the ball and the letter cards.

Explain: ***When I toss this ball to you, say the blend /cl/ twice. Then say a word that begins with that blend and toss the ball to a classmate.***

Model: **/cl/, /cl/, clock.** Demonstrate the sequence with a volunteer.

Toss the ball to a student. Provide prompts as needed (e.g., Where do you hang up your clothes?). Continue until all students have had several turns.

Word bank: clock, closet, clay, claw, clue, climb, clown, cliff, cloud, class, clever, clothes, cloak, cloth, cleats

Check Progress: Letter Stack

Observe each student during practice and use the following activity to check progress on the target skill. If student can correctly identify the blend twice, consider the intervention successful.

Point to the appropriate letter card as you say the sound.

Say: ***Repeat the blends for these letters: /cl/, /cl/, /sc/, /sc/.***

Shuffle letter cards for *cl* and *sc* together in a stack.

Say: ***Choose a card and tell me the blend.***

Have students draw a card from the stack, say the sound, and put the card on the bottom of the stack. Repeat until every student has had several opportunities to demonstrate knowledge of the target blend */cl/*.

The Sound for sc Is /sc/

Grade K

10 Min.

CCSS.RF.K.3a
TEKS 110.11.3.A

LEARNING OBJECTIVE: Demonstrate letter-sound correspondence by blending two consonant sounds.

LANGUAGE OBJECTIVE: Produce the sounds in a consonant blend when shown a visual grapheme.

Lesson Overview

Introduce the consonant blend, play a game to practice identifying the consonant blend, and assess students' ability to associate a consonant blend with a specific letter combination.

Materials	Preparation
• Letter and Picture Cards for *sc* • Letter and Picture Cards for *cl* • Paper bag	• Cut out all letter and picture cards.

Teach and Model

Show students the upper- and lowercase letter cards for *sc*.

Say: ***This is /sc/. The letters* s *and* c *blend together to stand for the sound /sc/. Make the blend with me: /sc/***. Have students produce the sound with you.

Point to the letter card.

Say: ***Make the blend /sc/ every time I put my finger on it.*** Have students produce the sound. Point to the card several times. Mix up the practice by asking individual students to say the sound.

Hold up a picture card.

Say: ***This word is* scarf*. It begins with the blend /sc/. What is this?*** Have students repeat the name of the picture.

Say: ***What sound does* scarf *begin with?*** Have students produce the */sc/* sound independently.

Repeat questions above with each picture card for */sc/*.

Picture cards for /sc/: scooter, scale, scorpion, scarecrow, scuba diver, scared, scarf, scoreboard

Connect Sound/Spelling: Letter Sound Bag

Put all letter and picture cards for *sc* in the paper bag.

Explain: ***The pictures on these cards start with /sc/. If you pull a letter card from the bag, tell me the blend. Then tell me a word that starts with that blend.***

Model: ***If I pull out* score*, I say /sc/, /sc/,* score.**

Explain: ***If you pull a picture card, tell me the blend it starts with and what the picture is.***

Model: ***If I pull out a picture of a* scooter*, I say /sc/, /sc/,* scooter.**

Have students take turns drawing cards from the paper bag.

Word bank: school, scoop, scooter, scale, scorpion, scarecrow, scuba diver, scared, scarf, scoreboard

Connect Sound/Spelling: Letter Sound Luggage

Show the letter cards.

Say: ***Let's pretend we are packing for a trip. Everything we take on the trip will start with the blend /sc/.***

Model: ***I'm going on a trip and I'm going to pack* a scooter *and* a scarf.**

Ask: ***What else can we pack that starts with the blend /sc/?*** Have students respond. Show flash cards or provide prompts as necessary (e.g., Can you think of a tool that starts with /sc/?).

Word bank: screwdriver, scale, scoop, school, school books, sculpture, scarecrow, schedule, scuba gear

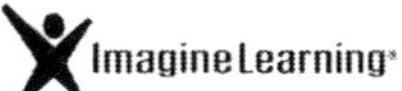

Check Progress: Letter Flip

Observe each student during practice and use the following activity to check progress on the target skill. If student can correctly identify the blend twice, consider the intervention successful.

Point to the appropriate letter card as you say the sound.

Say: ***Repeat the blends for these letters: /sc/, /cl/.***

Put all the flash cards face down on the table and mix them up.

Say: ***Choose a card and tell me the blend.***

Have students choose a card and say the sound, mixing the cards between student turns. Give every student a turn, repeating until each student has had the opportunity to demonstrate knowledge on the target blend */sc/*.

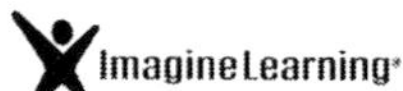

Reteaching Lessons

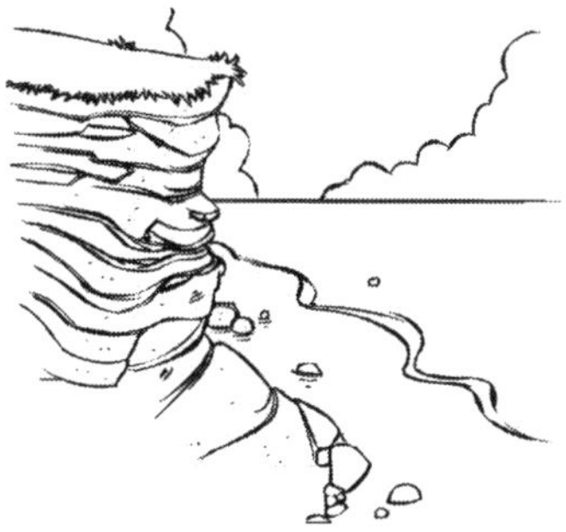

Cl

cl

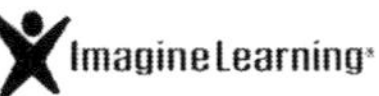

Sc	sc

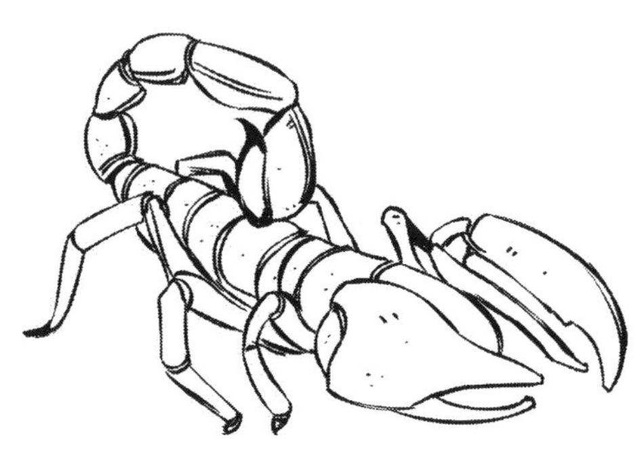	
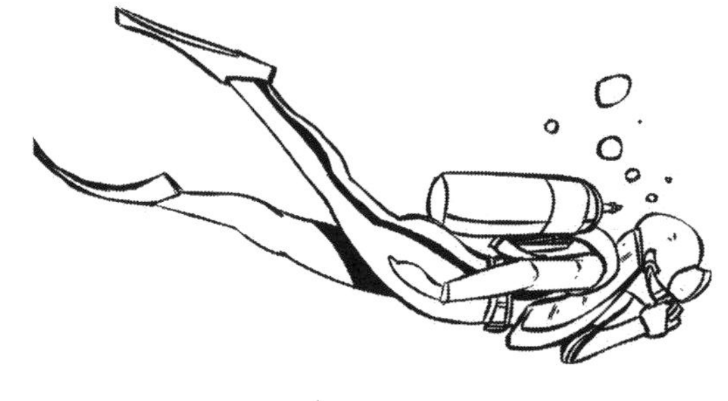	

Reteaching Lessons ✓

The Sound for cr Is /cr/

LEARNING OBJECTIVE: Demonstrate letter-sound correspondence by blending two consonant sounds.

LANGUAGE OBJECTIVE: Produce the sounds in a consonant blend when shown a visual grapheme.

Lesson Overview

Introduce the consonant blend, play a game to practice identifying the consonant blend, and assess students' ability to associate a consonant blend with a specific letter combination.

Materials	Preparation
• Letter and Picture Cards for *cr* • Letter and Picture Cards for *fr* • Paper Bag	• Cut out all letter and picture cards.

Teach and Model

Show students the upper- and lowercase letter cards for *cr*.

Say: ***This is /cr/. The letters* c *and* r *blend together to stand for the sound /cr/. Make the blend with me: /cr/***. Have students produce the sound with you.

Point to the letter card.

Say: ***Make the blend /cr/ every time I put my finger on it.*** Have students produce the sound. Point to the card several times. Mix up the practice by asking individual students to say the sound.

Hold up a picture card.

Say: ***This word is* crown. *It begins with the blend /cr/. What is this?*** Have students repeat the name of the picture.

Say: ***What sound does* crown *begin with?*** Have students produce the */cr/* sound independently.

Repeat questions above with each picture card for */cr/*.

Picture cards for /cr/: crab, crocodile, crackers, crayon, crown, credit card, cry, crack

Connect Sound/Spelling: Letter Sound Bag

Put all letter and picture cards for *cr* in the paper bag.

Explain: ***The pictures on these cards start with /cr/. If you pull a letter card from the bag, tell me the blend. Then tell me a word that starts with that blend.***

Model: ***If I pull out* crawl, *I say /cr/, /cr/,* crawl.**

Explain: ***If you pull a picture card, tell me the blend it starts with and what the picture is.***

Model: ***If I pull out a picture of a crown, I say /cr/, /cr/,* crown.**

Have students take turns drawing cards from the paper bag.

Word bank: crawl, creak, crib, crumb, crow, crab, craft, cricket, cry

Connect Sound/Spelling: Thumbs Up, Thumbs Down for Beginning Sounds

Say: ***Show me thumbs up.*** Model what thumbs up looks like and help students show their thumbs up.

Explain: ***When you hear a word that begins with the blend /cr/, make a thumbs up and say the blend. If the word doesn't start with the blend /cr/, give me a thumbs down.*** Model thumbs down for students and help students show their thumbs down.

Say each word from the word bank below, alternating between words that begin with */cr/* and words that don't.

Words that begin with /cr/: create, crops, crash, crime, crystal, crazy, crush, crooked

Words that don't begin with /cr/: leaf, cat, rock, jumping

Check Progress: Letter Flip

Observe each student during practice and use the following activity to check progress on the target skill. If student can correctly identify the blend twice, consider the intervention successful.

Point to the appropriate letter card as you say the sound.

Say: ***Repeat the blends for these letters: /cr/, /fr/.***

Put all the flash cards face down on the table and mix them up.

Say: ***Choose a card and tell me the blend.***

Have students choose a card and say the sound, mixing the cards between student turns. Give every student a turn, repeating until each student has had the opportunity to demonstrate knowledge on the target blend */cr/*.

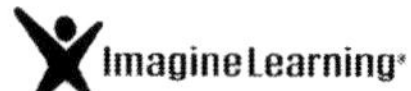

The Sound for fr Is /fr/

Grade K
10 Min.

CCSS.RF.K.3a
TEKS 110.11.3.A

LEARNING OBJECTIVE: Demonstrate letter-sound correspondence by blending two consonant sounds.

LANGUAGE OBJECTIVE: Produce the sounds in a consonant blend when shown a visual grapheme.

Lesson Overview

Introduce the consonant blend, play a game to practice identifying the consonant blend, and assess students' ability to associate a consonant blend with a specific letter combination.

Materials	Preparation
• Letter and Picture Cards for *fr* • Letter and Picture Cards for *cr* • Small, soft ball or toy	• Cut out all letter and picture cards.

Teach and Model

Show students the upper- and lowercase letter cards for *fr*.

Say: ***This is /fr/. The letters* f *and* r *blend together to stand for the sound /fr/. Make the blend with me: /fr/***. Have students produce the sound with you.

Point to the letter card.

Say: ***Make the blend /fr/ every time I put my finger on it.*** Have students produce the sound. Point to the card several times. Mix up the practice by asking individual students to say the sound.

Hold up a picture card.

Say: ***This word is* frog. *It begins with the blend /fr/. What is this?*** Have students repeat the name of the picture.

Say: ***What sound does* frog *begin with?*** Have students produce the */fr/* sound independently.

Repeat questions above with each picture card for */fr/*.

Picture cards for /fr/: frog, fries, fruit, frown, frame, fridge, friends, front

Connect Sound/Spelling: Thumbs Up, Thumbs Down for Beginning Sounds

Say: ***Show me thumbs up.*** Model what thumbs up looks like and help students show their thumbs up.

Explain: ***When you hear a word that begins with the blend /fr/, make a thumbs up and say the blend. If the word doesn't start with the blend /fr/, give me a thumbs down.*** Model thumbs down for students and help students show their thumbs down.

Say each word from the word bank below, alternating between words that begin with */fr/* and words that don't.

Words that begin with /fr/: fresh, frozen, frost, freezer, frying pan, fries, front, free

Words that don't begin with /fr/: dress, bright, flipped, ready, film

EXTENSION ACTIVITY: Ask students to think of other words that begin with /fr/.

Connect Sound/Spelling: Letter Sound Toss

Show the ball and the letter cards.

Explain: ***When I toss this ball to you, say the blend /fr/ twice. Then say a word that begins with that blend and toss the ball to a classmate.***

Model: **/fr/, /fr/, frozen.** Demonstrate the sequence with a volunteer.

Toss the ball to a student. Provide prompts as needed (e.g., What do you eat with a hamburger?). Continue until all students have had several turns.

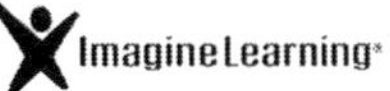

Word bank: frozen, French fries, fruit, frown, frame, fridge, friends, free, freezer, frying pan

Check Progress: Letter Flip

Observe each student during practice and use the following activity to check progress on the target skill. If student can correctly identify the blend twice, consider the intervention successful.

Point to the appropriate letter card as you say the sound.

Say: ***Repeat the blends for these letters: /fr/, /cr/.***

Put all the flash cards face down on the table and mix them up.

Say: ***Choose a card and tell me the blend.***

Have students choose a card and say the sound, mixing the cards between student turns. Give every student a turn, repeating until each student has had the opportunity to demonstrate knowledge on the target blend */fr/*.

Cr

cr

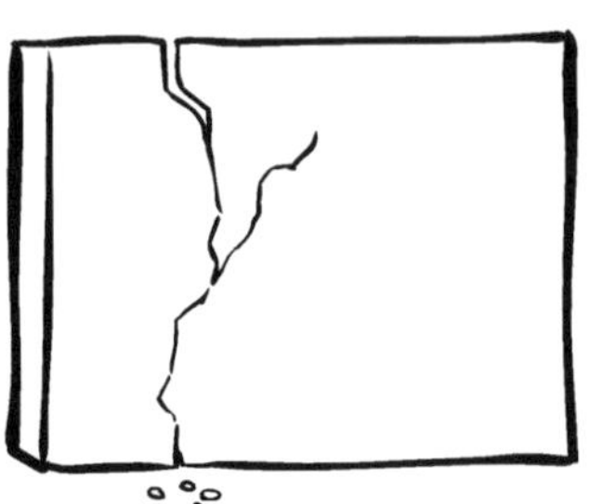

Letter and Picture Cards for cr

Fr

fr

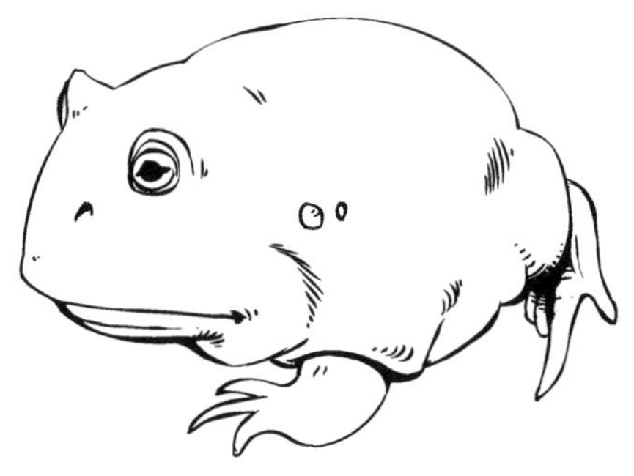

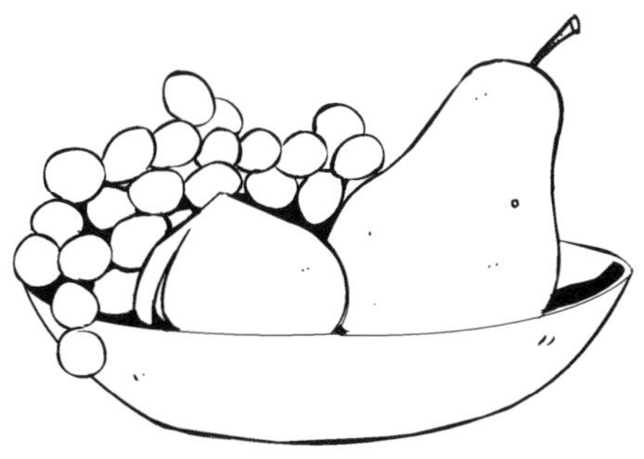

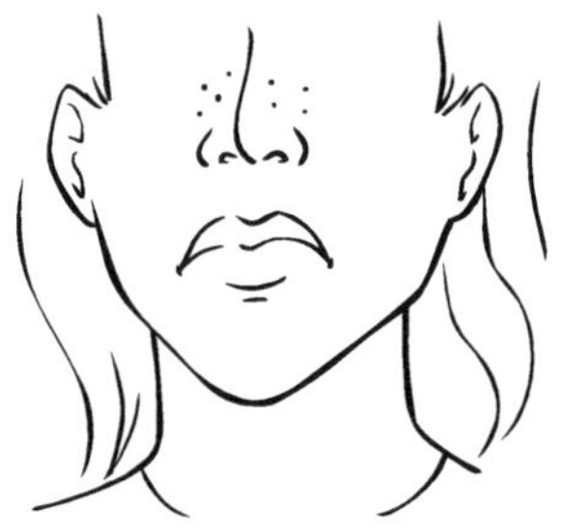

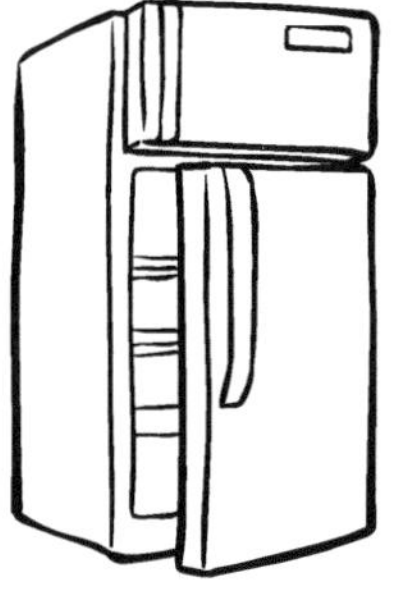

Letter Sounds

The Sound for fl Is /fl/

Grade K | 10 Min. | CCSS.RF.K.3a TEKS 110.11.3.A

LEARNING OBJECTIVE: Demonstrate letter-sound correspondence by blending two consonant sounds.

LANGUAGE OBJECTIVE: Produce the sounds in a consonant blend when shown a visual grapheme.

Lesson Overview

Introduce the consonant blend, play a game to practice identifying the consonant blend, and assess students' ability to associate a consonant blend with a specific letter combination.

Materials	Preparation
• Letter and Picture Cards for *fl* • Letter and Picture Cards for *wh*	• Cut out all letter and picture cards.

Teach and Model

Show students the upper- and lowercase letter cards for *fl*.

Say: ***This is /fl/. The letters* f *and* l *blend together to stand for the sound /fl/. Make the blend with me: /fl/***. Have students produce the sound with you.

Point to the letter card.

Say: ***Make the blend /fl/ every time I put my finger on it.*** Have students produce the sound. Point to the card several times. Mix up the practice by asking individual students to say the sound.

Hold up a picture card.

Say: ***This word is* flower. *It begins with the blend /fl/. What is this?*** Have students repeat the name of the picture.

Say: ***What sound does* flower *begin with?*** Have students produce the */fl/* sound independently.

Repeat questions above with each picture card for */fl/*.

Picture cards for /fl/: flamingo, fly, flower, flute, flag, flame, flight attendant, floss

Connect Sound/Spelling: Letter Sound Sort

Shuffle picture cards for *fl* and *wh* together. Display letter cards for *fl* on a table, allowing enough space for a column of picture cards below the letter cards. Display letter cards for *wh* next to the letter cards for *fl*.

Say: ***This are the letters* w *and* h. Wh *stands for the sound /wh/. Everyone say /wh/.*** Have students produce the sound.

Show the stack of picture cards.

Explain: ***The pictures on these cards begin with the letter sound /fl/ or /wh/. We are going to put them with their matching letter.***

Show the first picture card.

Demonstrate: **Flower*. This picture begins with the letter sound /fl/: /fl/, /fl/,* flower*. Say /fl/, /fl/,* flower.** Have students repeat the sound and word.

Demonstrate: **Flower *goes with this card, /fl/.*** Place the picture card below the letter cards for *fl*.

Have students draw the remaining picture cards from the stack and place them in a column under the matching letter card. As each card is added, direct students to say the letter sound twice and then name the picture: */fl/*, */fl/*, flag; */wh/*, */wh/*, wheel.

Picture cards for /wh/: whale, whisker, whistle, wheel, whisk, wheelchair, wheat, whisper

EXTENSION ACTIVITY: Randomly point to pictures in the two columns and instruct students to repeat the letter sound and name the picture.

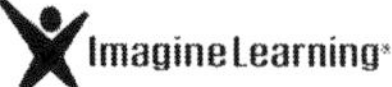

Connect Sound/Spelling: Thumbs Up, Thumbs Down for Beginning Sounds

Say: ***Show me thumbs up.*** Model what thumbs up looks like and help students show their thumbs up.

Explain: ***When you hear a word that begins with the blend /fl/, make a thumbs up and say the blend. If the word doesn't start with the blend /fl/, give me a thumbs down.*** Model thumbs down for students and help students show their thumbs down.

Say each word from the word bank below, alternating between words that begin with */fl/* and words that don't.

Words that begin with /fl/: floss, flannel, flashcard, fleece, flake, flame, fluoride, flash, flat, Florida, flood, float

Words that don't begin with /fl/: cloud, block, sled, plant, slide

EXTENSION ACTIVITY: Ask students to think of other words that start with /fl/.

Check Progress: Letter Stack

Observe each student during practice and use the following activity to check progress on the target skill. If student can correctly identify the blend twice, consider the intervention successful.

Point to the appropriate letter card as you say the sound.

Say: ***Repeat the blends for these letters: /fl/, /fl/, /wh/, /wh/.***

Shuffle letter cards for *fl* and *wh* together in a stack.

Say: ***Choose a card and tell me the blend.***

Have students draw a card from the stack, say the sound, and put the card on the bottom of the stack. Repeat until every student has had several opportunities to demonstrate knowledge of the target blend */fl/*.

Reteaching Lessons

The Sound for wh Is /wh/

Grade K | 10 Min. | CCSS.RF.K.3a TEKS 110.11.3.A

LEARNING OBJECTIVE: Demonstrate letter-sound correspondence by producing the most common sound for the digraph.

LANGUAGE OBJECTIVE: Produce the sound for each consonant digraph when shown a visual grapheme.

Lesson Overview

Introduce the digraph, play a game to practice identifying the digraph, and assess students' ability to associate a specific digraph with a consonant combination.

Materials	Preparation
• Letter and Picture Cards for *wh* • Letter and Picture Cards for *fl*	• Cut out all letter and picture cards.

Teach and Model

Show students the upper- and lowercase letter cards for *wh*.

Say: ***This is /wh/. The letters* w *and* h *stand for the letter sound /wh/. Make the letter sound with me: /wh/.*** Have students produce the letter sound with you.

Point to the letter card.

Say: ***Make the letter sound /wh/ every time I put my finger on it: /wh/.*** Have students produce the letter sound. Point to the card several times. Mix up the practice by asking individual students to say the letter sound.

Hold up a picture card.

Say: ***This word is* whale. *It begins with /wh/. What is this?*** Have students repeat the name of the picture.

Say: ***What letter sound does* whale *begin with?*** Have students produce the */wh/* sound independently.

Repeat questions above with each picture card.

Picture cards for /wh/: whale, whisker, whistle, wheel, whisk, wheelchair, wheat, whisper

Connect Sound/Spelling: Thumbs Up, Thumbs Down for Beginning Sounds

Say: ***Show me thumbs up.*** Model what thumbs up looks like and help students show their thumbs up.

Explain: ***When you hear a word that begins with the letter sound /wh/, make a thumbs up and say the letter sound. If the word doesn't start with the letter sound /wh/, give me a thumbs down.*** Model thumbs down for students and help students show their thumbs down.

Say each word from the word bank below, alternating between words that begin with */wh/* and words that don't.

Words that begin with /wh/: wheelbarrow, whiff, whisper, white, whatever, when, why, where, whiz, which, whip cream

Words that don't begin with /wh/: sandwich, cloud, log, jungle

EXTENSION ACTIVITY: Ask students to think of other words that begin with */wh/*.

Connect Sound/Spelling: Letter Sound Toss

Show the ball and the letter cards.

Explain: ***When I toss this ball to you, say the letter sound /wh/ twice. Then say a word that begins with that letter sound and toss the ball to a classmate.***

Model: **/wh/, /wh/, whale.** Demonstrate the sequence with a volunteer.

Toss the ball to a student. Provide prompts as needed (e.g., What starts with */wh/* and can be made into bread?). Continue until all students have had several turns.

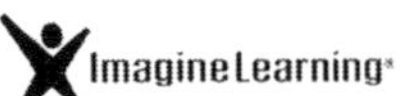

Prompt as needed using words from the word bank.

Word bank: why, wheel, white, when, whisker, wheel, whistle

Check Progress: Letter Flip

Observe each student during practice and use the following activity to check progress on the target skill. If student can correctly identify the digraph twice, consider the intervention successful.

Point to the appropriate letter card as you say the sound.

Say: ***Repeat the sounds for these letters: /wh/, /tr/.***

Put all the flash cards face down on the table and mix them up.

Say: ***Choose a card and tell me the letter sound.***

Have students choose a card and say the sound, mixing the cards between student turns. Give every student a turn, repeating until each student has had the opportunity to demonstrate knowledge on the target digraph */wh/*.

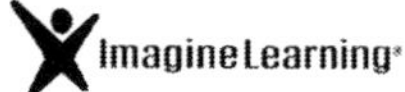

Fl	

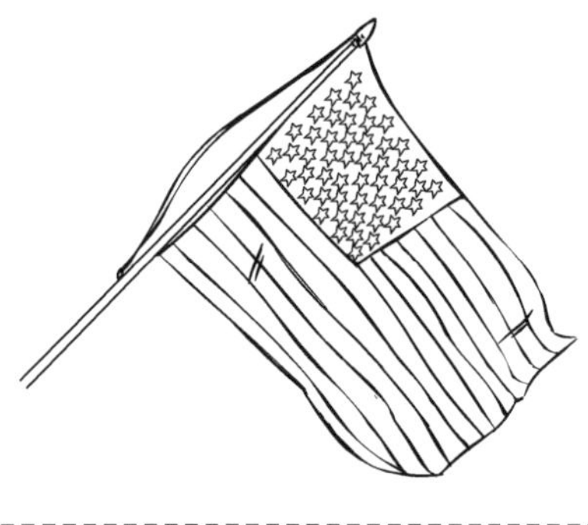	

Wh	wh

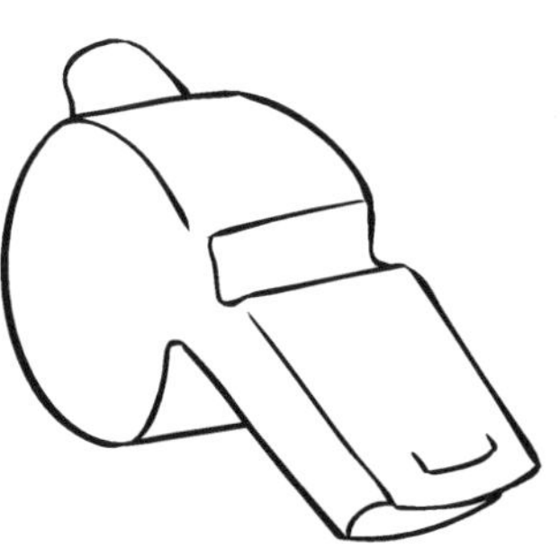	
	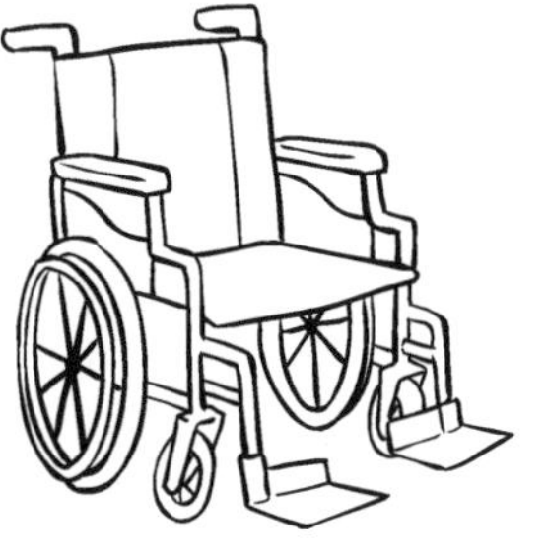

Reteaching Lessons ✓

The Sound for gl Is /gl/

Grade K

10 Min.

CCSS.RF.K.3a
TEKS 110.11.3.A

LEARNING OBJECTIVE: Demonstrate letter-sound correspondence by blending two consonant sounds.

LANGUAGE OBJECTIVE: Produce the sounds in a consonant blend when shown a visual grapheme.

Lesson Overview

Introduce the consonant blend, play a game to practice identifying the consonant blend, and assess students' ability to associate a consonant blend with a specific letter combination.

Materials	Preparation
• Letter and Picture Cards for *gl* • Letter and Picture Cards for *th*	• Cut out all letter and picture cards.

Teach and Model

Show students the upper- and lowercase letter cards for *gl*.

Say: ***This is* /gl/*. The letters* g *and* l *blend together to stand for the sound* /gl/*. Make the blend with me:* /gl/**. Have students produce the sound with you.

Point to the letter card.

Say: ***Make the blend* /gl/ *every time I put my finger on it.*** Have students produce the sound. Point to the card several times. Mix up the practice by asking individual students to say the sound.

Hold up a picture card.

Say: ***This word is* glove*. It begins with the blend* /gl/*. What is this?*** Have students repeat the name of the picture.

Say: ***What sound does* glove *begin with?*** Have students produce the */gl/* sound independently.

Repeat questions above with each picture card for */gl/*.

Picture cards for /gl/: gloves, glue, globe, glasses, glass, glacier, glider, gladiator

Connect Sound/Spelling: Letter Sound Sort

Shuffle picture cards for *gl* and *th* together. Display letter cards for *gl* on a table, allowing enough space for a column of picture cards below the letter cards. Display letter cards for *th* next to the letter cards for *gl*.

Say: ***These are the letters* t *and* h*.* Th *stands for the sound* /th/*. Everyone say* /th/*.*** Have students produce the sound.

Show the stack of picture cards.

Explain: ***The pictures on these cards begin with the letter sound* /gl/ *or* /th/*. We are going to put them with their matching letter.***

Show the first picture card.

Demonstrate: **Glue*. This picture begins with the letter sound* /gl/: /gl/, /gl/, glue*. Say* /gl/, /gl/, glue.** Have students repeat the sound and word.

Demonstrate: **Glue *goes with this card,* /gl/*.*** Place the picture card below the letter cards for *gl*.

Have students draw the remaining picture cards from the stack and place them in a column under the matching letter card. As each card is added, direct students to say the letter sound twice and then name the picture: */gl/*, */gl/*, glasses; */th/*, */th/*, thumb.

Picture cards for /th/: thirteen, three, thermometer, thumb, thread, thimble, thief, theater

EXTENSION ACTIVITY: Randomly point to pictures in the two columns and instruct students to repeat the letter sound and name the picture.

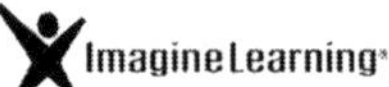

Connect Sound/Spelling: Thumbs Up, Thumbs Down for Beginning Sounds

Say: ***Show me thumbs up.*** Model what thumbs up looks like and help students show their thumbs up.

Explain: ***When you hear a word that begins with the blend /gl/, make a thumbs up and say the blend. If the word doesn't start with the blend /gl/, give me a thumbs down.*** Model thumbs down for students and help students show their thumbs down.

Say each word from the word bank below, alternating between words that begin with */gl/* and words that don't.

Words that begin with /gl/: glad, glasses, gloss, glass, glue

Words that don't begin with /gl/: photo, carrot, tractor, drill

EXTENSION ACTIVITY: Ask students to think of other words that begin with /gl/.

Check Progress: Letter Flip

Observe each student during practice and use the following activity to check progress on the target skill. If student can correctly identify the blend twice, consider the intervention successful.

Point to the appropriate letter card as you say the sound.

Say: ***Repeat the blends for these letters: /gl/, /th/.***

Put all the flash cards face down on the table and mix them up.

Say: ***Choose a card and tell me the blend.***

Have students choose a card and say the sound, mixing the cards between student turns. Give every student a turn, repeating until each student has had the opportunity to demonstrate knowledge on the target blend */gl/*.

Reteaching Lessons ✓

The Sound for th Is /th/

LEARNING OBJECTIVE: Demonstrate letter-sound correspondence by producing the most common sound for the digraph.

LANGUAGE OBJECTIVE: Produce the sound for each consonant digraph when shown a visual grapheme.

Lesson Overview

Introduce the digraph, play a game to practice identifying the digraph, and assess students' ability to associate a specific digraph with a consonant combination.

Materials	Preparation
• Letter and Picture Cards for *th* • Letter and Picture Cards for *gl* • Paper Bag	• Cut out all letter and picture cards.

Teach and Model

Show students the upper- and lowercase letter cards for *th*.

Say: ***This is /th/. The letters* t *and* h *stand for the letter sound /th/. Make the letter sound with me: /th/.*** Have students produce the letter sound with you.

Point to the letter card.

Say: ***Make the letter sound /th/ every time I put my finger on it: /th/.*** Have students produce the letter sound. Point to the card several times. Mix up the practice by asking individual students to say the letter sound.

Hold up a picture card.

Say: ***This word is* thumb. *It begins with /th/. What is this?*** Have students repeat the name of the picture.

Say: ***What letter sound does* thumb *begin with?*** Have students produce the */th/* sound independently.

Repeat questions above with each picture card.

Picture cards for /th/: thirteen, three, thermometer, thumb, thread, thimble, thief, theater

Connect Sound/Spelling: Letter Sound Bag

Put all letter and picture cards for *th* in the paper bag.

Explain: ***The pictures on these cards start with /th/. If you pull a letter card from the bag, tell me the letter sound. Then tell me a word that starts with that letter sound.***

Model: ***If I pull out* third, *I say /th/, /th/,* third.**

Explain: ***If you pull a picture card, tell me the letter sound it starts with and what the picture is.***

Model: ***If I pull out a picture of a three, I say /th/, /th/,* three.**

Have students take turns drawing cards from the paper bag.

Word bank: third, think, throat, thin, thunder, thanks,

Connect Sound/Spelling: Stand Up, Sit Down

Show the letter card.

Explain: ***When I say a word, listen carefully to the beginning and the ending sounds of the word. When you hear /th/ at the beginning of the word, stand up. When you hear /th/ at the end of the word, sit down. Let's try one.***

Ask: ***Where do you hear /th/ in* thumb?** Students should stand up.

Say: ***Yes!* Thumb *has /th/ at the beginning of the word, so you stand up. Let's try another one:* math.** Students should sit down.

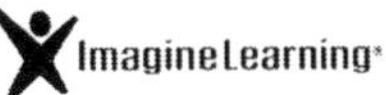

Say: ***Good!* Math *has* /th/ *at the end of the word, so you sit down.***

Alternate between words beginning and ending with */th/* from the lists below.

Words that begin with /th/: theme, think, thirty, thunder, thank, thaw, throat, thick, thing, thin

Words that end with /th/: math, dishcloth, labyrinth, teeth, path, birdbath, breath, sleuth, mouth, fifth, month, tenth, both, with

Check Progress: Letter Flip

Observe each student during practice and use the following activity to check progress on the target skill. If student can correctly identify the digraph twice, consider the intervention successful.

Point to the appropriate letter card as you say the sound.

Say: ***Repeat the sounds for these letters:* /th/, /gl/.**

Put all the flash cards face down on the table and mix them up.

Say: ***Choose a card and tell me the letter sound.***

Have students choose a card and say the sound, mixing the cards between student turns. Give every student a turn, repeating until each student has had the opportunity to demonstrate knowledge on the target digraph */th/*.

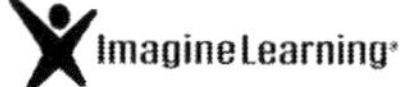

Gl gl

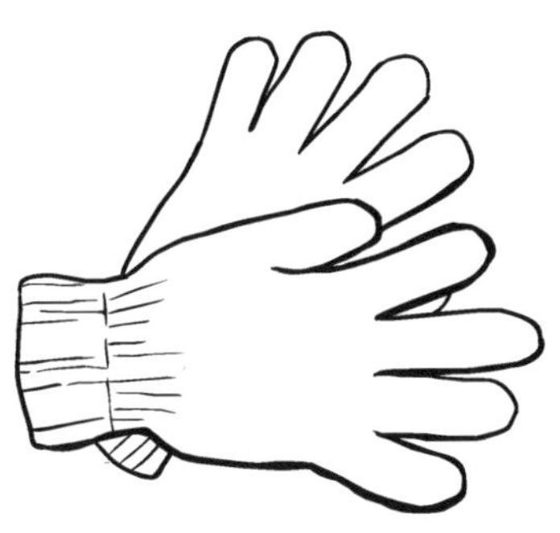

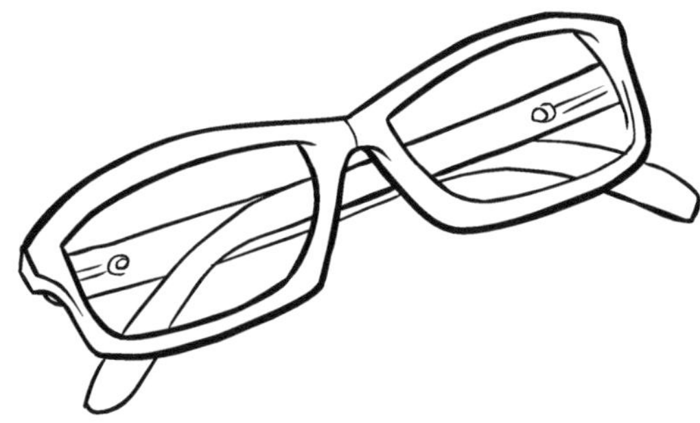

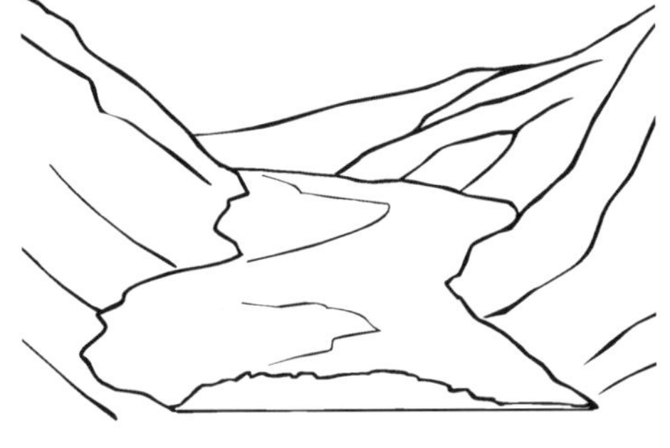

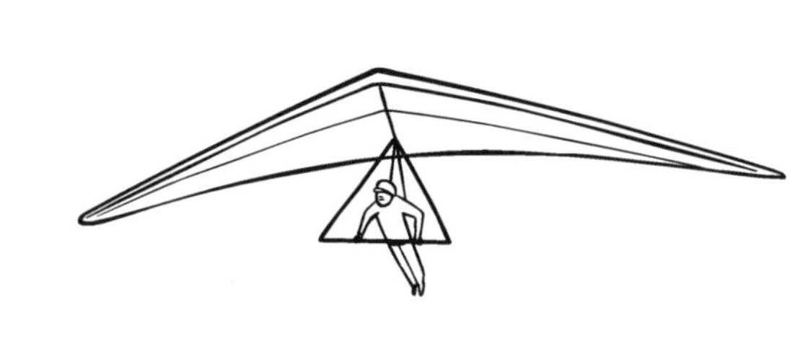

Reteaching Lessons

Th	th
13	3
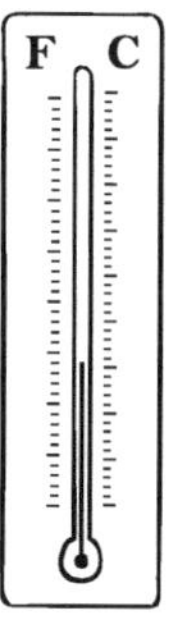	
	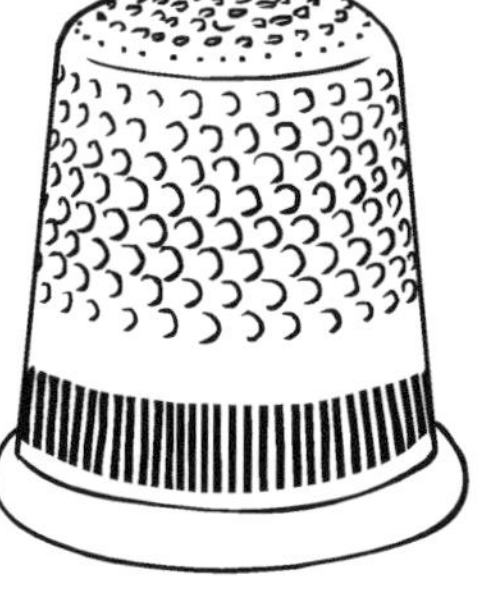

Reteaching Lessons

The Sound for pl Is /pl/

Grade K

10 Min.

CCSS.RF.K.3a
TEKS 110.11.3.A

LEARNING OBJECTIVE: Demonstrate letter-sound correspondence by blending two consonant sounds.

LANGUAGE OBJECTIVE: Produce the sounds in a consonant blend when shown a visual grapheme.

Lesson Overview

Introduce the consonant blend, play a game to practice identifying the consonant blend, and assess students' ability to associate a consonant blend with a specific letter combination.

Materials	Preparation
• Letter and Picture Cards for *pl* • Letter and Picture Cards for *tr*	• Cut out all letter and picture cards.

Teach and Model

Show students the upper- and lowercase letter cards for *pl*.

Say: ***This is /pl/. The letters* p *and* l *blend together to stand for the sound /pl/. Make the blend with me: /pl/.*** Have students produce the sound with you.

Point to the letter card.

Say: ***Make the blend /pl/ every time I put my finger on it.*** Have students produce the sound. Point to the card several times. Mix up the practice by asking individual students to say the sound.

Hold up a picture card.

Say: ***This word is* plum. *It begins with the blend /pl/. What is this?*** Have students repeat the name of the picture.

Say: ***What sound does* plum *begin with?*** Have students produce the */pl/* sound independently.

Repeat questions above with each picture card for */pl/*.

Picture cards for /pl/: platypus, plum, planet, plate, plant, plane, pliers, plug

Connect Sound/Spelling: Letter Sound Sort

Shuffle picture cards for *pl* and *tr* together. Display letter cards for *pl* on a table, allowing enough space for a column of picture cards below the letter cards. Display letter cards for *tr* next to the letter cards for *pl*.

Say: ***These are the letters* t *and* r. Tr *stands for the sound /tr/. Everyone say /tr/.*** Have students produce the sound.

Show the stack of picture cards.

Explain: ***The pictures on these cards begin with the letter sound /pl/ or /tr/. We are going to put them with their matching letter.***

Show the first picture card.

Demonstrate: **Plate. *This picture begins with the letter sound /pl/: /pl/, /pl/, plate. Say /pl/, /pl/, plate.*** Have students repeat the sound and word.

Demonstrate: **Plate *goes with this card, /pl/.*** Place the picture card below the letter cards for *pl*.

Have students draw the remaining picture cards from the stack and place them in a column under the matching letter card. As each card is added, direct students to say the letter sound twice and then name the picture: */pl/*, */pl/*, plug; */tr/*, */tr/*, trash.

Picture cards for /tr/: triangle, tree, train, trophy, trail, track, trampoline, trash

EXTENSION ACTIVITY: Randomly point to pictures in the two columns and instruct students to repeat the letter sound and name the picture.

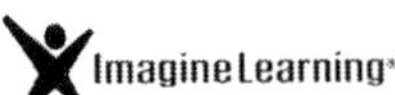

Connect Sound/Spelling: Letter Sound Luggage

Show the letter cards.

Say: ***Let's pretend we are packing for a trip. Everything we take on the trip will start with the blend /pl/.***

Model: ***I'm going on a trip and I'm going to pack* a plant and pliers.**

Ask: ***What else can we pack that starts with the blend /pl/?*** Have students respond. Show flash cards or provide prompts as necessary (e.g., What do you put your food on that starts with /pl/?).

Word bank: plate, plug, planter, plastic plate, plane, plaid pack, plow, plunger, plywood

Check Progress: Letter Flip

Observe each student during practice and use the following activity to check progress on the target skill. If student can correctly identify the blend twice, consider the intervention successful.

Point to the appropriate letter card as you say the sound.

Say: ***Repeat the blends for these letters: /pl/, /tr/.***

Put all the flash cards face down on the table and mix them up.

Say: ***Choose a card and tell me the blend.***

Have students choose a card and say the sound, mixing the cards between student turns. Give every student a turn, repeating until each student has had the opportunity to demonstrate knowledge on the target blend */pl/*.

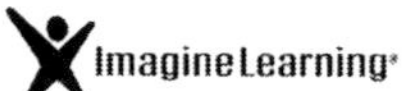

The Sound for tr Is /tr/

LEARNING OBJECTIVE: Demonstrate letter-sound correspondence by blending two consonant sounds.

LANGUAGE OBJECTIVE: Produce the sounds in a consonant blend when shown a visual grapheme.

Lesson Overview

Introduce the consonant blend, play a game to practice identifying the consonant blend, and assess students' ability to associate a consonant blend with a specific letter combination.

Materials	Preparation
• Letter and Picture Cards for *tr* • Letter and Picture Cards for *pl* • Small, soft ball or toy	• Cut out all letter and picture cards.

Teach and Model

Show students the upper- and lowercase letter cards for *tr*.

Say: ***This is /tr/. The letters* t *and* r *blend together to stand for the sound /tr/. Make the blend with me: /tr/***. Have students produce the sound with you.

Point to the letter card.

Say: ***Make the blend /tr/ every time I put my finger on it.*** Have students produce the sound. Point to the card several times. Mix up the practice by asking individual students to say the sound.

Hold up a picture card.

Say: ***This word is* train. *It begins with the blend /tr/. What is this?*** Have students repeat the name of the picture.

Say: ***What sound does* train *begin with?*** Have students produce the */tr/* sound independently.

Repeat questions above with each picture card for */tr/*.

Picture cards for /tr/: triangle, tree, train, trophy, trail, track, trampoline, trash

Connect Sound/Spelling: Thumbs Up, Thumbs Down for Beginning Sounds

Say: ***Show me thumbs up.*** Model what thumbs up looks like and help students show their thumbs up.

Explain: ***When you hear a word that begins with the blend /tr/, make a thumbs up and say the blend. If the word doesn't start with the blend /tr/, give me a thumbs down.*** Model thumbs down for students and help students show their thumbs down.

Say each word from the word bank below, alternating between words that begin with */tr/* and words that don't.

Words that begin with /tr/: train, trophy, trade, traffic, trampoline, tree, trail, triangle, track, trash

Words that don't begin with /tr/: guard, lion, ten, hand

EXTENSION ACTIVITY: Ask students to think of other words that begin with /tr/.

Connect Sound/Spelling: Letter Sound Toss

Show the ball and the letter cards.

Explain: ***When I toss this ball to you, say the blend /tr/ twice. Then say a word that begins with that blend and toss the ball to a classmate.***

Model: **/tr/, /tr/, tree.** Demonstrate the sequence with a volunteer.

Toss the ball to a student. Provide prompts as needed (e.g., What shape starts with /tr/?). Continue until all students have had several turns.

Word bank: triangle, tree, train, trophy, trail, track, trampoline, trash

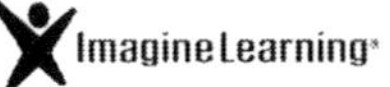

Check Progress: Letter Stack

Observe each student during practice and use the following activity to check progress on the target skill. If student can correctly identify the blend twice, consider the intervention successful.

Point to the appropriate letter card as you say the sound.

Say: ***Repeat the blends for these letters: /tr/, /tr/, /pl/, /pl/.***

Shuffle letter cards for *tr* and *pl* together in a stack.

Say: ***Choose a card and tell me the blend.***

Have students draw a card from the stack, say the sound, and put the card on the bottom of the stack. Repeat until every student has had several opportunities to demonstrate knowledge of the target blend */tr/*.

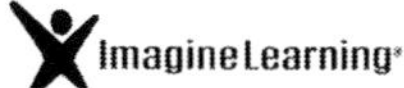

Pl	pl

	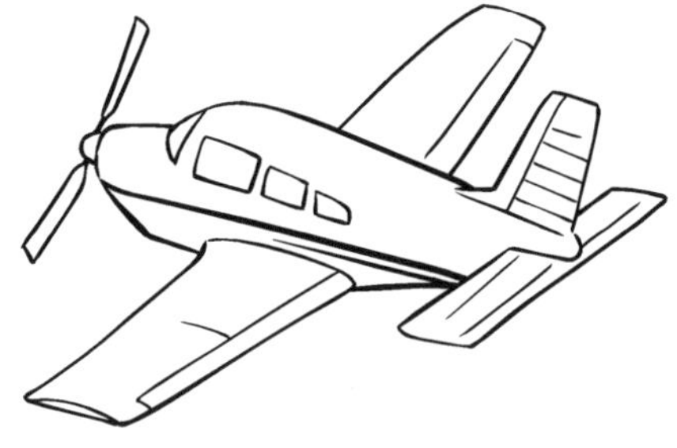
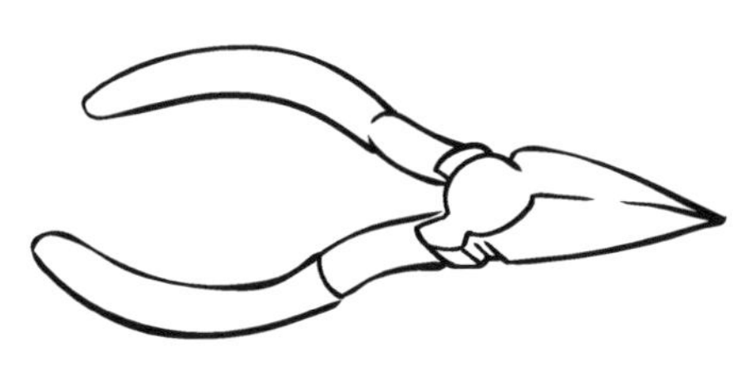	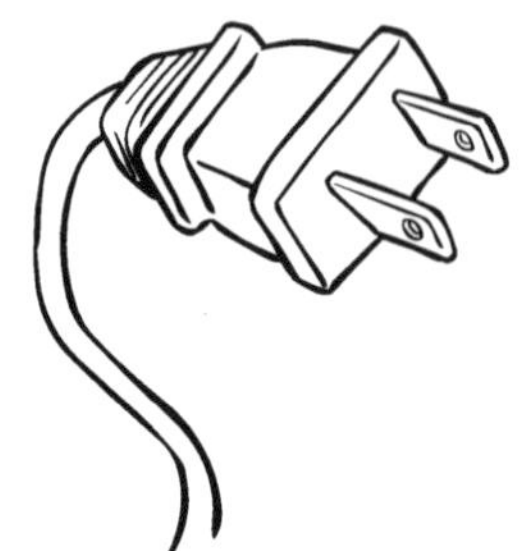

Tr	tr

	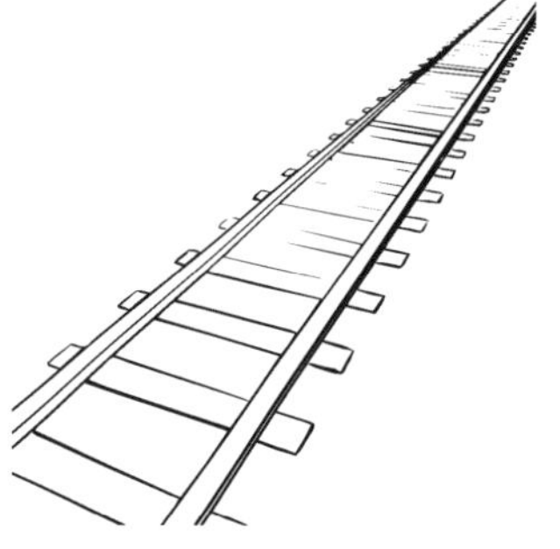
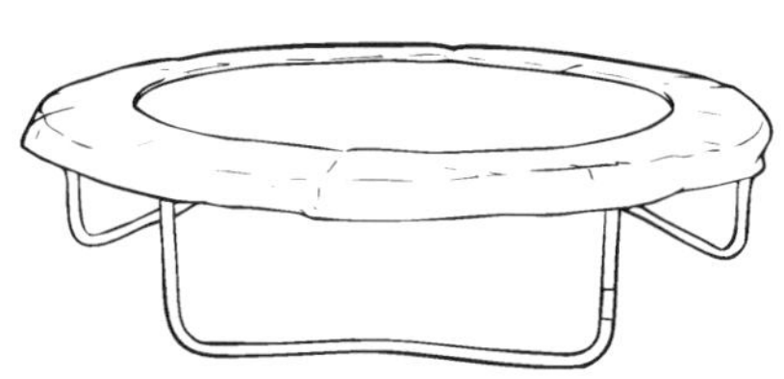	

The Sound for pr Is /pr/

LEARNING OBJECTIVE: Demonstrate letter-sound correspondence by blending two consonant sounds.

LANGUAGE OBJECTIVE: Produce the sounds in a consonant blend when shown a visual grapheme.

Lesson Overview

Introduce the consonant blend, play a game to practice identifying the consonant blend, and assess students' ability to associate a consonant blend with a specific letter combination.

Materials	Preparation
• Letter and Picture Cards for *pr* • Letter and Picture Cards for *sh* • Paper bag	• Cut out all letter and picture cards.

Teach and Model

Show students the upper- and lowercase letter cards for *pr*.

Say: ***This is /pr/. The letters* p *and* r *blend together to stand for the sound /pr/. Make the blend with me: /pr/***. Have students produce the sound with you.

Point to the letter card.

Say: ***Make the blend /pr/ every time I put my finger on it.*** Have students produce the sound. Point to the card several times. Mix up the practice by asking individual students to say the sound.

Hold up a picture card.

Say: ***This word is* pretzel*. It begins with the blend /pr/. What is this?*** Have students repeat the name of the picture.

Say: ***What sound does* pretzel *begin with?*** Have students produce the */pr/* sound independently.

Repeat questions above with each picture card for */pr/*.

Picture cards for /pr/: pretzel, princess, president, present, propeller, prize, professor, price tag

Connect Sound/Spelling: Thumbs Up, Thumbs Down for Beginning Sounds

Say: ***Show me thumbs up.*** Model what thumbs up looks like and help students show their thumbs up.

Explain: ***When you hear a word that begins with the blend /pr/, make a thumbs up and say the blend. If the word doesn't start with the blend /pr/, give me a thumbs down.*** Model thumbs down for students and help students show their thumbs down.

Say each word from the word bank below, alternating between words that begin with */pr/* and words that don't.

Words that begin with /pr/: prairie, preschool, prize, practice, price, program, princess, predict, project, program, prince

Words that don't begin with /pr/: trail, crunch, photo, glasses

EXTENSION ACTIVITY: Ask students to think of other words that begin with /pr/.

Connect Sound/Spelling: Letter Sound Bag

Put all letter and picture cards for *pr* in the paper bag.

Explain: ***The pictures on these cards start with /pr/. If you pull a letter card from the bag, tell me the blend. Then tell me a word that starts with that blend.***

Model: ***If I pull out* practice*, I say /pr/, /pr/,* practice*.***

Explain: ***If you pull a picture card, tell me the blend it starts with and what the picture is.***

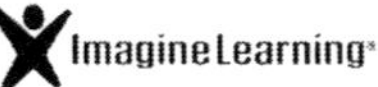

Model: ***If I pull out a picture of a prize, I say /pr/, /pr/, prize.***

Have students take turns drawing cards from the paper bag.

Word bank: practice, pretzel, prince, project, program, problem

Check Progress: Letter Stack

Observe each student during practice and use the following activity to check progress on the target skill. If student can correctly identify the blend twice, consider the intervention successful.

Point to the appropriate letter card as you say the sound.

Say: ***Repeat the blends for these letters: /pr/, /pr/, /sh/, /sh/.***

Shuffle letter cards for *pr* and *sh* together in a stack.

Say: ***Choose a card and tell me the blend.***

Have students draw a card from the stack, say the sound, and put the card on the bottom of the stack. Repeat until every student has had several opportunities to demonstrate knowledge of the target blend */pr/*.

Reteaching Lessons ✓

The Sound for sh is /sh/

Grade K

10 Min.

CCSS.RF.K.3a
TEKS 110.11.3.A

LEARNING OBJECTIVE: Demonstrate letter-sound correspondence by producing the most common sound for the digraph.

LANGUAGE OBJECTIVE: Produce the sound for each consonant digraph when shown a visual grapheme.

Lesson Overview

Introduce the digraph, play a game to practice identifying the digraph, and assess students' ability to associate a specific digraph with a consonant combination.

Materials	Preparation
• Letter and Picture Cards for *sh* • Letter and Picture Cards for *pr* • Paper bag	• Cut out all letter and picture cards.

Teach and Model

Show students the upper- and lowercase letter cards for *sh*.

Say: ***This is /sh/. The letters* s *and* h *stand for the letter sound /sh/. Make the letter sound with me: /sh/.*** Have students produce the letter sound with you.

Point to the letter card.

Say: ***Make the letter sound /sh/ every time I put my finger on it: /sh/.*** Have students produce the letter sound. Point to the card several times. Mix up the practice by asking individual students to say the letter sound.

Hold up a picture card.

Say: ***This word is* shirt. *It begins with /sh/. What is this?*** Have students repeat the name of the picture.

Say: ***What letter sound does* shirt *begin with?*** Have students produce the */sh/* sound independently.

Repeat questions above with each picture card.

Picture cards for /sh/: shirt, shoes, shark, sheep, shadow, shamrock, shell, shower

Connect Sound/Spelling: Letter Sound Bag

Put all letter and picture cards for *sh* in the paper bag.

Explain: ***The pictures on these cards start with /sh/. If you pull a letter card from the bag, tell me the letter sound. Then tell me a word that starts with that letter sound.***

Model: ***If I pull out* sheep, *I say /sh/, /sh/,* sheep.**

Explain: ***If you pull a picture card, tell me the letter sound it starts with and what the picture is.***

Model: ***If I pull out a picture of a sheep, I say /sh/, /sh/,* sheep.**

Have students take turns drawing cards from the paper bag.

Word bank: sheep, shin, ship, short, shake, show, shell, shadow

Connect Sound/Spelling: Stand Up, Sit Down

Show the letter card.

Explain: ***When I say a word, listen carefully to the beginning and the ending sounds of the word. When you hear /sh/ at the beginning of the word, stand up. When you hear /sh/ at the end of the word, sit down. Let's try one.***

Ask: ***Where do you hear /sh/ in* shark?** Students should stand up.

Say: ***Yes!* Shark *has /sh/ at the beginning of the word, so you stand up. Let's try another one:* fish.** Students should sit down.

Say: ***Good!* Fish *has /sh/ at the end of the word, so you sit down.***

Alternate between words beginning and ending with */sh/* from the lists below.

Words that begin with /sh/: shop, shade, shampoo, shark, ship, shelf, shallow, shoelace, sharpen, shaken, shrinking, shaped, shin

Words that end with /sh/: fish, hairbrush, wash, selfish, finish, squish, splash, squash, crush, slush, fresh, flash, trash, push, wish

Check Progress: Letter Flip

Observe each student during practice and use the following activity to check progress on the target skill. If student can correctly identify the digraph twice, consider the intervention successful.

Point to the appropriate letter card as you say the sound.

Say: ***Repeat the sounds for these letters: /sh/, /pr/.***

Put all the flash cards face down on the table and mix them up.

Say: ***Choose a card and tell me the letter sound.***

Have students choose a card and say the sound, mixing the cards between student turns. Give every student a turn, repeating until each student has had the opportunity to demonstrate knowledge on the target digraph */sh/*.

Pr pr

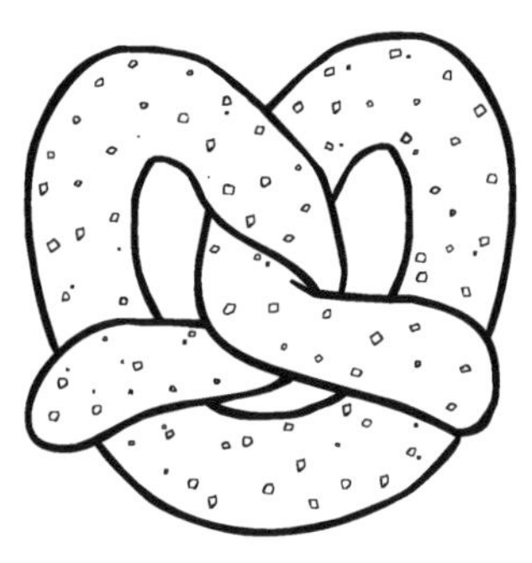

Letter and Picture Cards for pr

Sh	sh

	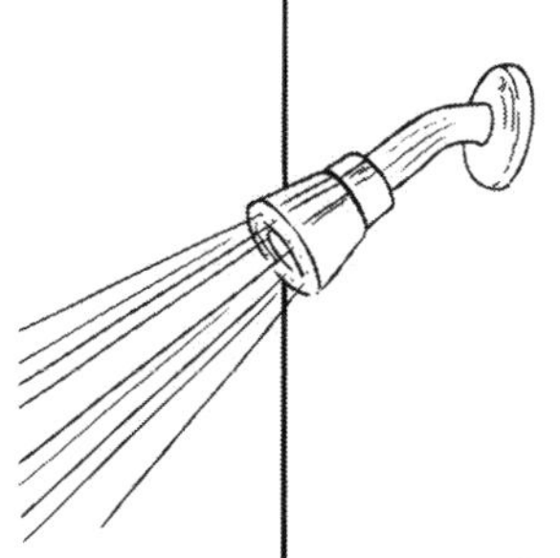

Reteaching Lessons ✓

Letter and Picture Cards for sh

The Sound for scr Is /scr/

Grade K

10 Min.

CCSS.RF.K.3a
TEKS 110.11.3.A

LEARNING OBJECTIVE: Demonstrate letter-sound correspondence by blending two consonant sounds.

LANGUAGE OBJECTIVE: Produce the sounds in a consonant blend when shown a visual grapheme.

Lesson Overview

Introduce the consonant blend, play a game to practice identifying the consonant blend, and assess students' ability to associate a consonant blend with a specific letter combination.

Materials	Preparation
• Letter and Picture Cards for *scr* • Letter and Picture Cards for *sn* • Paper bag	• Cut out all letter and picture cards.

Teach and Model

Show students the upper- and lowercase letter cards for *scr*.

Say: ***This is /scr/. The letters* s, c, *and* and r *blend together to stand for the sound /scr/. Make the blend with me: /scr/***. Have students produce the sound with you.

Point to the letter card.

Say: ***Make the blend /scr/ every time I put my finger on it.*** Have students produce the sound. Point to the card several times. Mix up the practice by asking individual students to say the sound.

Hold up a picture card.

Say: ***This word is* scrapbook. *It begins with the blend /scr/. What is this?*** Have students repeat the name of the picture.

Say: ***What sound does* scrapbook *begin with?*** Have students produce the */scr/* sound independently.

Repeat questions above with each picture card for */scr/*.

Picture cards for /scr/: scrape, scream, scratch, screen, screw, scrub, scrap, scrapbook

Connect Sound/Spelling: Letter Sound Bag

Put all letter and picture cards for *scr* in the paper bag.

Explain: ***The pictures on these cards start with /scr/. If you pull a letter card from the bag, tell me the blend. Then tell me a word that starts with that blend.***

Model: ***If I pull out* scrub, *I say /scr/, /scr/,* scrub.**

Explain: ***If you pull a picture card, tell me the blend it starts with and what the picture is.***

Model: ***If I pull out a picture of a scrapbook, I say /scr/, /scr/,* scrapbook.**

Have students take turns drawing cards from the paper bag.

Word bank: scrub, scribble, scream, scratch, screw, scrap

Connect Sound/Spelling: Thumbs Up, Thumbs Down for Beginning Sounds

Say: ***Show me thumbs up.*** Model what thumbs up looks like and help students show their thumbs up.

Explain: ***When you hear a word that begins with the blend /scr/, make a thumbs up and say the blend. If the word doesn't start with the blend /scr/, give me a thumbs down.*** Model thumbs down for students and help students show their thumbs down.

Say each word from the word bank below, alternating between words that begin with */scr/* and words that don't.

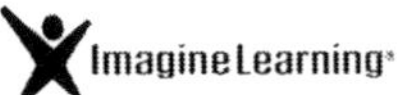

Words that begin with /scr/: screw, scrub, scream, scrambled egg, scrap, scrape, scratch, screen, scrub, script, scribe

Words that don't begin with /scr/: nine, sandwich, untie, soup

Check Progress: Letter Stack

Observe each student during practice and use the following activity to check progress on the target skill. If student can correctly identify the blend twice, consider the intervention successful.

Point to the appropriate letter card as you say the sound.

Say: ***Repeat the blends for these letters: /scr/, /scr/, /sn/, /sn/.***

Shuffle letter cards for *scr* and *sn* together in a stack.

Say: ***Choose a card and tell me the blend.***

Have students draw a card from the stack, say the sound, and put the card on the bottom of the stack. Repeat until every student has had several opportunities to demonstrate knowledge of the target blend */scr/*.

The Sound for sn Is /sn/

Grade K

10 Min.

CCSS.RF.K.3a
TEKS 110.11.3.A

LEARNING OBJECTIVE: Demonstrate letter-sound correspondence by blending two consonant sounds.

LANGUAGE OBJECTIVE: Produce the sounds in a consonant blend when shown a visual grapheme.

Lesson Overview

Introduce the consonant blend, play a game to practice identifying the consonant blend, and assess students' ability to associate a consonant blend with a specific letter combination.

Materials	Preparation
• Letter and Picture Cards for *sn* • Letter and Picture Cards for *scr* • Small, soft ball or toy	• Cut out all letter and picture cards.

Teach and Model

Show students the upper- and lowercase letter cards for *sn*.

Say: ***This is /sn/. The letters* s *and* n *blend together to stand for the sound /sn/. Make the blend with me: /sn/***. Have students produce the sound with you.

Point to the letter card.

Say: ***Make the blend /sn/ every time I put my finger on it.*** Have students produce the sound. Point to the card several times. Mix up the practice by asking individual students to say the sound.

Hold up a picture card.

Say: ***This word is* snail. *It begins with the blend /sn/. What is this?*** Have students repeat the name of the picture.

Say: ***What sound does* snail *begin with?*** Have students produce the */sn/* sound independently.

Repeat questions above with each picture card for */sn/*.

Picture cards for /sn/: snail, snake, snack, snow, snap, snore, sneakers, snowman

Connect Sound/Spelling: Thumbs Up, Thumbs Down for Beginning Sounds

Say: ***Show me thumbs up.*** Model what thumbs up looks like and help students show their thumbs up.

Explain: ***When you hear a word that begins with the blend /sn/, make a thumbs up and say the blend. If the word doesn't start with the blend /sn/, give me a thumbs down.*** Model thumbs down for students and help students show their thumbs down.

Say each word from the word bank below, alternating between words that begin with */sn/* and words that don't.

Words that begin with /sn/: snorkel, sniff, sneeze, snowy, snowman, snort, snag, sniffle, snakeskin

Words that don't begin with /sn/: spring, faster, drink, thumb

EXTENSION ACTIVITY: Ask students to think of other words that begin with /sn/.

Connect Sound/Spelling: Letter Sound Toss

Show the ball and the letter cards.

Explain: ***When I toss this ball to you, say the blend /sn/ twice. Then say a word that begins with that blend and toss the ball to a classmate.***

Model: **/sn/, /sn/, snail.** Demonstrate the sequence with a volunteer.

Toss the ball to a student. Provide prompts as needed (e.g., What do you eat between meals?). Continue until all students have had several turns.

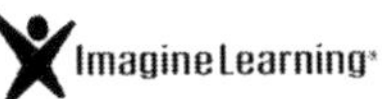

Word bank: snail, snack, snap, sneakers, snort, snore, sniff, sneeze, snow, snowman, snoop, snout

Check Progress: Letter Flip

Observe each student during practice and use the following activity to check progress on the target skill. If student can correctly identify the blend twice, consider the intervention successful.

Point to the appropriate letter card as you say the sound.

Say: ***Repeat the blends for these letters: /sn/, /scr/.***

Put all the flash cards face down on the table and mix them up.

Say: ***Choose a card and tell me the blend.***

Have students choose a card and say the sound, mixing the cards between student turns. Give every student a turn, repeating until each student has had the opportunity to demonstrate knowledge on the target blend */sn/*.

Scr

scr

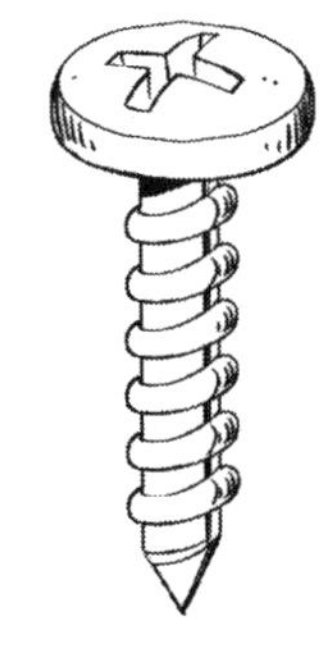

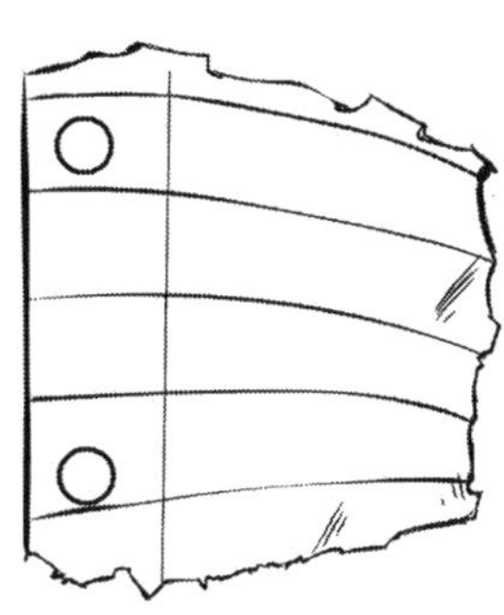

Letter and Picture Cards for scr

Sn	sn

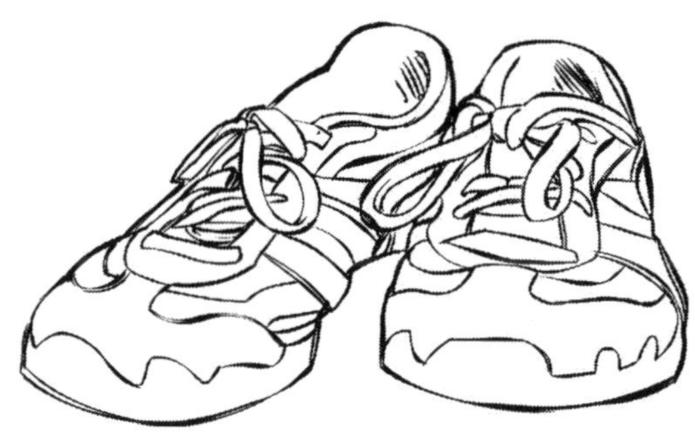	

The Sound for sk Is /sk/

Grade K

10 Min.

CCSS.RF.K.3a
TEKS 110.11.3.A

LEARNING OBJECTIVE: Demonstrate letter-sound correspondence by blending two consonant sounds.

LANGUAGE OBJECTIVE: Produce the sounds in a consonant blend when shown a visual grapheme.

Lesson Overview

Introduce the consonant blend, play a game to practice identifying the consonant blend, and assess students' ability to associate a consonant blend with a specific letter combination.

Materials	Preparation
• Letter and Picture Cards for *sk* • Letter and Picture Cards for *ph*	• Cut out all letter and picture cards.

Teach and Model

Show students the upper- and lowercase letter cards for *sk*.

Say: ***This is /sk/. The letters* s *and* k *blend together to stand for the sound /sk/. Make the blend with me: /sk/.*** Have students produce the sound with you.

Point to the letter card.

Say: ***Make the blend /sk/ every time I put my finger on it.*** Have students produce the sound. Point to the card several times. Mix up the practice by asking individual students to say the sound.

Hold up a picture card.

Say: ***This word is* skate. *It begins with the blend /sk/. What is this?*** Have students repeat the name of the picture.

Say: ***What sound does* skate *begin with?*** Have students produce the */sk/* sound independently.

Repeat questions above with each picture card for */sk/*.

Picture cards for /sk/: skunk, skirt, sky, skate, skeleton, skis, skyscraper, sketch

Connect Sound/Spelling: Thumbs Up, Thumbs Down for Beginning Sounds

Say: ***Show me thumbs up.*** Model what thumbs up looks like and help students show their thumbs up.

Explain: ***When you hear a word that begins with the blend /sk/, make a thumbs up and say the blend. If the word doesn't start with the blend /sk/, give me a thumbs down.*** Model thumbs down for students and help students show their thumbs down.

Say each word from the word bank below, alternating between words that begin with */sk/* and words that don't.

Words that begin with /sk/: skate, skydiver, skull, skid, skill, sketch, skyline

Words that don't begin with /sk/: key, triangle, flag, garden.

Connect Sound/Spelling: Letter Sound Sort

Shuffle picture cards for *sk* and *ph* together. Display letter cards for *sk* on a table, allowing enough space for a column of picture cards below the letter cards. Display letter cards for *ph* next to the letter cards for *sk*.

Say: ***These are the letters* p *and* h. Ph *stands for the sound /ph/. Everyone say /ph/.*** Have students produce the sound.

Show the stack of picture cards.

Explain: ***The pictures on these cards begin with the letter sound /sk/ or /ph/. We are going to put them with their matching letter.***

Show the first picture card.

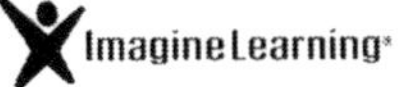

Demonstrate: **Skunk.** ***This picture begins with the letter sound /sk/: /sk/, /sk/, skunk. Say /sk/, /sk/, skunk.*** Have students repeat the sound and word.

Demonstrate: **Skunk *goes with this card, /sk/.*** Place the picture card below the letter cards for *sk*.

Have students draw the remaining picture cards from the stack and place them in a column under the matching letter card. As each card is added, direct students to say the letter sound twice and then name the picture: */sk/, /sk/*, skeleton; */ph/, /ph/*, phone.

Picture cards for /ph/: phone, photo, pharmacy, physician, photographer, pheasant, phonics, pharaoh

EXTENSION ACTIVITY: Randomly point to pictures in the two columns and instruct students to repeat the letter sound and name the picture.

Check Progress: Letter Stack

Observe each student during practice and use the following activity to check progress on the target skill. If student can correctly identify the blend twice, consider the intervention successful.

Point to the appropriate letter card as you say the sound.

Say: ***Repeat the blends for these letters: /sk/, /sk/, /ph/, /ph/.***

Shuffle letter cards for *sk* and *ph* together in a stack.

Say: ***Choose a card and tell me the blend.***

Have students draw a card from the stack, say the sound, and put the card on the bottom of the stack. Repeat until every student has had several opportunities to demonstrate knowledge of the target blend */sk/*.

The Sound for ph Is /f/

Grade K

10 Min.

CCSS.RF.K.3a
TEKS 110.11.3.A

LEARNING OBJECTIVE: Demonstrate letter-sound correspondence by producing the most common sound for the digraph.

LANGUAGE OBJECTIVE: Produce the sound for each consonant digraph when shown a visual grapheme.

Lesson Overview

Introduce the digraph, play a game to practice identifying the digraph, and assess students' ability to associate a specific digraph with a consonant combination.

Materials	Preparation
• Letter and Picture Cards for *ph* • Letter and Picture Cards for *sk*	• Cut out all letter and picture cards.

Teach and Model

Show students the upper- and lowercase letter cards for *ph*.

Say: ***This is /f/. The letters* p *and* h *stand for the letter sound /f/. Make the letter sound with me: /f/.*** Have students produce the letter sound with you.

Point to the letter card.

Say: ***Make the letter sound /f/ every time I put my finger on it: /f/.*** Have students produce the letter sound. Point to the card several times. Mix up the practice by asking individual students to say the letter sound.

Hold up a picture card.

Say: ***This word is* phone. *It begins with /f/. What is this?*** Have students repeat the name of the picture.

Say: ***What letter sound does* phone *begin with?*** Have students produce the */f/* sound independently.

Repeat questions above with each picture card.

Picture cards for /f/: phone, photo, pharmacy, physician, photographer, pheasant, phonics, pharaoh

Connect Sound/Spelling: Letter Sound Sort

Shuffle picture cards for *ph* and *sk* together. Display letter cards for *ph* on a table, allowing enough space for a column of picture cards below the letter cards. Display letter cards for *sk* next to the letter cards for *ph*.

Say: ***This is letter* sk. Sk *stands for the letter sound /sk/. Everyone say /sk/.*** Have students produce the letter sound.

Show the stack of picture cards.

Explain: ***The pictures on these cards begin with the sound /f/ or /sk/. We are going to put them with their matching letter.***

Show the first picture card.

Demonstrate: **Phone. *This picture begins with the letter sound /f/: /f/, /f/,* phone. *Say /f/, /f/,* phone.** Have students repeat the letter sound and word.

Demonstrate: **Phone *goes with this card, /f/.*** Place the picture card below the letter cards for *ph*.

Have students draw the remaining picture cards from the stack and place them in a column under the matching letter card. As each card is added, direct students to say the digraph twice and then name the picture: */f/*, */f/*, phonics; */sk/*, */sk/*, sky.

Picture cards for /sk/: skunk, skirt, sky, skate, skeleton, ski, skyscraper, sketch

EXTENSION ACTIVITY: Randomly point to pictures in the two columns and instruct students to repeat the digraph and name the picture.

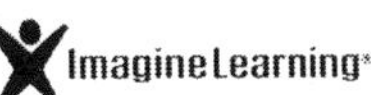

Connect Sound/Spelling: Stand Up, Sit Down

Show the letter card.

Explain: ***When I say a word, listen carefully to the beginning and the ending sounds of the word. When you hear /f/ at the beginning of the word, stand up. When you hear /f/ at the end of the word, sit down. Let's try one.***

Ask: ***Where do you hear /f/ in* photo?** Students should stand up.

Say: ***Yes!* Photo *has /f/ at the beginning of the word, so you stand up. Let's try another one:* autograph.** Students should sit down.

Say: ***Good!* Autograph *has /f/ at the end of the word, so you sit down.***

Alternate between words beginning and ending with */f/* from the lists below.

Words that begin with /f/: photo, phantom, pharaoh, phone, phonics, pharmacy, phase, photographer, pharmacist, physician

Words that end with /f/: graph, morph, triumph, monograph, paragraph, photograph, telegraph, Joseph, Ralph

Check Progress: Letter Flip

Observe each student during practice and use the following activity to check progress on the target skill. If student can correctly identify the digraph twice, consider the intervention successful.

Point to the appropriate letter card as you say the sound.

Say: ***Repeat the sounds for these letters: /f/, /sk/.***

Put all the flash cards face down on the table and mix them up.

Say: ***Choose a card and tell me the letter sound.***

Have students choose a card and say the sound, mixing the cards between student turns. Give every student a turn, repeating until each student has had the opportunity to demonstrate knowledge on the target digraph */f/*.

Reteaching Lessons

Sk

sk

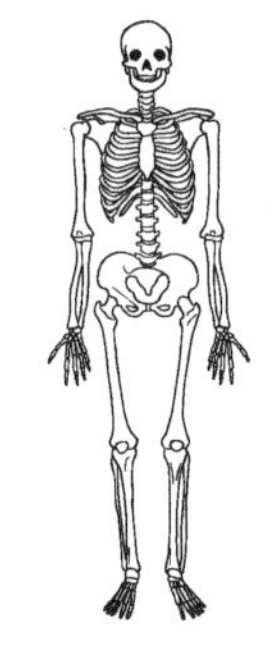

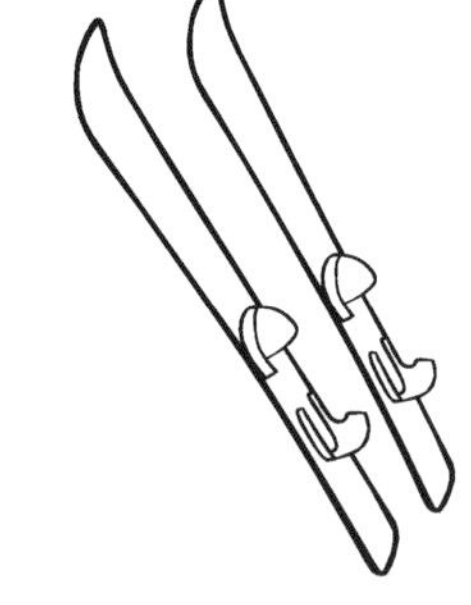

Ph

ph

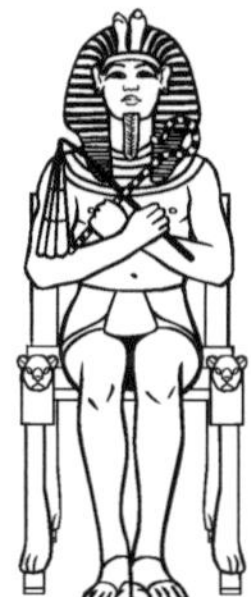

Reteaching Lessons

The Sound for sp is /sp/

Grade K

10 Min.

CCSS.RF.K.3a
TEKS 110.11.3.A

LEARNING OBJECTIVE: Demonstrate letter-sound correspondence by blending two consonant sounds.

LANGUAGE OBJECTIVE: Produce the sounds in a consonant blend when shown a visual grapheme.

Lesson Overview

Introduce the consonant blend, play a game to practice identifying the consonant blend, and assess students' ability to associate a consonant blend with a specific letter combination.

Materials	Preparation
• Letter and Picture Cards for *sp* • Letter and Picture Cards for *sw* • Small, soft ball or toy	• Cut out all letter and picture cards.

Teach and Model

Show students the upper- and lowercase letter cards for *sp*.

Say: ***This is /sp/. The letters* s *and* p *blend together to stand for the sound /sp/. Make the blend with me: /sp/***. Have students produce the sound with you.

Point to the letter card.

Say: ***Make the blend /sp/ every time I put my finger on it.*** Have students produce the sound. Point to the card several times. Mix up the practice by asking individual students to say the sound.

Hold up a picture card.

Say: ***This word is* spoon. *It begins with the blend /sp/. What is this?*** Have students repeat the name of the picture.

Say: ***What sound does* spoon *begin with?*** Have students produce the */sp/* sound independently.

Repeat questions above with each picture card for */sp/*.

Picture cards for /sp/: spider, spaghetti, spoon, sponge, spot, speedboat, spark, spout

Connect Sound/Spelling: Letter Sound Toss

Show the ball and the letter cards.

Explain: ***When I toss this ball to you, say the blend /sp/ twice. Then say a word that begins with that blend and toss the ball to a classmate.***

Model: **/sp/, /sp/, spider.** Demonstrate the sequence with a volunteer.

Toss the ball to a student. Provide prompts as needed (e.g., What do you use to eat soup?). Continue until all students have had several turns.

Word bank: spider, spoon, spaghetti, sponge, spot, speedboat, spark, spout

Connect Sound/Spelling: Stand Up, Sit Down

Show the letter card.

Explain: ***When I say a word, listen carefully to the beginning and the ending sounds of the word. When you hear /sp/ at the beginning of the word, stand up. When you hear /sp/ at the end of the word, sit down. Let's try one.***

Ask: ***Where do you hear /sp/ in* spoon?** Students should stand up.

Say: ***Yes!* Spoon *has /sp/ at the beginning of the word, so you stand up. Let's try another one:* wisp.** Students should sit down.

Say: ***Good!* Wisp *has /sp/ at the end of the word, so you sit down.***

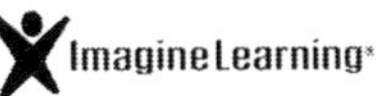

Alternate between words beginning and ending with /sp/ from the lists below.

Words that begin with /sp/: sponge, spoon, spark, spout, speed, spell, spill, spool, space

Words that end with /sp/: clasp, gasp, wasp, wisp, crisp, lisp

Check Progress: Letter Stack

Observe each student during practice and use the following activity to check progress on the target skill. If student can correctly identify the blend twice, consider the intervention successful.

Point to the appropriate letter card as you say the sound.

Say: ***Repeat the blends for these letters: /sp/, /sp/, /sw/, /sw/.***

Shuffle letter cards for *sp* and *sw* together in a stack.

Say: ***Choose a card and tell me the blend.***

Have students draw a card from the stack, say the sound, and put the card on the bottom of the stack. Repeat until every student has had several opportunities to demonstrate knowledge of the target blend */sp/*.

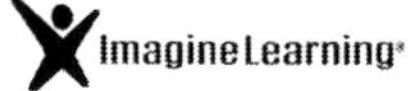

The Sound for sw is /sw/

LEARNING OBJECTIVE: Demonstrate letter-sound correspondence by blending two consonant sounds.

LANGUAGE OBJECTIVE: Produce the sounds in a consonant blend when shown a visual grapheme.

Lesson Overview

Introduce the consonant blend, play a game to practice identifying the consonant blend, and assess students' ability to associate a consonant blend with a specific letter combination.

Materials	Preparation
• Letter and Picture Cards for *sw* • Letter and Picture Cards for *sp*	• Cut out all letter and picture cards.

Teach and Model

Show students the upper- and lowercase letter cards for *sw*.

Say: ***This is /sw/. The letters* s *and* w *blend together to stand for the sound /sw/. Make the blend with me: /sw/***. Have students produce the sound with you.

Point to the letter card.

Say: ***Make the blend /sw/ every time I put my finger on it.*** Have students produce the sound. Point to the card several times. Mix up the practice by asking individual students to say the sound.

Hold up a picture card.

Say: ***This word is* swing. *It begins with the blend /sw/. What is this?*** Have students repeat the name of the picture.

Say: ***What sound does* swing *begin with?*** Have students produce the */sw/* sound independently.

Repeat questions above with each picture card for */sw/*.

Picture cards for /sw/: swing, swim, swan, sweater, sword, swirl, sweaty, sweep

Reteaching Lessons

Connect Sound/Spelling: Thumbs Up, Thumbs Down for Beginning Sounds

Say: ***Show me thumbs up.*** Model what thumbs up looks like and help students show their thumbs up.

Explain: ***When you hear a word that begins with the blend /sw/, make a thumbs up and say the blend. If the word doesn't start with the blend /sw/, give me a thumbs down.*** Model thumbs down for students and help students show their thumbs down.

Say each word from the word bank below, alternating between words that begin with */sw/* and words that don't.

Words that begin with /sw/: swing, swim, sweep, swift, swirl, swamp, sweet, sweat, swipe, swallow, swollen, swing, sweater

Words that don't begin with /sw/: hat, farmer, square, goldfish

EXTENSION ACTIVITY: Ask students to think of other words that begin with /sw/.

Connect Sound/Spelling: Letter Sound Sort

Shuffle picture cards for *sw* and *sp* together. Display letter cards for *sw* on a table, allowing enough space for a column of picture cards below the letter cards. Display letter cards for *sp* next to the letter cards for *sw*.

Say: ***This is letter* sp. sp *stands for the sound /sp/. Everyone say /sp/.*** Have students produce the sound.

Show the stack of picture cards.

Explain: ***The pictures on these cards begin with the letter sound /sw/ or /sp/. We are going to put them with their matching letter.***

Show the first picture card.

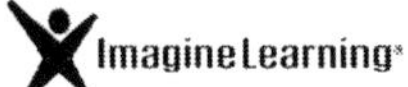

Demonstrate: **Swan*. This picture begins with the letter sound* /sw/: /sw/, /sw/, swan. *Say* /sw/, /sw/, swan.** Have students repeat the sound and word.

Demonstrate: **Swan *goes with this card,* /sw/.** Place the picture card below the letter cards for *sw*.

Have students draw the remaining picture cards from the stack and place them in a column under the matching letter card. As each card is added, direct students to say the letter sound twice and then name the picture: */sw/*, */sw/*, swim; */sp/*, */sp/*, spider.

Picture cards for /sp/: spider, spaghetti, spoon, sponge, spot, speedboat, spark, spout

EXTENSION ACTIVITY: Randomly point to pictures in the two columns and instruct students to repeat the letter sound and name the picture.

Check Progress: Letter Flip

Observe each student during practice and use the following activity to check progress on the target skill. If student can correctly identify the blend twice, consider the intervention successful.

Point to the appropriate letter card as you say the sound.

Say: ***Repeat the blends for these letters: /sw/, /sp/.***

Put all the flash cards face down on the table and mix them up.

Say: ***Choose a card and tell me the blend.***

Have students choose a card and say the sound, mixing the cards between student turns. Give every student a turn, repeating until each student has had the opportunity to demonstrate knowledge on the target blend */sw/*.

Sp

sp

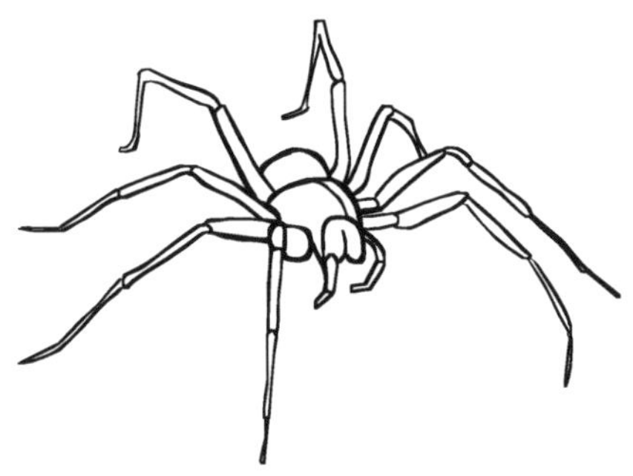

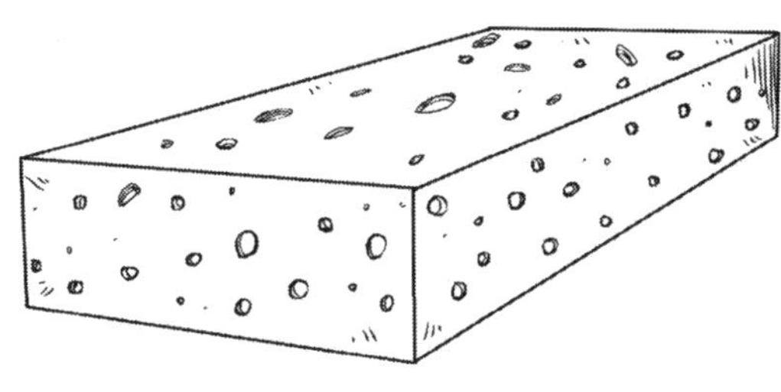

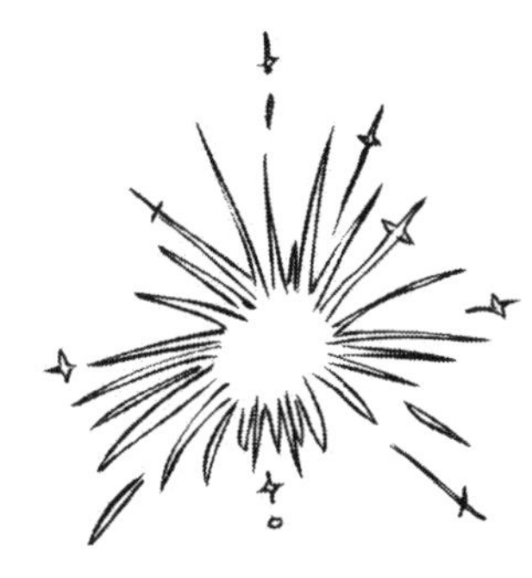

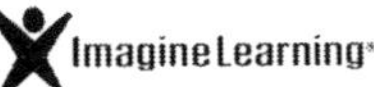

Sw

The Sound for st Is /st/

CCSS.RF.K.3a
TEKS 110.11.3.A

LEARNING OBJECTIVE: Demonstrate letter-sound correspondence by blending two consonant sounds.

LANGUAGE OBJECTIVE: Produce the sounds in a consonant blend when shown a visual grapheme.

Lesson Overview

Introduce the consonant blend, play a game to practice identifying the consonant blend, and assess students' ability to associate a consonant blend with a specific letter combination.

Materials	Preparation
• Letter and Picture Cards for *st* • Letter and Picture Cards for *ch* • Paper bag	• Cut out all letter and picture cards.

Teach and Model

Show students the upper- and lowercase letter cards for *st*.

Say: ***This is /st/. The letters* s *and* t *blend together to stand for the sound /st/. Make the blend with me: /st/***. Have students produce the sound with you.

Point to the letter card.

Say: ***Make the blend /st/ every time I put my finger on it.*** Have students produce the sound. Point to the card several times. Mix up the practice by asking individual students to say the sound.

Hold up a picture card.

Say: ***This word is* star. *It begins with the blend /st/. What is this?*** Have students repeat the name of the picture.

Say: ***What sound does* star *begin with?*** Have students produce the */st/* sound independently.

Repeat questions above with each picture card for */st/*.

Picture cards for /st/: stingray, strawberry, steak, string, stapler, star, stop, stairs

Connect Sound/Spelling: Letter Sound Bag

Put all letter and picture cards for *st* in the paper bag.

Explain: ***The pictures on these cards start with /st/. If you pull a letter card from the bag, tell me the blend. Then tell me a word that starts with that blend.***

Model: ***If I pull out* string, *I say /st/, /st/,* string.**

Explain: ***If you pull a picture card, tell me the blend it starts with and what the picture is.***

Model: ***If I pull out a picture of a star, I say /st/, /st/,* star.**

Have students take turns drawing cards from the paper bag.

Word bank: string, star, story, start, state, stage, stack, sticky, storm, step

Connect Sound/Spelling: Stand Up, Sit Down

Show the letter card.

Explain: ***When I say a word, listen carefully to the beginning and the ending sounds of the word. When you hear /st/ at the beginning of the word, stand up. When you hear /st/ at the end of the word, sit down. Let's try one.***

Ask: ***Where do you hear /st/ in* star?** Students should stand up.

Say: ***Yes!* Star *has /st/ at the beginning of the word, so you stand up. Let's try another one:* toast.** Students should sit down.

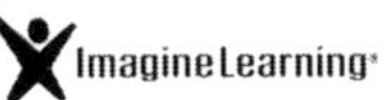

Say: ***Good!* Toast *has* /st/ *at the end of the word, so you sit down.***

Alternate between words beginning and ending with /st/ from the lists below.

Words that begin with /st/: stop, stool, stairs, store, street, string, stapler, star, stone

Words that end with /st/: last, must, rust, fast, checklist, lost, dentist, gymnast, chest, boost, waist, burst, wrist, west

Check Progress: Letter Flip

Observe each student during practice and use the following activity to check progress on the target skill. If student can correctly identify the blend twice, consider the intervention successful.

Point to the appropriate letter card as you say the sound.

Say: ***Repeat the blends for these letters:* /st/, /ch/.**

Put all the flash cards face down on the table and mix them up.

Say: ***Choose a card and tell me the blend.***

Have students choose a card and say the sound, mixing the cards between student turns. Give every student a turn, repeating until each student has had the opportunity to demonstrate knowledge on the target blend /st/.

Reteaching Lessons

The Sound for ch Is /ch/

Grade K

10 Min.

CCSS.RF.K.3a
TEKS 110.11.3.A

LEARNING OBJECTIVE: Demonstrate letter-sound correspondence by producing the most common sound for the digraph.

LANGUAGE OBJECTIVE: Produce the sound for each consonant digraph when shown a visual grapheme.

Lesson Overview

Introduce the digraph, play a game to practice identifying the digraph, and assess students' ability to associate a specific digraph with a consonant combination.

Materials	Preparation
• Letter and Picture Cards for *ch* • Letter and Picture Cards for *st*	• Cut out all letter and picture cards.

Teach and Model

Show students the upper- and lowercase letter cards for *ch*.

Say: ***This is /ch/. The letters* c *and* h *stand for the letter sound /ch/. Make the letter sound with me: /ch/.*** Have students produce the letter sound with you.

Point to the letter card.

Say: ***Make the letter sound /ch/ every time I put my finger on it: /ch/.*** Have students produce the letter sound. Point to the card several times. Mix up the practice by asking individual students to say the letter sound.

Hold up a picture card.

Say: ***This word is* chair. *It begins with /ch/. What is this?*** Have students repeat the name of the picture.

Say: ***What letter sound does* chair *begin with?*** Have students produce the */ch/* sound independently.

Repeat questions above with each picture card.

Picture cards for /ch/: chicken, chair, chipmunk, cheese, cherry, chips, chin, chain

Connect Sound/Spelling: Letter Sound Sort

Shuffle picture cards for *ch* and *st* together. Display letter cards for *ch* on a table, allowing enough space for a column of picture cards below the letter cards. Display letter cards for *st* next to the letter cards for *ch*.

Say: ***This is letter* st. St *stands for the letter sound /st/. Everyone say /st/.*** Have students produce the letter sound.

Show the stack of picture cards.

Explain: ***The pictures on these cards begin with the sound /ch/ or /st/. We are going to put them with their matching letter.***

Show the first picture card.

Demonstrate: **Chair. *This picture begins with the letter sound /ch/: /ch/, /ch/,* chair. *Say /ch/, /ch/,* chair.** Have students repeat the letter sound and word.

Demonstrate: **Chair *goes with this card, /ch/.*** Place the picture card below the letter cards for *ch*.

Have students draw the remaining picture cards from the stack and place them in a column under the matching letter card. As each card is added, direct students to say the digraph twice and then name the picture: */ch/*, */ch/*, chin; */st/*, */st/*, stop.

Picture cards for /st/: stingray, strawberry, steak, string, stapler, star, stop, stairs

EXTENSION ACTIVITY: Randomly point to pictures in the two columns and instruct students to repeat the digraph and name the picture.

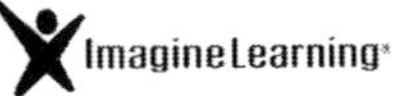

Connect Sound/Spelling: Stand Up, Sit Down

Show the letter card.

Explain: ***When I say a word, listen carefully to the beginning and the ending sounds of the word. When you hear /ch/ at the beginning of the word, stand up. When you hear /ch/ at the end of the word, sit down. Let's try one.***

Ask: ***Where do you hear /ch/ in* chin?** Students should stand up.

Say: ***Yes!* Chin *has /ch/ at the beginning of the word, so you stand up. Let's try another one:* teach.** Students should sit down.

Say: ***Good!* Teach *has /ch/ at the end of the word, so you sit down.***

Alternate between words beginning and ending with */ch/* from the lists below.

Words that begin with /ch/: chilly, chase, charm, child, chart, chalk, chance, charcoal, charger, cheerful, chewed, chart

Words that end with /ch/: cockroach, teach, workbench, research, sandwich, spinach, branch, crunch, wrench, speech, search, peach, bench, coach, lunch, touch, each

Check Progress: Letter Flip

Observe each student during practice and use the following activity to check progress on the target skill. If student can correctly identify the digraph twice, consider the intervention successful.

Point to the appropriate letter card as you say the sound.

Say: ***Repeat the sounds for these letters: /ch/, /st/.***

Put all the flash cards face down on the table and mix them up.

Say: ***Choose a card and tell me the letter sound.***

Have students choose a card and say the sound, mixing the cards between student turns. Give every student a turn, repeating until each student has had the opportunity to demonstrate knowledge on the target digraph */ch/*.

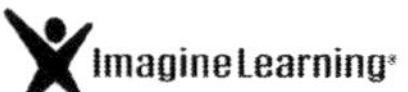

St	st
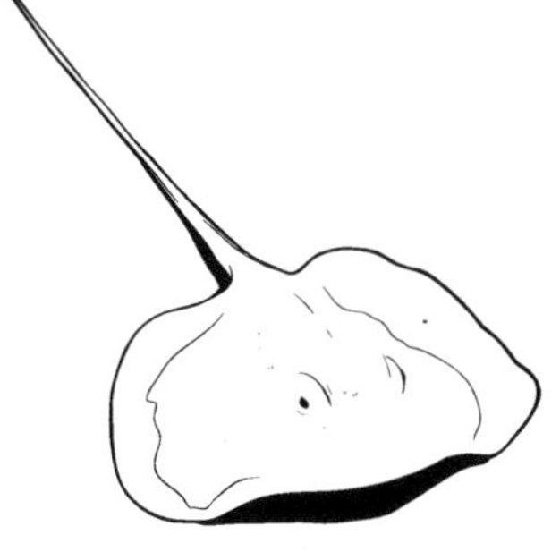	
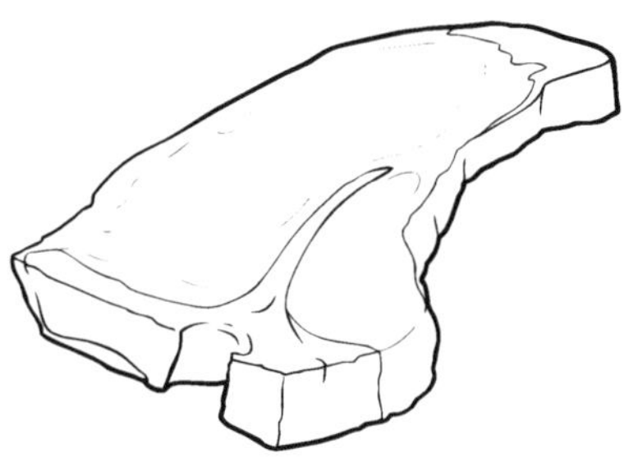	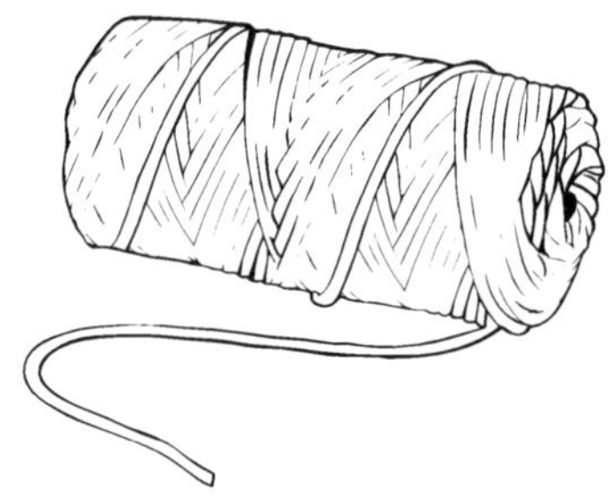
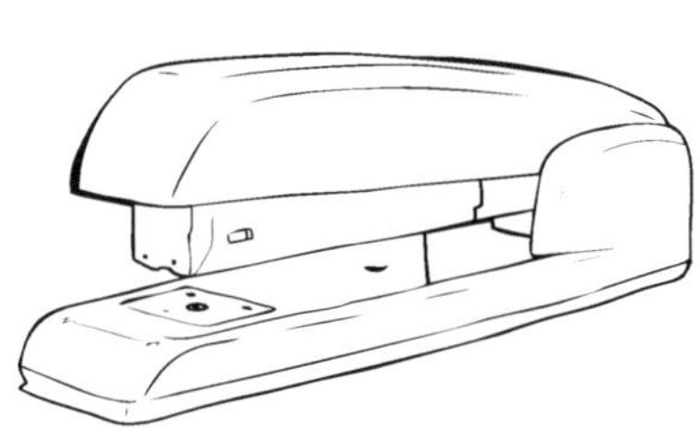	

Letter and Picture Cards for st

Ch	ch

	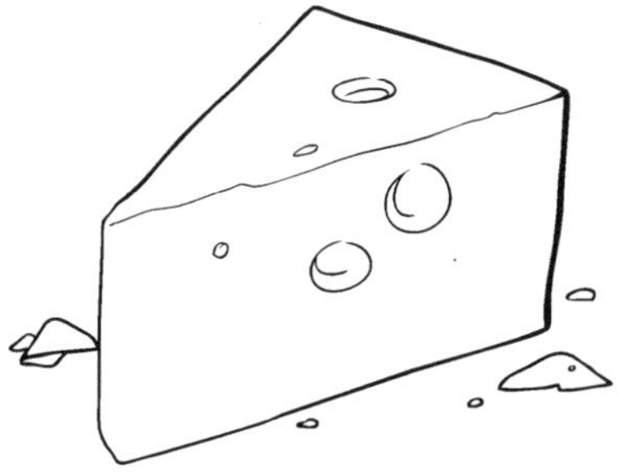

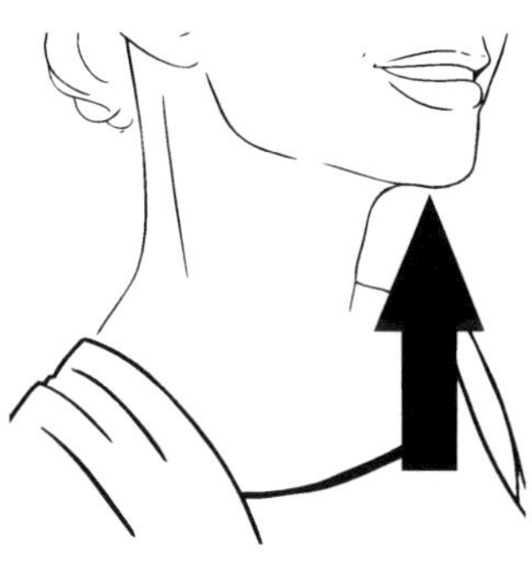	

Reteaching Lessons

The Sound for kn Is /n/

Grade K

10 Min.

CCSS.RF.K.3a
TEKS 110.11.3.A

LEARNING OBJECTIVE: Demonstrate letter-sound correspondence by producing the sound associated with the consonants k (silent) and n.

LANGUAGE OBJECTIVE: Produce the correct letter sound when shown a visual grapheme.

Lesson Overview

Introduce the letter sound, play a game to practice identifying the letter sound, and assess students' ability to associate a specific letter sound with a specific letter.

Materials	Preparation
• Letter and Picture Cards for *kn* • Letter and Picture Cards for *wr*	• Cut out all letter and picture cards.

Teach and Model

Show students the upper- and lowercase letter cards for *kn*.

Say: ***This is* kn. *The letters* k *and* n *together stand for the sound /n/. Make the sound with me: /n/.*** Have students produce the sound with you.

Point to the letter card.

Say: ***Make the /n/ sound every time I put my finger on it.*** Have students produce the sound. Point to the card several times. Mix up the practice by asking individual students to say the sound.

Hold up a picture card.

Say: ***This is* knit. *It begins with /n/. What is this?*** Have students repeat the name of the picture.

Say: ***What sound does* knit *begin with?*** Have students produce the /n/ sound independently.

Repeat questions above with each picture card.

Picture cards for /n/: knit, knee, knob, knot, knife, kneel, knuckle, knight

Connect Sound/Spelling: Thumbs Up, Thumbs Down for Beginning Sounds

Say: ***Show me thumbs up.*** Model what thumbs up looks like and help students show their thumbs up.

Explain: ***When you hear a word that begins with the letter sound /n/, make a thumbs up and say the letter sound. If the word doesn't start with the letter sound /n/, give me a thumbs down.*** Model thumbs down for students and help students show their thumbs down.

Say each word from the word bank below, alternating between words that begin with /n/ and words that don't.

Words that begin with /n/: knot, knife, knee, knit, knob, kneel, knuckle, knight, knapsack, knock

Words that don't begin with /n/: snack, pan, rock, rabbit

Connect Sound/Spelling: Letter Sound Sort

Shuffle picture cards for *kn* and *wr* together. Display letter cards for *kn* on a table, allowing enough space for a column of picture cards below the letter cards. Display letter cards for *wr* next to the letter cards for *kn*.

Say: ***This is letter* wr. Wr *stands for the sound /r/. Everyone say /r/.*** Have students produce the sound.

Show the stack of picture cards.

Explain: ***The pictures on these cards begin with the letter sounds /n/ or /r/. We are going to put them with their matching letter.***

Show the first picture card.

Demonstrate: **Kneel. *This picture begins with the letter sound /n/: /n/, /n/,* kneel. *Say /n/, /n/,* kneel.** Have students repeat the sound and word.

Demonstrate: **Kneel *goes with this card, /n/.*** Place the picture card below the letter cards for *kn*.

Have students draw the remaining picture cards from the stack and place them in a column under the matching letter card. As each card is added, direct students to say the sound twice and then name the picture: */n/, /n/, knot; /r/, /r/, wren*.

Picture cards for /r/: wren, wrap, wrist, write, wreath, wristband, wrinkle, wrench

EXTENSION ACTIVITY: Randomly point to pictures in the two columns and instruct students to repeat the letter sound and name the picture.

Check Progress: Letter Flip

Observe each student during practice and use the following activity to check progress on the target skill. If student can correctly identify the letter sound twice, consider the intervention successful.

Point to the appropriate letter card as you say the sound.

Say: ***Repeat the letter sounds for these letters: /n/, /r/.***

Put all the flash cards face down on the table and mix them up.

Say: ***Choose a card and tell me the letter sound.***

Have students choose a card and say the sound, mixing the cards between student turns. Give every student a turn, repeating until each student has had the opportunity to demonstrate knowledge on the target letter sound */kn/*.

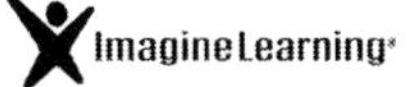

The Sound for wr Is /r/

LEARNING OBJECTIVE: Demonstrate letter-sound correspondence by producing the sound associated with the consonants w (silent) and r.

LANGUAGE OBJECTIVE: Produce the correct letter sound when shown a visual grapheme.

Lesson Overview

Introduce the letter sound, play a game to practice identifying the letter sound, and assess students' ability to associate a specific letter sound with a specific letter.

Materials	Preparation
• Letter and Picture Cards for *wr* • Letter and Picture Cards for *kn*	• Cut out all letter and picture cards.

Teach and Model

Show students the upper- and lowercase letter cards for *wr*.

Say: ***This is* wr. *The letters* w *and* r *together stand for the sound /ɾ/. Make the sound with me: /ɾ/.*** Have students produce the sound with you.

Point to the letter card.

Say: ***Make the /ɾ/ sound every time I put my finger on it.*** Have students produce the sound. Point to the card several times. Mix up the practice by asking individual students to say the sound.

Hold up a picture card.

Say: ***This is* wreath. *It begins with /ɾ/. What is this?*** Have students repeat the name of the picture.

Say: ***What sound does* wreath *begin with?*** Have students produce the /r/ sound independently.

Repeat questions above with each picture card.

Picture cards for /ɾ/: wren, wrap, wrist, write, wreath, wristband, wrinkle, wrench

Connect Sound/Spelling: Letter Sound Sort

Shuffle picture cards for *wr* and *kn* together. Display letter cards for *wr* on a table, allowing enough space for a column of picture cards below the letter cards. Display letter cards for *kn* next to the letter cards for *wr*.

Say: ***This is letter* kn. Kn *stands for the sound /n/. Everyone say /n/.*** Have students produce the sound.

Show the stack of picture cards.

Explain: ***The pictures on these cards begin with the letter sounds /ɾ/ or /n/. We are going to put them with their matching letter.***

Show the first picture card.

Demonstrate: **Wrist. *This picture begins with the letter sound /ɾ/: /ɾ/, /ɾ/,* wrist. *Say /ɾ/, /ɾ/,* wrist.** Have students repeat the sound and word.

Demonstrate: **Wrist *goes with this card, /ɾ/.*** Place the picture card below the letter cards for *wr*.

Have students draw the remaining picture cards from the stack and place them in a column under the matching letter card. As each card is added, direct students to say the sound twice and then name the picture: /r/, /r/, *wrist*; /n/, /n/, *knit*.

Picture cards for /n/: knit, knee, knob, knot, knife, kneel, knuckle, knight

EXTENSION ACTIVITY: Randomly point to pictures in the two columns and instruct students to repeat the letter sound and name the picture.

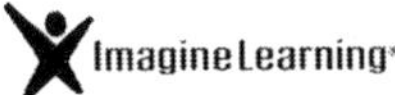

Connect Sound/Spelling: Thumbs Up, Thumbs Down for Beginning Sounds

Say: ***Show me thumbs up.*** Model what thumbs up looks like and help students show their thumbs up.

Explain: ***When you hear a word that begins with the letter sound /r/, make a thumbs up and say the letter sound. If the word doesn't start with the letter sound /r/, give me a thumbs down.*** Model thumbs down for students and help students show their thumbs down.

Say each word from the word bank below, alternating between words that begin with /r/ and words that don't.

Words that begin with /r/: wrist, wreath, wreck, wrong, wrinkle, write, wrestle, wrapped, wriggled, wrench

Words that don't begin with /r/: fix, stop, wagon, year

Check Progress: Letter Stack

Observe each student during practice and use the following activity to check progress on the target skill. If student can correctly identify the letter sound twice, consider the intervention successful.

Point to the appropriate letter card as you say the sound.

Say: ***Repeat the letter sounds for these letters: /r/, /r/, /n/, /n/.***

Shuffle letter cards for *wr* and *kn* together in a stack.

Say: ***Choose a card and tell me the letter sound.***

Have students draw a card from the stack, say the sound, and put the card on the bottom of the stack. Repeat until every student has had several opportunities to demonstrate knowledge of the target letter sound /r/.

Reteaching Lessons

Kn	kn
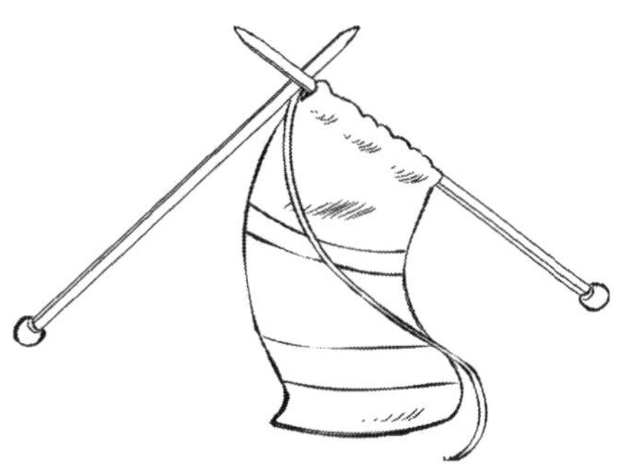	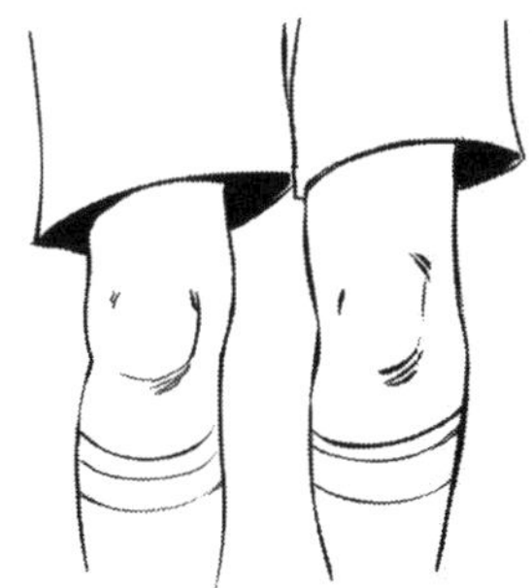
	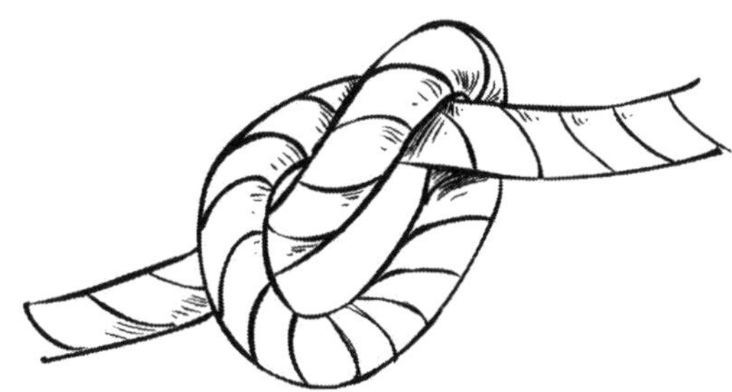
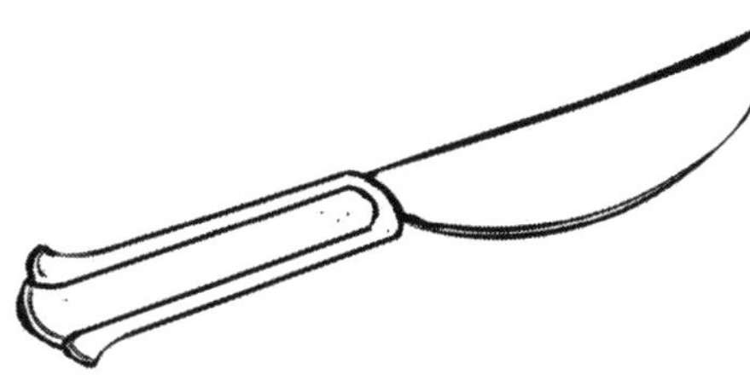	

Letter and Picture Cards for kn

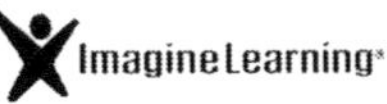

Wr	wr

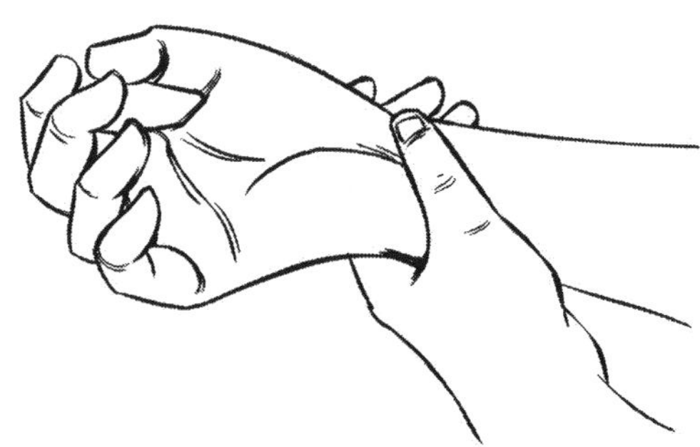	

	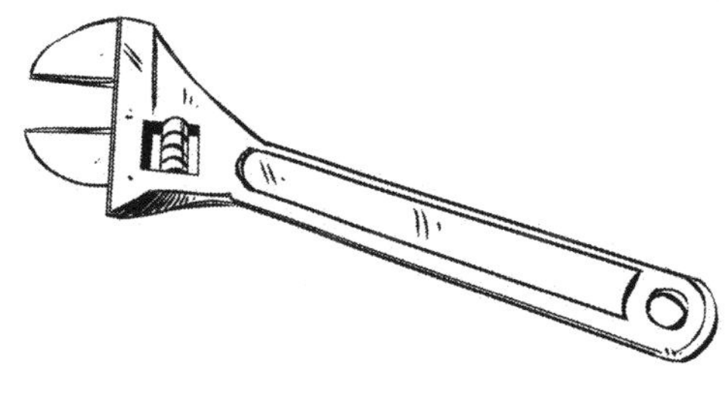

Short Vowels: a, i, o

Grade K

15 Min.

CCSS.RF.K.3.B
TEKS 110.11.b.3.A

LEARNING OBJECTIVE: Identify the short vowel sound of the vowels *a*, *i*, and *o*.
LANGUAGE OBJECTIVE: Produce the short vowel sounds when shown a visual grapheme.

Lesson Overview

Students review short vowels *a*, *i*, and *o* with a game similar to bingo.

Materials	Preparation
• Short Vowel Flash Cards • Short Vowel Bingo game boards (one for each student) • Game pieces (12 per student)	• Cut out short vowel flash cards. • Cut out short vowel bingo game boards.

Teach and Model

Write or display three CVC words, one for each short vowel: *cat*, *wig*, and *mop*. Teach students the short vowel sound for each word:

Point to and read aloud the word *cat*, emphasizing the short vowel sound.

Say: ***The short vowel sound in* cat *is /ă/.***

Model: **Cat, /ă/.** Have students repeat the word and the vowel sound with you.

Point to the letter *a*.

Model: ***The letter* a *makes the sound /ă/.*** Have students repeat the vowel sound.

Repeat for short *i* (/ĭ/ and *fish*) and short *o* (/ŏ/ and *mop*).

Connect Letters to Sounds: Short Vowel Search

Distribute Short Vowel Bingo game boards to students.

Say: ***Put your finger on the short vowel as I say it. Find /ă/ as in* man.**

Have students point to an *a* on their bingo card and repeat the short vowel and the word: */ă/, man.*

Repeat for short *i* (/ĭ/ and *big*) and short *o* (/ŏ/ and *mom*).

Say: ***Now put your finger on the short vowel that matches the vowel sounds in the words I say:* his, pack, not.**

Monitor student responses. Repeat words with emphasized vowel sound as needed.

Connect Letters to Sounds: Short Vowel Bingo

Say: ***We are going to play Short Vowel Bingo.***

Distribute 12 game pieces to each student. Place short vowel picture flash cards face down in a stack.

Play bingo. Take a card from the top of the stack. Say the name of the picture, say the short vowel, and say the name of the picture again.

Model: **Doll, /ŏ/, doll.**

Have students repeat the model with you.

Say: ***Find any short vowel /ŏ/ on your bingo card and put a game piece on it.*** Show students how to put game pieces on their card.

Instruct students to say "Bingo!" when they have four vowels in a row covered and to say "Blackout!" when they have covered the whole board.

Place card in discard stack. Have students take turns selecting a card from the top of the stack. The student should name the picture, repeat the short vowel, and then name the picture again.

Continue playing until one student has a completed card and says,"Blackout!"

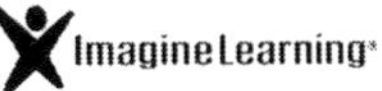

Flash cards for a: pan, hat, flag, van, jam, plant, snack, hand

Flash cards for i: six, swim, quilt, knit, wrist, kick, chin, kit

Flash cards for o: doll, moth, off, rock, box, floss, sloth, knob

Check Progress

Observe each student during practice and use the following activity to check progress made on the target skill. If student can correctly identify each short vowel (a, i, o) twice, consider the intervention successful.

Place a bingo card in front of students.

Say: ***Put your finger on short* a *and tell me the sound.***

Repeat for *i* and *o*. Alternate between students.

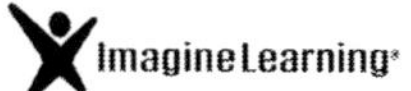

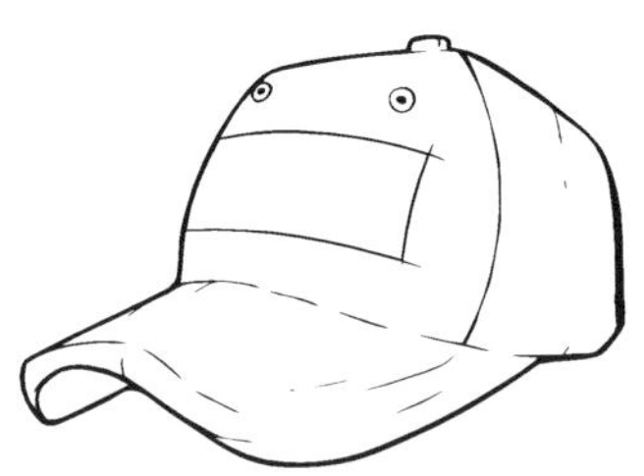

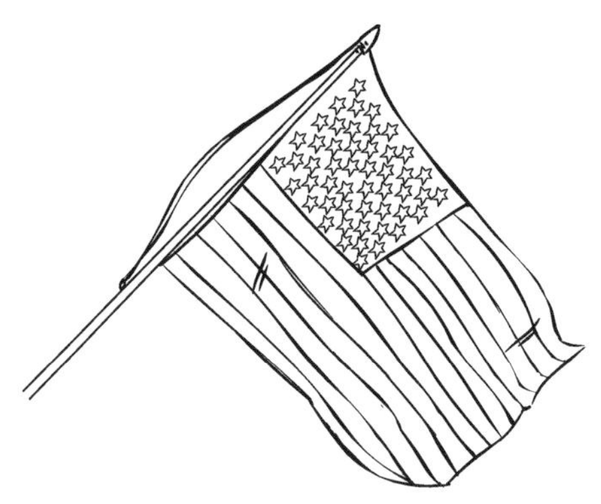

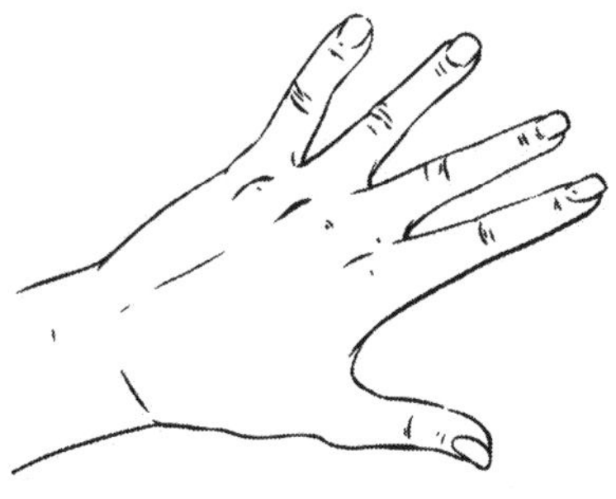

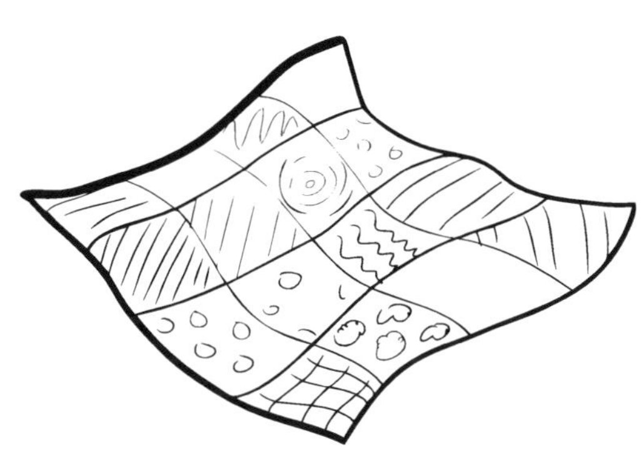

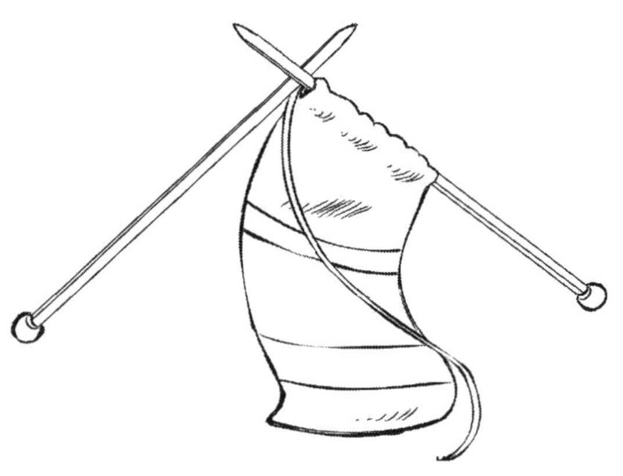

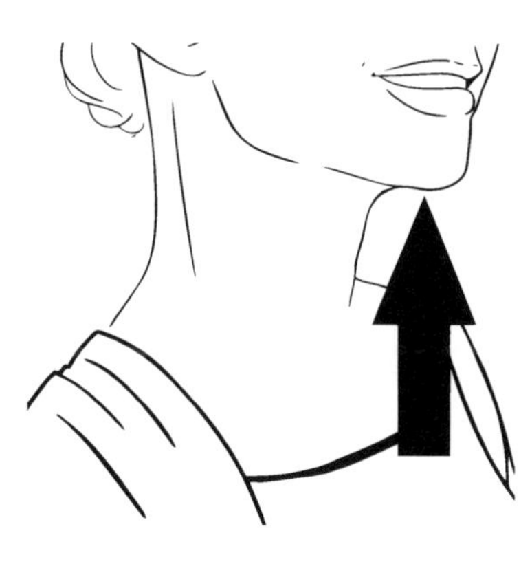

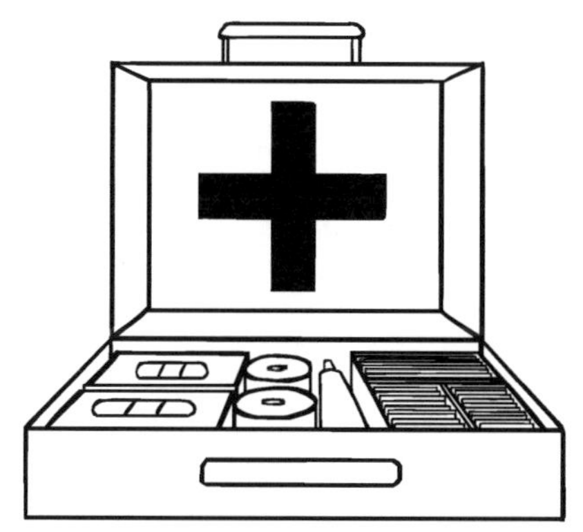

Reteaching Lessons ✓

OFF

o	a	i	o
o	i	a	a
i	a	a	i
a	o	i	o

i	a	o	i
a	i	a	o
o	o	i	a
i	o	a	i

Short Vowel Bingo game board

i	o	a	o
i	a	i	a
o	i	a	i
o	a	o	i

i	a	a	i
a	o	i	o
i	o	o	i
a	i	a	o

Short Vowel Bingo game board

Short Vowels: a, i, o, u

Grade K

15 Min.

CCSS.RF.K.3.B
TEKS 110.11.b.3.A

LEARNING OBJECTIVE: Identify the short vowel sound of the vowels *a*, *i*, *o*, and *u*.
LANGUAGE OBJECTIVE: Produce the short vowel sounds when shown a visual grapheme.

Lesson Overview

Students review short vowels *a*, *i*, *o*, and *u* with a game similar to bingo.

Materials	Preparation
• Short Vowel Flash Cards • Short Vowel Bingo game boards (one for each student) • Game pieces (12 per student)	• Cut out short vowel flash cards • Cut out short vowel bingo game boards

Teach and Model

Write or display three CVC words, one for each short vowel: *hat*, *fish*, *fox*, and *rug*. Teach students the short vowel sound for each word:

Point to and read aloud the word *hat*, emphasizing the short vowel sound.

Say: ***The short vowel sound in* hat *is* /ă/.**

Model: **Hat, /ă/.** Have students repeat the word and the vowel sound with you.

Point to the letter *a*.

Model: ***The letter* a *makes the sound /ă/.*** Have students repeat the vowel sound.

Repeat for short *i* (/ĭ/ and *fish*), short *o* (/ŏ/ and *mop*), and short *u* (/ŭ/ and *rug*).

Connect Letters to Sounds: Short Vowel Search

Distribute Short Vowel Bingo game boards to students.

Say: ***Put your finger on the short vowel as I say it. Find /ă/ as in* sad.**

Have students point to an *a* on their bingo card and repeat the short vowel and the word: /ă/, *sad*.

Repeat for short *i* (/ĭ/ and *lid*), short *o* (/ŏ/ and *sock*), and short *u* (/ŭ/ and *tug*).

Say: ***Now put your finger on the short vowel that matches the vowel sounds in the words I say:* fit, had, not, fun.**

Monitor student responses. Repeat words with emphasized vowel sound as needed.

Connect Letters to Sounds: Short Vowel Bingo

Say: ***We are going to play Short Vowel Bingo.***

Distribute 12 game pieces to each student. Place short vowel picture flash cards face down in a stack.

Play bingo. Take a card from the top of the stack. Say the name of the picture, say the short vowel, and say the name of the picture again.

Model: **Nut, /ŭ/, nut.**

Have students repeat the model with you.

Say: ***Find any short vowel /ŭ/ on your bingo card and put a game piece on it.*** Show students how to put game pieces on their card.

Instruct students to say "Bingo!" when they have four vowels in a row covered and to say "Blackout!" when they have covered the whole board.

Place card in discard stack. Have students take turns selecting a card from the top of the stack. The student should name the picture, repeat the short vowel, and then name the picture again.

Continue playing until one student has a completed card and says,"Blackout!"

Flash cards for a: cat, van, hand, yam, crab, scrap

Flash cards for i: fish, kid, wig, quiz, mix, kit

Flash cards for o: dog, ox, frog, stop, clock, knot

Flash cards for u: sun, plum, duck, rug, brush, skunk

Check Progress

Observe each student during practice and use the following activity to check progress made on the target skill. If student can correctly identify each short vowel (a, i, o, u) twice, consider the intervention successful.

Place a bingo card in front of students.

Say: ***Put your finger on short* a *and tell me the sound.***

Repeat for *i, o,* and *u*. Alternate between students.

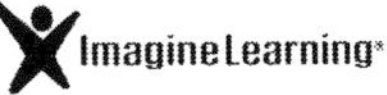

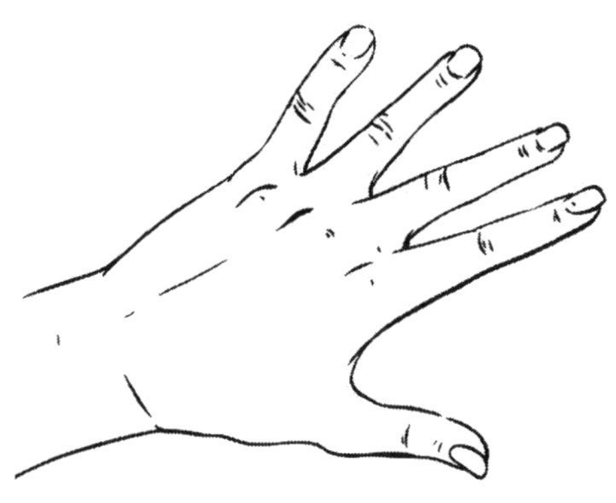

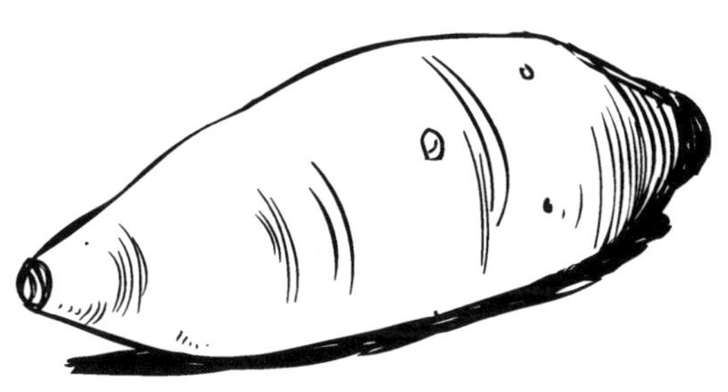

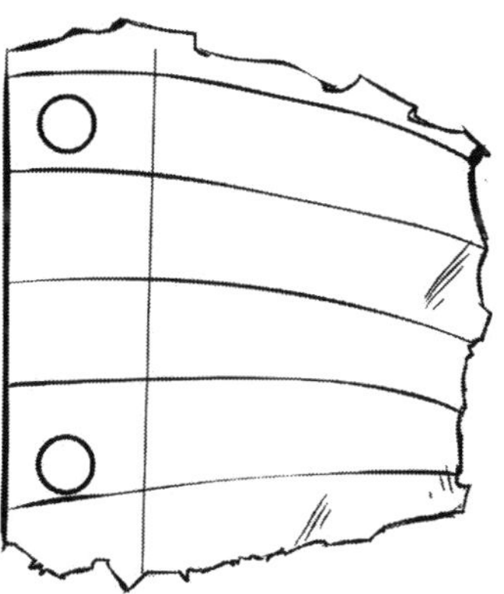

Reteaching Lessons ✓

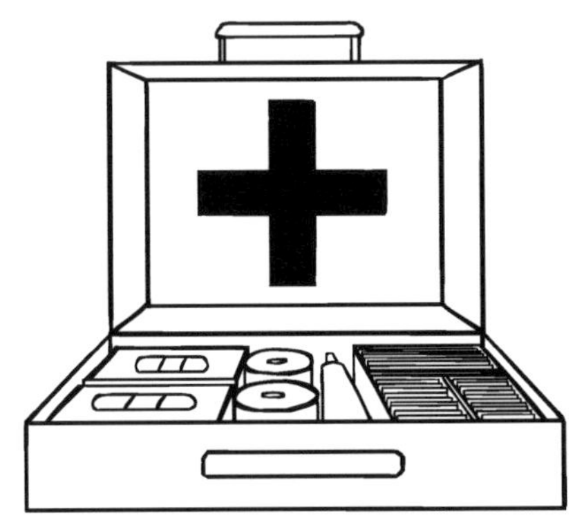

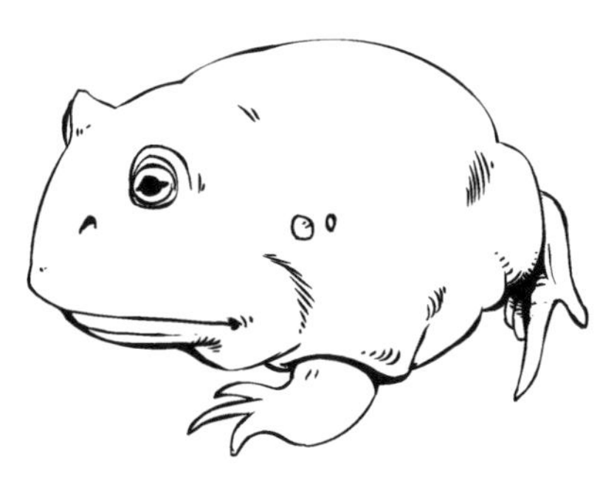

STOP

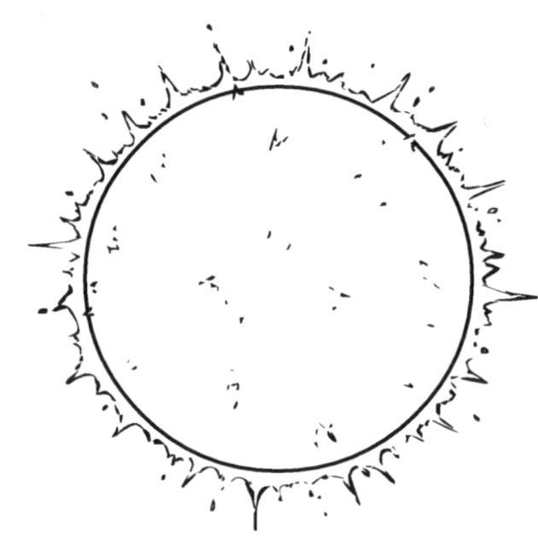

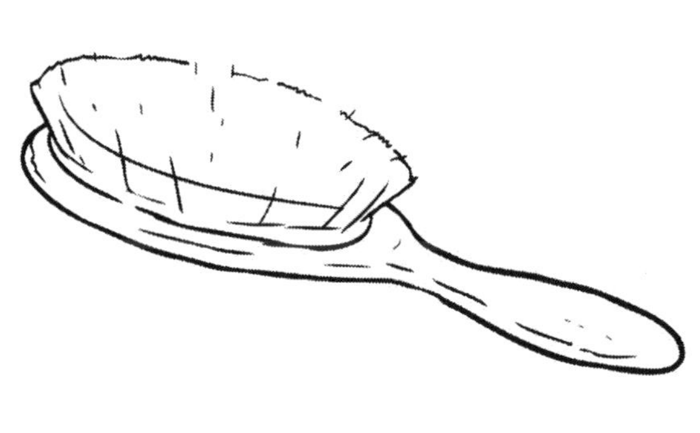

Reteaching Lessons

o	o	i	a
a	u	o	u
i	i	i	o
u	a	u	a

i	a	u	i
a	o	i	u
u	a	u	a
o	i	o	u

Short Vowel Bingo game board

i	u	o	i
o	i	u	a
u	a	o	a
a	o	i	u

u	o	i	o
u	a	u	a
a	i	i	o
o	a	u	i

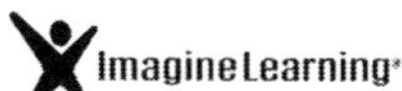

Letter Sounds

Short Vowels: a, e, i, o, u

Grade K

15 Min.

CCSS.RF.K.3.B
TEKS 110.11.b.3.A

LEARNING OBJECTIVE: Identify the short vowel sound of the vowels *a, e, i, o,* and *u.*
LANGUAGE OBJECTIVE: Produce the short vowel sounds when shown a visual grapheme.

Lesson Overview

Students review short vowels *a, e, i, o,* and *u* with a game similar to bingo.

Materials	Preparation
• Short Vowel Flash Cards • Short Vowel Bingo game boards (one for each student) • Game pieces (12 per student)	• Cut out short vowel flash cards • Cut out short vowel bingo game boards

Teach and Model

Write or display three CVC words, one for each short vowel: *van, jet, kit, dog,* and *sun*. Teach students the short vowel sound for each word:

Point to and read aloud the word *van*, emphasizing the short vowel sound.

Say: ***The short vowel sound in* van *is* /ă/.**

Model: **Van, /ă/.** Have students repeat the word and the vowel sound with you.

Point to the letter *a*.

Model: ***The letter* a *makes the sound* /ă/.** Have students repeat the vowel sound.

Repeat for short *e* (/ĕ/ and *jet*), short *i* (/ĭ/ and *kit*), short *o* (/ŏ/ and *dog*), and short *u* (/ŭ/ and *sun*).

Connect Letters to Sounds: Short Vowel Search

Distribute Short Vowel Bingo game boards to students.

Say: ***Put your finger on the short vowel as I say it. Find /ă/ as in* bag.**

Have students point to an *a* on their bingo card and repeat the short vowel and the word: */ă/, bag*.

Repeat for *short i* (/ĭ/ and *rip*), short *o* (/ŏ/ and *mom*), short *u* (/ŭ/ and *cub*), and short *e* (/ĕ/ and *leg*).

Say: ***Now put your finger on the short vowel that matches the vowel sounds in the words I say:* bug, dad, pin, mop, run.**

Monitor student responses. Repeat words with emphasized vowel sound as needed.

Connect Letters to Sounds: Short Vowel Bingo

Say: ***We are going to play Short Vowel Bingo.***

Distribute 12 game pieces to each student. Place short vowel picture flash cards face down in a stack.

Play bingo. Take a card from the top of the stack. Say the name of the picture, say the short vowel, and say the name of the picture again.

Model: **Ten, /ĕ/, ten.**

Have students repeat the model with you.

Say: ***Find any short vowel /ĕ/ on your bingo card and put a game piece on it.*** Show students how to put game pieces on their card.

Instruct students to say "Bingo!" when they have four vowels in a row covered and to say "Blackout!" when they have covered the whole board.

Place card in discard stack. Have students take turns selecting a card from the top of the stack. The student should name the picture, repeat the short vowel, and then name the picture again.

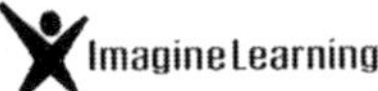

Continue playing until one student has a completed card and says,"Blackout!"

Flash cards for a: flag, hat, yak, snap

Flash cards for e: net, hen, jet, web, shell, sled

Flash cards for i: six, chin, slip, drill

Flash cards for o: on, fox, log, knob

Flash cards for u: duck, rug, tux, skunk, plug, brush

Check Progress

*Observe each student during practice and use the following activity to check progress made on the target skill. If student can correctly identify each short vowel (*a, i, o, u, e*) twice, consider the intervention successful.*

Place a bingo card in front of students.

Say: ***Put your finger on short* e *and tell me the sound.***

Repeat for *a, i, o,* and *u*. Alternate between students.

Short Vowel Flash Cards

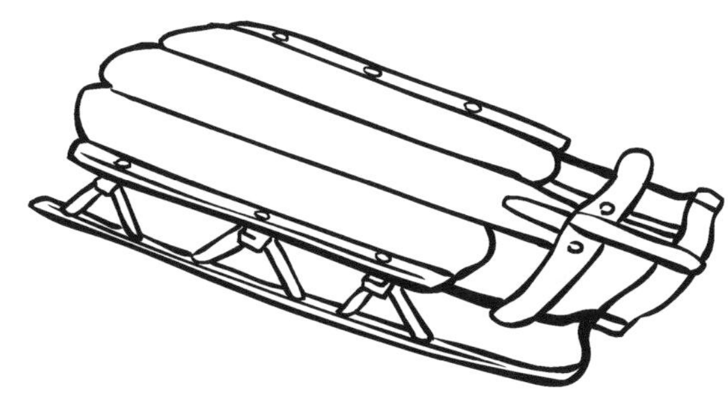

6

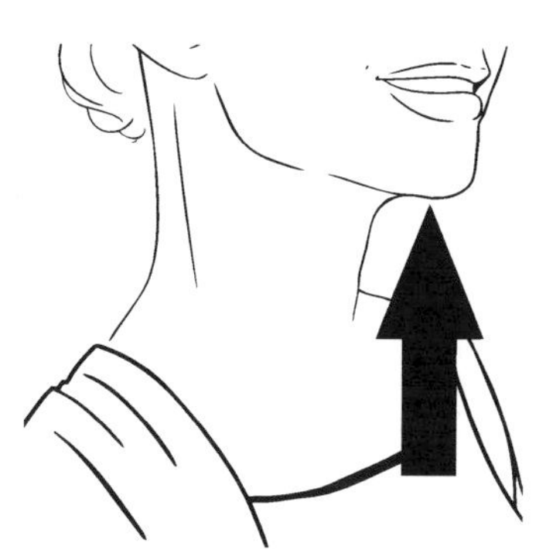

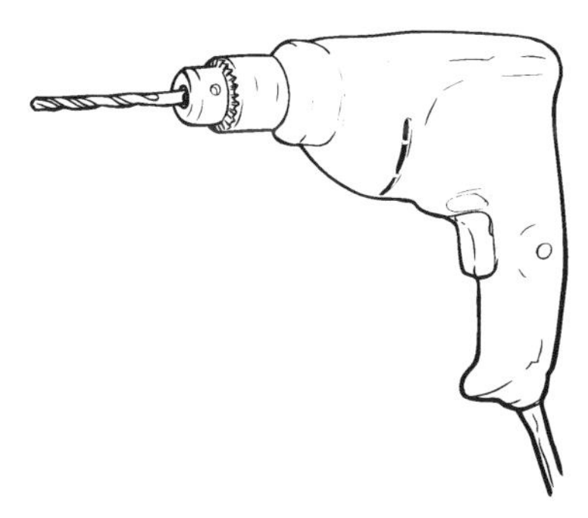

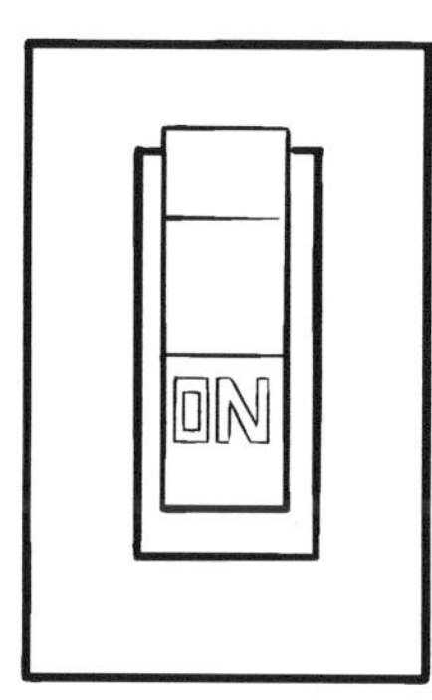

u	e	u	o
i	o	e	i
e	o	a	u
a	u	i	e

e	a	u	i
u	i	e	o
i	e	u	a
o	u	o	a

Short Vowel Bingo game board

a	u	i	e
o	i	e	a
i	u	a	e
e	o	i	u

i	u	e	u
a	a	i	e
o	e	a	i
e	u	e	u

Short Vowel Bingo game board

Long a, Short a

LEARNING OBJECTIVE: Distinguish between the long and short *a* sound.
LANGUAGE OBJECTIVE: Sort images by the vowel sounds found in their names.

Lesson Overview

Students distinguish between short and long vowel sounds for letter *a*, then sort picture cards into long *a* and short *a* columns.

Materials	Preparation
• Alphabet Chart • Picture Cards Sets 1 and 2	• Print the Alphabet Chart. Color the vowels red. • Cut out picture cards. Set aside *can*, *cane*, *cat*, and *gate*. Keep remaining cards from set 1 separate from set 2 cards.

Teach and Model

Display the Alphabet Chart and ask: ***Who can tell me why some of these letters are red?***

If needed, prompt students to say that the red letters are vowels.

Say: ***Every vowel has two sounds. One is called the short sound and the other is called the long sound. Who can tell me the short vowel sound for the letter* a**?

If needed, prompt students to say /ă/.

Say: ***It's in words like* cat, man, *and* class.**

Have students repeat the short *a* sound.

Say: ***The letter* a *also has a long sound. The long sound of each vowel is the same as its name.***

Point to the letter *a* on the Alphabet Chart.

Ask: ***What is the name of this letter?***

Say: ***The long* a *sound is in words like* late, same, *and* place.**

Have students repeat the long *a* sound.

Say: ***I'm going to look around and name some things I see. Each time you hear the long* a *sound, give me a thumbs up and say /ā/.***

Say these words, pausing after each word to allow time for responses: **nose, face, back, feet, table, smile, name, hand, blue, page.**

Explain: ***The difference between long and short* a *is very important. If you change the sound of the vowel, it can change the meaning of the word.***

Ask: ***Do you hear the short* a *in* can? *Listen:* can. *Do you hear the long* a *in* cane? *Listen:* cane.**

Ask: ***Which one could you use to help you walk? Which one could hold soup?***

After students answer, remind them that changing the vowel sound can change the meaning of a word.

Practice and Apply

Use Picture Card Set 1. Place the *can* and *cane* picture cards on the table with enough room for a column of cards to be placed below each of them.

Say: ***Let's practice long* a *and short* a *with pictures. This is a* can. *It has the short vowel sound /ă/:* can. *This is a* cane. *It has the long vowel sound /ā/:* cane.**

Display the picture card *cat*.

Model: ***Here is a cat. Listen to the vowel sound in the middle of the word:* cat. Cat *has a short vowel sound, so I will put it under the picture of the* can.**

Display the picture card *gate*.

Reteaching Lessons

Model: ***This is a*** **gate.** ***Listen to the vowel sound in the middle of the word:*** **gate. Gate** ***has a long vowel sound, so I will put it under the picture of the*** **cane.**

Invite students to take turns sorting the remaining picture cards. Have students draw a card, say the word out loud, and place the card in the matching vowel sound column. Have the student point to and name the picture cards in the entire column starting at the top.

If students use a name other than the intended word for each picture, remind them that all the words have either a short *a* or long *a* sound. Help them choose the right name.

When all picture cards have been sorted, point to the long vowel sound column

Ask: ***Do all of these words have a long*** **a** ***sound? Let's check by naming all the pictures in the long*** **a** ***column.*** With the students, name each picture out loud. Repeat with short vowel column.

Picture Cards Set 1: can, cane, cat, gate, bag, map, bat, fan, hat, plate, snake, game, vase, tape, grape

Check Progress

Observe each student during practice and use the following activity to check progress made on the target skill. If student can correctly sort each sound, consider the intervention successful.

Use Picture Cards Set 2. Retain the header cards (*can* and *cane*) from set 1.

Say: ***I'll show you a card from this stack and say the name of the picture. You repeat the word and then place it in the correct column.***

Give each student the opportunity to place at least one card for each sound.

Picture Cards Set 2: face, cake, whale, wave, maze, skate, rake, shapes, jam, lamb, crab, van, man, pan, hand

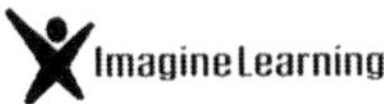

Alphabet Chart

Alphabet Chart			Aa	Bb	Cc
Dd	Ee	Ff	Gg	Hh	Ii
Jj	Kk	Ll	Mm	Nn	Oo
Pp	Qq	Rr	Ss	Tt	Uu
Vv	Ww	Xx	Yy	Zz	

Picture Cards (Set 2)

Long e, Short e

Grade 1

10 Min.

CCSS.RF.K.3c
TEKS 110.12.3.A

LEARNING OBJECTIVE: Distinguish between the long and short e sound.
LANGUAGE OBJECTIVE: Sort images by the vowel sounds found in their names.

Lesson Overview

Students distinguish between short and long vowel sounds for letter *e*, then sort picture cards into long *e* and short *e* columns.

Materials	Preparation
• Alphabet Chart • Picture Cards Sets 1 and 2	• Print the Alphabet Chart. Color the vowels red. • Cut out picture cards. Set aside *bed*, *bead*, *shell*, and *wheel*. Keep remaining cards from set 1 separate from set 2 cards.

Teach and Model

Display the Alphabet Chart and ask: ***Who can tell me why some of these letters are red?***

If needed, prompt students to say that the red letters are vowels.

Say: ***Every vowel has two sounds. One is called the short sound and the other is called the long sound. Who can tell me the short vowel sound for the letter* e?**

If needed, prompt students to say /ĕ/.

Say: ***It's in words like* let, send, *and* yes.**

Have students repeat the short *e* sound.

Say: ***The letter* e *also has a long sound. The long sound of each vowel is the same as its name.***

Point to the letter *e* on the Alphabet Chart.

Ask: ***What is the name of this letter?***

Say: ***The long* e *sound is in words like* nice, line, *and* write.**

Have students repeat the long *e* sound.

Say: ***I'm going to look around and name some things I see. Each time you hear the long* e *sound, give me a thumbs up and say /ē/.***

Say these words, pausing after each word to allow time for responses: **nose, pen, feet, red, teeth, hat, hand, desk, green, heads.**

Explain: ***The difference between long and short* e *is very important. If you change the sound of the vowel, it can change the meaning of the word.***

Ask: ***Do you hear the short* e *in* bed*? Listen:* bed. *Do you hear the long* e *in* bead*? Listen:* bead.**

Ask: ***Which one could you wear around your neck? Which one would be nice to sleep on?***

After students answer, remind them that changing the vowel sound can change the meaning of a word.

Practice and Apply

Use Picture Card Set 1. Place the *bed* and *bead* picture cards on the table with enough room for a column of cards to be placed below each of them.

Say: ***Let's practice long* e *and short* e *with pictures. This is a* bed. *It has the short vowel sound /ĕ/:* bed. *This is a* bead. *It has the long vowel sound /ē/:* bead.**

Display the picture card *shell*.

Model: ***Here is a* shell. *Listen to the vowel sound in the middle of the word:* shell. Shell *has a short vowel sound, so I will put it under the picture of the* bed.**

Display the picture card *wheel*.

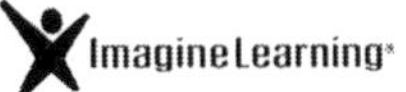

Model: ***This is a* wheel. *Listen to the vowel sound in the middle of the word:* wheel. Wheel *has a long vowel sound, so I will put it under the picture of the* bead.**

Invite students to take turns sorting the remaining picture cards. Have students draw a card, say the word out loud, and place the card in the matching vowel sound column. Have the student point to and name the picture cards in the entire column starting at the top.

If students use a name other than the intended word for each picture, remind them that all the words have either a short *e* or long *e* sound. Help them choose the right name.

When all picture cards have been sorted, point to the long vowel sound column

Ask: ***Do all of these words have a long* e *sound? Let's check by naming all the pictures in the long* e *column.*** With the students, name each picture out loud. Repeat with short vowel column.

Picture cards in set 1: bed, bead, shell, wheel, bench, hen, jet, vest, check, bee, leaf, cheese, feet, seal, tree

Check Progress

Observe each student during practice and use the following activity to check progress made on the target skill. If student can correctly sort each sound, consider the intervention successful.

Use Picture Cards Set 2. Retain the header cards (*bed* and *bead*) from set 1.

Say: ***I'll show you a card from this stack and say the name of the picture. You repeat the word and then place it in the correct column.***

Give each student the opportunity to place at least one card for each sound.

Picture Card Set 2: bell, nest, pen, tent, net, belt, ten, flea, seeds, street, meat, three, sheep, sleeve, jeep

Alphabet Chart

Alphabet Chart			Aa	Bb	Cc
Dd	Ee	Ff	Gg	Hh	Ii
Jj	Kk	Ll	Mm	Nn	Oo
Pp	Qq	Rr	Ss	Tt	Uu
Vv	Ww	Xx	Yy	Zz	

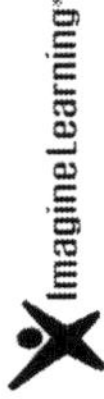

Reteaching Lessons ✓

Picture Cards (Set 2)

Long i, Short i

Grade 1

10 Min.

CCSS.RF.K.3c
TEKS 110.12.3.A

LEARNING OBJECTIVE: Distinguish between the long and short *i* sound.
LANGUAGE OBJECTIVE: Sort images by the vowel sounds found in their names.

Lesson Overview

Students distinguish between short and long vowel sounds for letter *i*, then sort picture cards into long *i* and short *i* columns.

Materials	Preparation
• Alphabet Chart • Picture Cards Sets 1 and 2	• Print the Alphabet Chart. Color the vowels red. • Cut out picture cards. Set aside *pin*, *pines*, *brick*, and *light*. Keep remaining cards from set 1 separate from set 2 cards.

Teach and Model

Display the Alphabet Chart and ask: ***Who can tell me why some of these letters are red?***

If needed, prompt students to say that the red letters are vowels.

Say: ***Every vowel has two sounds. One is called the short sound and the other is called the long sound. Who can tell me the short vowel sound for the letter* i*?***

If needed, prompt students to say /ĭ/.

Say: ***It's in words like* kid, miss, *and* list.**

Have students repeat the short *i* sound.

Say: ***The letter* i *also has a long sound. The long sound of each vowel is the same as its name.***

Point to the letter *i* on the Alphabet Chart.

Ask: ***What is the name of this letter?***

Say: ***The long* i *sound is in words like* teach, feel, *and* read.**

Have students repeat the long *i* sound.

Say: ***I'm going to look around and name some things I see. Each time you hear the long* i *sound, give me a thumbs up and say /ī/.***

Say these words, pausing after each word to allow time for responses: **light, face, table, white, feet, window, smile, lid, hand, tile, page.**

Explain: ***The difference between long and short* i *is very important. If you change the sound of the vowel, it can change the meaning of the word.***

Ask: ***Do you hear the short* i *in* pins*? Listen:* pins*. Do you hear the long* i *in* pines*? Listen:* pines.**

Ask: ***Which of these would you sit under to have a picnic? Which of these could hold your socks together?***

After students answer, remind them that changing the vowel sound can change the meaning of a word.

Practice and Apply

Use Picture Card Set 1. Place the *pins* and *pines* picture cards on the table with enough room for a column of cards to be placed below each of them.

Say: ***Let's practice long* i *and short* i *with pictures. This is a* pin*. It has the short vowel sound /ĭ/:* pin*. This is a* pine*. It has the long vowel sound /ī/:* pine.**

Display the picture card *brick*.

Model: ***Here is a* brick*. Listen to the vowel sound in the middle of the word:* brick*.* Brick *has a short vowel sound, so I will put it under the picture of the* pins.**

Display the picture card *light*.

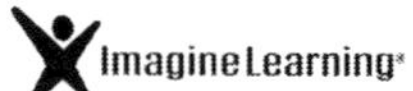

Model: ***This is a* light. *Listen to the vowel sound in the middle of the word:* light. Light *has a long vowel sound, so I will put it under the picture of the* pines.**

Invite students to take turns sorting the remaining picture cards. Have students draw a card, say the word out loud, and place the card in the matching vowel sound column. Have the student point to and name the picture cards in the entire column starting at the top.

If students use a name other than the intended word for each picture, remind them that all the words have either a short *i* or long *i* sound. Help them choose the right name.

When all picture cards have been sorted, point to the long vowel sound column

Ask: ***Do all of these words have a long* i *sound? Let's check by naming all the pictures in the long* i *column.*** With the students, name each picture out loud. Repeat with short vowel column.

Picture Cards Set 1: pin, pine, brick, light, chicks, stick, fin, wig, fish, dime, nine, bike, kite, tie, knife

Check Progress

Observe each student during practice and use the following activity to check progress made on the target skill. If student can correctly sort each sound, consider the intervention successful.

Use Picture Cards Set 2. Retain the header cards (*pins* and *pines*) from set 1.

Say: ***I'll show you a card from this stack and say the name of the picture. You repeat the word and then place it in the correct column.***

Give each student the opportunity to place at least one card for each sound.

Picture Cards Set 2: bib, rip, pills, lips, hill, ship, fig, mitt, slide, rice, pie, fire, mice, vine, five

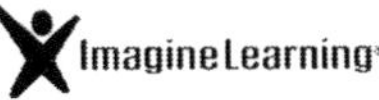

Alphabet Chart			Aa	Bb	Cc
Dd	Ee	Ff	Gg	Hh	Ii
Jj	Kk	Ll	Mm	Nn	Oo
Pp	Qq	Rr	Ss	Tt	Uu
Vv	Ww	Xx	Yy	Zz	

Picture Cards (Set 1)

Reteaching Lessons

Long o, Short o

Grade 1

10 Min.

CCSS.RF.K.3c
TEKS 110.12.3.A

LEARNING OBJECTIVE: Distinguish between the long and short *o* sound.
LANGUAGE OBJECTIVE: Sort images by the vowel sounds found in their names.

Lesson Overview

Students distinguish between short and long vowel sounds for letter *o*, then sort picture cards into long *o* and short *o* columns.

Materials	Preparation
• Alphabet Chart • Picture Cards Sets 1 and 2	• Print the Alphabet Chart. Color the vowels red. • Cut out picture cards. Set aside *knot, note, pot,* and *bone*. Keep remaining cards from set 1 separate from set 2 cards.

Teach and Model

Display the Alphabet Chart and ask: ***Who can tell me why some of these letters are red?***

If needed, prompt students to say that the red letters are vowels.

Say: ***Every vowel has two sounds. One is called the short sound and the other is called the long sound. Who can tell me the short vowel sound for the letter* o*?***

If needed, prompt students to say /ŏ/.

Say: ***It's in words like* not, block, *and* hop.**

Have students repeat the short *o* sound.

Say: ***The letter* o *also has a long sound. The long sound of each vowel is the same as its name.***

Point to the letter *o* on the Alphabet Chart.

Ask: ***What is the name of this letter?***

Say: ***The long* o *sound is in words like* hope, road, *and* no.**

Have students repeat the long *o* sound.

Say: ***I'm going to look around and name some things I see. Each time you hear the long* o *sound, give me a thumbs up and say /ō/.***

Say these words, pausing after each word to allow time for responses: **nose, arm, clothes, feet, lock, name, hand, note, throat.**

Explain: ***The difference between long and short* o *is very important. If you change the sound of the vowel, it can change the meaning of the word.***

Ask: ***Do you hear the short* o *in* knot*? Listen:* knot. *Do you hear the long* o *in* note*? Listen:* note.**

Ask: ***Which one could help you sing music? Which one could help you keep your shoes on your feet?***

After students answer, remind them that changing the vowel sound can change the meaning of a word.

Practice and Apply

Use Picture Card Set 1. Place the *knot* and *note* picture cards on the table with enough room for a column of cards to be placed below each of them.

Say: ***Let's practice long* o *and short* o *with pictures. This is a* knot. *It has the short vowel sound /ŏ/:* knot. *This is a* note. *It has the long vowel sound /ō/:* note.**

Display the picture card *pot*.

Model: ***Here is a* pot. *Listen to the vowel sound in the middle of the word:* pot. Pot *has a short vowel sound, so I will put it under the picture of the* knot.**

Display the picture card *bone*.

Model: ***This is a* bone. *Listen to the vowel sound in the middle of the word:* bone. Bone *has a long vowel sound, so I will put it under the picture of the* note.**

Invite students to take turns sorting the remaining picture cards. Have students draw a card, say the word out loud, and place the card in the matching vowel sound column. Have the student point to and name the picture cards in the entire column starting at the top.

If students use a name other than the intended word for each picture, remind them that all the words have either a short *o* or long *o* sound. Help them choose the right name.

When all picture cards have been sorted, point to the long vowel sound column

Ask: ***Do all of these words have a long o sound? Let's check by naming all the pictures in the long o column.*** With the students, name each picture out loud. Repeat with short vowel column.

Picture Cards Set 1: knot, note, pot, bone, fox, dog, lock, socks, mop, bow, stove, boat, phone, comb, snow

Check Progress

Observe each student during practice and use the following activity to check progress made on the target skill. If student can correctly sort each sound, consider the intervention successful.

Use Picture Cards Set 2. Retain the header cards (*knot* and *note*) from set 1.

Say: ***I'll show you a card from this stack and say the name of the picture. You repeat the word and then place it in the correct column.***

Give each student the opportunity to place at least one card for each sound.

Picture Cards Set 2: clock, bot, log, rock, cop, stop, box, coat, bowl, soap, toad, globe, rose, cone, robe

Reteaching Lessons

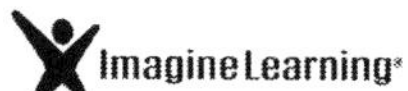

Alphabet Chart

Alphabet Chart			Aa	Bb	Cc
Dd	Ee	Ff	Gg	Hh	Ii
Jj	Kk	Ll	Mm	Nn	Oo
Pp	Qq	Rr	Ss	Tt	Uu
Vv	Ww	Xx	Yy	Zz	

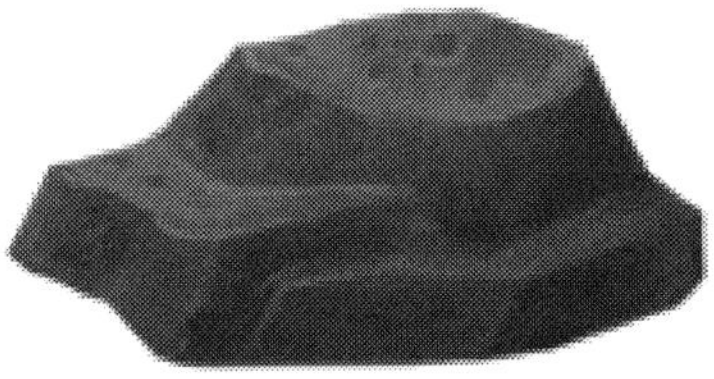

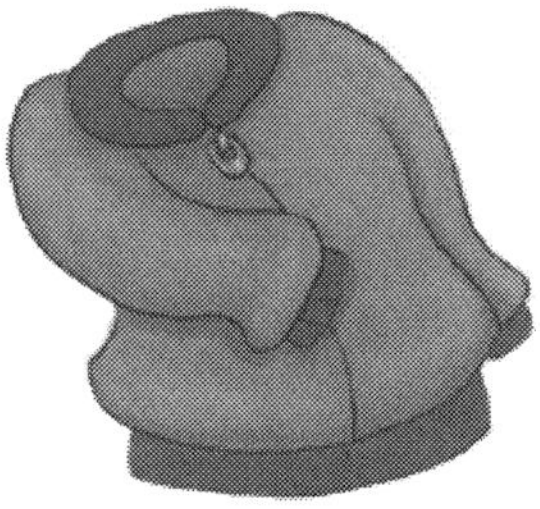

Picture Cards (Set 2)

Letter Sounds

Long u, Short u

Grade 1

10 Min.

CCSS.RF.K.3c
TEKS 110.12.3.A

LEARNING OBJECTIVE: Distinguish between the long and short *u* sound.
LANGUAGE OBJECTIVE: Sort images by the vowel sounds found in their names.

Lesson Overview

Students distinguish between short and long vowel sounds for letter *u,* then sort picture cards into long *u* and short *u* columns.

Materials	Preparation
• Alphabet Chart • Picture Cards Sets 1 and 2	• Print the Alphabet Chart. Color the vowels red. • Cut out picture cards. Set aside *tub, tube, plug,* and *glue*. Keep remaining cards from set 1 separate from set 2 cards.

Teach and Model

Display the Alphabet Chart and ask: ***Who can tell me why some of these letters are red?***

If needed, prompt students to say that the red letters are vowels.

Say: ***Every vowel has two sounds. One is called the short sound and the other is called the long sound. Who can tell me the short vowel sound for the letter* u*?***

If needed, prompt students to say /ŭ/.

Say: ***It's in words like* fun, cut, *and* hug.**

Have students repeat the short *u* sound.

Say: ***The letter* u *also has a long sound. The long sound of each vowel is the same as its name.***

Point to the letter *u* on the Alphabet Chart.

Ask: ***What is the name of this letter?***

Say: ***The long* u *sound is in words like* rule, new, *and* suit.**

Have students repeat the long *u* sound.

Say: ***I'm going to look around and name some things I see. Each time you hear the long* u *sound, give me a thumbs up and say /ū/.***

Say these words, pausing after each word to allow time for responses: **blue, face, buttons, feet, shoes, numbers, school, smiles, students.**

Explain: ***The difference between long and short* u *is very important. If you change the sound of the vowel, it can change the meaning of the word.***

Ask: ***Do you hear the short* u *in* tub*? Listen:* tub. *Do you hear the long* u *in* tube*? Listen:* tube.**

Ask: ***Which one would help you float in the water? Which one would help your rubber ducky float?***

After students answer, remind them that changing the vowel sound can change the meaning of a word.

Practice and Apply

Use Picture Card Set 1. Place the *tub* and *tube* picture cards on the table with enough room for a column of cards to be placed below each of them.

Say: ***Let's practice long* u *and short* u *with pictures. This is a* tub. *It has the short vowel sound /ŭ/:* tub. *This is a* tube. *It has the long vowel sound /ū/:* tube.**

Display the picture card *plug.*

Model: ***Here is a* plug. *Listen to the vowel sound in the middle of the word:* plug. Plug *has a short vowel sound, so I will put it under the picture of the* tub.**

Display the picture card *glue.*

Reteaching Lessons

Model: ***This is a* glue. *Listen to the vowel sound in the middle of the word:* glue. Glue *has a long vowel sound, so I will put it under the picture of the* tube.**

Invite students to take turns sorting the remaining picture cards. Have students draw a card, say the word out loud, and place the card in the matching vowel sound column. Have the student point to and name the picture cards in the entire column starting at the top.

If students use a name other than the intended word for each picture, remind them that all the words have either a short *u* or long *u* sound. Help them choose the right name.

When all picture cards have been sorted, point to the long vowel sound column

Ask: ***Do all of these words have a long* u *sound? Let's check by naming all the pictures in the long* u *column.*** With the students, name each picture out loud. Repeat with short vowel column.

Picture Cards Set 1: tub, tube, plug, glue, cup, bugs, skunk, sun, duck, boots, moon, cube, fruit, shoes, soup

Check Progress

Observe each student during practice and use the following activity to check progress made on the target skill. If student can correctly sort each sound, consider the intervention successful.

Use Picture Cards Set 2. Retain the header cards (*tub* and *tube*) from set 1.

Say: ***I'll show you a card from this stack and say the name of the picture. You repeat the word and then place it in the correct column.***

Give each student the opportunity to place at least one card for each sound.

Picture Cards Set 2: hut, nut, bus, drum, rug, trunk, plum, truck, two, spoon, moose, juice, goose, screw, mule

Alphabet Chart			Aa	Bb	Cc
Dd	Ee	Ff	Gg	Hh	Ii
Jj	Kk	Ll	Mm	Nn	Oo
Pp	Qq	Rr	Ss	Tt	Uu
Vv	Ww	Xx	Yy	Zz	

Picture Cards (Set 1)

Reteaching Lessons ✓

Vowel Teams ai and ay

Grade 1

10 Min.

CCSS.RF.1.3.C
TEKS 110.12.3.A

LEARNING OBJECTIVE: Identify the long *a* sound in words formed with the vowel teams *ai* and *ay*.
LANGUAGE OBJECTIVE: Match long *a* vowel sound to print by pointing to vowel teams *ai* and *ay* in words

Lesson Overview

Students hear and recognize the long *a* sound (/ā/) first in isolation and then in words that contain the *ai* or *ay* vowel teams. Students then practice saying words with long *a* and sort words with long *a* vowel teams.

Materials	Preparation
• *ai* and *ay* Word Cards	• Cut out word cards.

NOTE: /ā/ (long *a*, as in *say*), /ē/ (long *e*, as in *she*), /ă/ (short *a*, as in *cat*), /ĭ/ (short *i*, as in *bit*)

Teach and Model

Remind students: ***Some letters stand for more than one sound. All vowels have a long sound and a short sound. Today we are going to practice long* a.**

Say: ***Listen to this sound: /ā/. That sound is called long* a. *I want to know if you can hear this sound. I'm going to say some different vowel sounds*.**

Hold up two fingers close together.

Say: ***When you hear long* a*, hold up your fingers up like this. If you don't hear long* a*, keep your hands down.***

Say the sounds below one at a time. Pause between sounds so that students have time to signal with their fingers. Increase the pace as students become more confident.

Sound bank:

/ā/ /ē/ /ă/ **/ā/** /ĭ/ **/ā/** /ă/ **/ā/** **/ā/**

/ĭ/ **/ā/** /ă/ /ă/ **/ā/** **/ā/** /ē/ **/ā/** /ă/

Practice and Apply: Listen for Long a

Say: ***Now practice making the long* a *sound. Watch my mouth. I'm going to say the /ā/ sound. When I make the /ā/ sound, my mouth is open and I can hold the sound for a long time.***

Model producing the sound. Then practice chorally with the students. Finally, have the students make the long *a* sound independently.

Say: **I'm going to say some words. If you hear the /ā/ sound in the word, hold up two fingers and say /ā/. If you don't hear the /ā/ sound, stay quiet and don't say anything.**

Say words from the word bank below. Have students listen for the long *a* sound and signal with two fingers together.

Word bank (words with long a *are bold)*: **aid**, **jay**, bat, **snail**, root, **say**, toss, **stain**, **ray**, ran, **plain**, hike, **play**, send, **laid**, **tray**, might, fast, **fail**, **gray**

Practice and Apply: Find ai and ay

Hold up two fingers.

Explain: ***When two letters work together to make one vowel sound, they are called vowel teams.***

Display *ai* and *ay* cards. Point to the *ai* card using two fingers together to illustrate that the two vowels work together.

Say: ***This is the* ai *team. It makes the long* a *sound: /ā/. This team is in words like* drain, rail, *and* paint.**

Point to the *ay* card using two fingers.

Say: ***This is the* ay *team. It also makes the long* a *sound: /ā/. This team is in words like* may, pay, *and* stray.**

Say: ***Let's see if we can find the long* a *vowel teams in words. I will show you some words. When you see a long* a *vowel team, point to it with two fingers—one for each letter in the team.***

Display word cards one at a time and have students identify long *a* words. Then read the word out loud and have students chorally repeat.

ai Word Cards: **braid**, **aim**, **train**, **jail**, mad, **rain**, seam, **wait**, like, **mail**, camp

ay Word Cards: **away**, **bay**, fly, **hay**, yak, **way**, ban, **stay**, boy, **tray**, key

Check Progress

Observe each student during practice and use the following activity to check progress made on the target skill. If student can correctly identify two words with long a*, consider the intervention successful.*

Say: ***I'll show each of you three words. When you see one with a long* a *team point to it and say the long* a *sound.***

Shuffle the word cards. Place three on the table in front of a student and read the words out loud as you point to them. Have students identify long *a* words. Rotate through the students until all have had a turn.

Reteaching Lessons

ay	away
bay	fly
hay	yak
way	ban
stay	boy
tray	key

ay Word Cards

ai	braid
aim	train
jail	mad
rain	seam
wait	like
mail	camp

Reteaching Lessons ✓

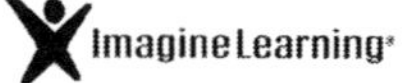

ai Word Cards

Vowel Teams ea and ee

Grade 1

10 Min.

CCSS.RF.1.3.C
TEKS 110.12.3.A

LEARNING OBJECTIVE: Decode and read advanced vocabulary words by analogy.

LANGUAGE OBJECTIVE: Use known words and patterns to sound out words formed with vowel teams.

Lesson Overview

Students hear and recognize the long e sound (/ē/) first in isolation and then in words that contain the *ea* or *ee* vowel teams. Students then practice saying words with long *e* and sort words with long *e* vowel teams.

Materials	Preparation
• *ea* and *ee* Word Cards	• Cut out word cards.

NOTE: /ē/ (long *e*, as in *she*), /ĕ/ (short *e*, as in *bed*), /ī/ (long *i*, as in *life*), /ō/ (long *o*, as in *say*)

Teach and Model

Remind students: ***Some letters stand for more than one sound. All vowels have a long sound and a short sound. Today we are going to practice long* e.**

Say: ***Listen to this sound: /ē/. That sound is called long* e. *I want to know if you can hear this sound. I'm going to say some different vowel sounds***.

Hold up two fingers close together.

Say: ***When you hear long* e, *hold up your fingers up like this. If you don't hear long* e, *keep your hands down.***

Say the sounds below one at a time. Pause between sounds so that students have time to signal with their fingers. Increase the pace as students become more confident.

Sound bank:

/ē/ /ĕ/ /ī/ **/ē/** **/ē/** /ō/ /ĕ/ **/ē/** /ī/

/ē/ **/ē/** /ō/ **/ē/** /ĕ/ **/ē/** /ī/ /ō/ **/ē/**

Practice and Apply: Listen for Long e

Say: ***Now practice making the long* e *sound. Watch my mouth. I'm going to say the /ē/ sound. When I make the /ē/ sound, my mouth is open and I can hold the sound for a long time.***

Model producing the sound. Then practice chorally with the students. Finally, have the students make the long *e* sound independently.

Say: ***I'm going to say some words. If you hear the /ē/ sound in the word, hold up two fingers and say /ē/. If you don't hear the /ē/ sound, stay quiet and don't say anything.***

Say words from the word bank below. Have students listen for the long *e* sound and signal with two fingers together.

Word bank (words with long e *are bold)*: **bee**, spin, **sea**, **greet**, met, **seem**, cape, **leaf**, **sleep**, late, **speak**, moon, **street**, rent, **please**, fry, **free**, **clean**, **peel**, post, big, **teen**

Practice and Apply: Find ea and ee

Hold up two fingers.

Explain: ***When two letters work together to make one vowel sound, they are called vowel teams.***

Display *ea* and *ee* cards. Point to the *ea* card using two fingers together to illustrate that the two vowels work together.

Say: ***This is the* ea *team. It makes the long* e *sound: /ē/. This team is in words like* flea, dream, *and* teach.**

Point to the *ee* card using two fingers.

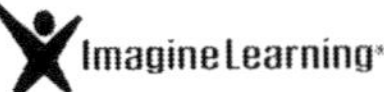

Say: ***This is the* ee *team. It also makes the long* e *sound: /ē/. This team is in words like* deep, feed, *and* sneeze.**

Say: ***Let's see if we can find the long* e *vowel teams in words. I will show you some words. When you see a long* e *vowel team, point to it with two fingers—one for each letter in the team.***

Display word cards one at a time and have students identify long *e* words. Then read the word out loud and have students chorally repeat.

ea Word Cards: **leaps**, **eat**, name, **team**, line, **beat**, fit, **stream**, mate, **each**, pledge

ee Word Cards: **green**, **tree**, **queen**, **feet**, loan, **seed**, plain, **sweet**, beg, **three**, pie

Check Progress

Observe each student during practice and use the following activity to check progress made on the target skill. If student can correctly identify two words with long e*, consider the intervention successful.*

Say: ***I'll show each of you three words. When you see one with a long* e *team point to it and say the long* e *sound.***

Shuffle the word cards. Place three on the table in front of a student and read the words out loud as you point to them. Have students identify long *e* words. Rotate through the students until all have had a turn.

ea	beat
leaps	fit
eat	stream
name	mate
team	each
line	pledge

✓ Reteaching Lessons

ea Word Cards

ee	seed
green	plain
tree	sweet
queen	beg
feet	three
loan	pie

Reteaching Lessons

Vowel Team igh

Grade 1

10 Min.

CCSS.RF.1.3.C
TEKS 110.12.3.A

LEARNING OBJECTIVE: Decode and read advanced vocabulary words by analogy.

LANGUAGE OBJECTIVE: Use known words and patterns to sound out words formed with vowel teams.

Lesson Overview

Students hear and recognize the long *i* sound (/ī/) first in isolation and then in words that contain the *igh* vowel team. Students then practice saying words with *igh* and sort words with the *igh* vowel team.

Materials	Preparation
• *igh* Word Cards	• Cut out word cards.

NOTE: /ī/ (long *i*, as in *life*), /ĭ/ (short *i*, as in *bit*), /ē/ (long *e*, as in *she*), /ū/ (long *u*, as in *blue*)

Teach and Model

Remind students: ***Some letters stand for more than one sound. All vowels have a long sound and a short sound. Today we are going to practice long* i.**

Say: ***Listen to this sound: /ī/. That sound is called long* i. *I want to know if you can hear this sound. I'm going to say some different vowel sounds*.**

Hold up three fingers close together.

Say: ***When you hear long* i, *hold up your fingers up like this. If you don't hear long* i, *keep your hands down.***

Say the sounds below one at a time. Pause between sounds so that students have time to signal with their fingers. Increase the pace as students become more confident.

Sound bank:

/ī/ /ē/ /ū/ **/ī/** /ĭ/ /ē/ **/ī/** /ū/ **/ī/**

/ē/ **/ī/** /ĭ/ /ū/ **/ī/** **/ī/** /ē/ /ĭ/ **/ī/**

Practice and Apply: Listen for Long i

Say: ***Now practice making the long* i *sound. Watch my mouth. I'm going to say the /ī/ sound. When I make the /ī/ sound, my mouth is open and I can hold the sound for a long time.***

Model producing the sound. Then practice chorally with the students. Finally, have the students make the long *i* sound independently.

Say: **I'm going to say some words. If you hear the /ī/ sound in the word, hold up three fingers and say /ī/. If you don't hear the /ī/ sound, stay quiet and don't say anything.**

Say words from the word bank below. Have students listen for the long *i* sound and signal with three fingers together.

Word bank (words with long i *are bold)*: **fright**, sit, **height**, hog, **fighter**, fruit, trip, meet, **might**, think, **thigh**, **wright**, **light**, stick, **right**, this, **sights**, fate, **flight**

Practice and Apply: Find ai and ay

Hold up three fingers.

Explain: ***When two or more letters work together to make one vowel sound, they are called vowel teams.***

Display *igh* card. Point to the *igh* card using three fingers together to illustrate that the three letters work together.

Say: ***This is the* igh *team. It makes the long* i *sound: /ī/. This team is in words like* high, right, *and* night.**

Say: ***Let's see if we can find the long* i *vowel team in words. I will show you some words. When you see the long* i *vowel team, point to it with three fingers—one for each letter in the team.***

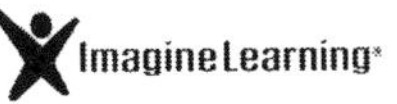

Display word cards one at a time and have students identify long *i* words. Then read the word out loud and have students chorally repeat.

igh Word Cards: bit, **high**, hid, **night**, fit, **right**, get, **flight**, train, **light**, wait, **sigh**, maid, **tight**, lint, point, **higher**, **brightly**, seat, tough, **delight**, laugh, wind

Check Progress

Observe each student during practice and use the following activity to check progress made on the target skill. If student can correctly identify two words with long i*, consider the intervention successful.*

Say: ***I'll show each of you three words. When you see one with the long* i *team point to it and say the long* i *sound.***

Shuffle the word cards. Place three on the table in front of a student and read the words out loud as you point to them. Have students identify long *i* words. Rotate through the students until all have had a turn.

igh	right
bit	get
high	flight
hid	train
night	light
fit	wait

Reteaching Lessons

sigh	brightly
maid	seat
tight	tough
lint	delight
point	laugh
higher	wind

Reteaching Lessons

Vowel Teams oa and ow

LEARNING OBJECTIVE: Decode and read advanced vocabulary words by analogy.

LANGUAGE OBJECTIVE: Use known words and patterns to sound out words formed with vowel teams.

Lesson Overview

Students hear and recognize the long *o* sound (/ō/) first in isolation and then in words that contain the *oa* or *ow* vowel teams. Students then practice saying words with long *o* and sort words with long *o* vowel teams.

Materials	Preparation
• *ew* and *ue* Word Cards	• Cut out word cards.

NOTE: /ō/ (long *o*, as in *no*), /ŏ/ (short *o*, as in *mom*), /ă/ (short *a*, as in *cat*), /ŭ/ (short *u*, as in *cup*)

Teach and Model

Remind students: ***Some letters stand for more than one sound. All vowels have a long sound and a short sound. Today we are going to practice long o.***

Say: ***Listen to this sound: /ō/. That sound is called long o. I want to know if you can hear this sound. I'm going to say some different vowel sounds.***

Hold up two fingers close together.

Say: ***When you hear long o, hold up your fingers up like this. If you don't hear long o, keep your hands down.***

Say the sounds below one at a time. Pause between sounds so that students have time to signal with their fingers. Increase the pace as students become more confident.

Sound bank:

/ō/ /ŏ/ **/ō/** /ă/ /ŭ/ **/ō/** **/ō/** /ă/ **/ō/**

/ŏ/ **/ō/** /ŭ/ **/ō/** /ă/ **/ō/** /ŏ/ **/ō/** /ŭ/

Practice and Apply: Listen for Long o

Say: ***Now practice making the long o sound. Watch my mouth. I'm going to say the /ō/ sound. When I make the /ō/ sound, my mouth is open and I can hold the sound for a long time.***

Model producing the sound. Then practice chorally with the students. Finally, have the students make the long *o* sound independently.

Say: **I'm going to say some words. If you hear the /ō/ sound in the word, hold up two fingers and say /ō/. If you don't hear the /ō/ sound, stay quiet and don't say anything.**

Say words from the word bank below. Have students listen for the long *o* sound and signal with two fingers together.

Word bank (words with long o are bold): **slow**, not, **coal**, mean, **show**, **toad**, job, **grow**, point, **soak**, **moat**, tub, barn, **flow**, **goal**, feed, **crow**, **toast**, golf, soup

Practice and Apply: Find oa and ow

Hold up two fingers.

Explain: ***When two letters work together to make one vowel sound, they are called vowel teams.***

Display *oa* and *ow* cards. Point to the *oa* card using two fingers together to illustrate that the two vowels work together.

Say: ***This is the oa team. It makes the long o sound: /ō/. This team is in words like* coat, roast, *and* oats.**

Point to the *ow* card using two fingers.

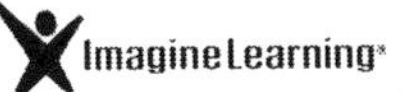

Say: ***This is the ow team. It also makes the long o sound: /ō/. This team is in words like* row, blow, *and* glow.**

Say: ***Let's see if we can find the long o vowel teams in words. I will show you some words. When you see a long o vowel team, point to it with two fingers—one for each letter in the team.***

Display word cards one at a time and have students identify long *o* words. Then read the word out loud and have students chorally repeat.

oa Word Cards: **boat**, **soap**, **road**, **foam**, **coach**, pond, loud, long, **coast**, **load**, land

ow Word Cards: **snow**, **own**, **slow**, **throw**, blew, tool, dog, yawn, **bowl**, **low**, wood

Check Progress

Observe each student during practice and use the following activity to check progress made on the target skill. If student can correctly identify two words with long o, consider the intervention successful.

Say: ***I'll show each of you three words. When you see one with a long o team point to it and say the long o sound.***

Shuffle the word cards. Place three on the table in front of a student and read the words out loud as you point to them. Have students identify long *o* words. Rotate through the students until all have had a turn.

Reteaching Lessons

oa	pond
boat	loud
soap	long
road	coast
foam	load
coach	land

oa Word Cards

Imagine Learning

ow	tool
snow	dog
own	yawn
slow	bowl
throw	low
blew	wood

Reteaching Lessons ✓

Vowel Teams ew and ue

Grade 1

10 Min.

CCSS.RF.1.3.C
TEKS 110.12.3.A

LEARNING OBJECTIVE: Decode and read advanced vocabulary words by analogy.

LANGUAGE OBJECTIVE: Use known words and patterns to sound out words formed with vowel teams.

Lesson Overview

Students hear and recognize the long *u* sound (/ū/) first in isolation and then in words that contain the *ai* or *ay* vowel teams. Students then practice saying words with long *u* and sort words with long *u* vowel teams.

Materials	Preparation
• *ew* and *ue* Word Cards	• Cut out word cards.

NOTE: /ū/ (long *u*, as in *blue*), /ŭ/ (short *u*, as in *cup*), /ē/ (long *e*, as in *she*), /ō/ (long *o*, as in *no*)

Teach and Model

Remind students: ***Some letters stand for more than one sound. All vowels have a long sound and a short sound. Today we are going to practice long* u.**

Say: ***Listen to this sound: /ū/. That sound is called long* u. *I want to know if you can hear this sound. I'm going to say some different vowel sounds*.**

Hold up two fingers close together.

Say: ***When you hear long* u, *hold up your fingers up like this. If you don't hear long* u, *keep your hands down.***

Say the sounds below one at a time. Pause between sounds so that students have time to signal with their fingers. Increase the pace as students become more confident.

Sound bank:

/ū/ /ē/ /ō/ **/ū/** /ŭ/ **/ū/ /ū/** /ŭ/ **/ō/**

/ū/ /ū/ /ŭ/ **/ū/** /ē/ /ō/ /ŭ/ **/ū/** /ŭ/

Practice and Apply: Listen for Long u

Say: ***Now practice making the long* u *sound. Watch my mouth. I'm going to say the /ū/ sound. When I make the /ū/ sound, my mouth is open and I can hold the sound for a long time.***

Model producing the sound. Then practice chorally with the students. Finally, have the students make the long *u* sound independently.

Say: **I'm going to say some words. If you hear the /ū/ sound in the word, hold up two fingers and say /ū/. If you don't hear the /ū/ sound, stay quiet and don't say anything.**

Say words from the word bank below. Have students listen for the long *u* sound and signal with two fingers together.

Word bank (words with long u *are bold)*: **new**, **blue**, fun, sheep, **grew**, book, **clue**, pot, **stew**, **glue**, join, hug, **drew**, **dew**, true, loan, **due**, **sue**, mud

Practice and Apply: Find ai and ay

Hold up two fingers.

Explain: ***When two letters work together to make one vowel sound, they are called vowel teams.***

Display *ai* and *ay* cards. Point to the *ai* card using two fingers together to illustrate that the two vowels work together.

Say: ***This is the* ai *team. It makes the long* u *sound: /ū/. This team is in words like* few, chew, *and* new.**

Point to the *ay* card using two fingers.

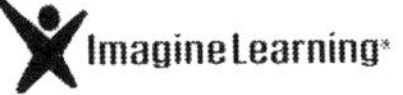

Say: ***This is the* ay *team. It also makes the long* u *sound: /ū/. This team is in words like* blue, glue, *and* true.**

Say: ***Let's see if we can find the long* u *vowel teams in words. I will show you some words. When you see a long* u *vowel team, point to it with two fingers—one for each letter in the team.***

Display word cards one at a time and have students identify long *u* words. Then read the word out loud and have students chorally repeat.

ue Word Cards: cut, clues, lump, blue, trust, true, bead, glue, goal, due, much

ew Word Cards: flow, few, how, chew, saw, blew, bug, view, when, stew, wet

Check Progress

Observe each student during practice and use the following activity to check progress made on the target skill. If student can correctly identify two words with long u*, consider the intervention successful.*

Say: ***I'll show each of you three words. When you see one with a long* u *team point to it and say the long* u *sound.***

Shuffle the word cards. Place three on the table in front of a student and read the words out loud as you point to them. Have students identify long *u* words. Rotate through the students until all have had a turn.

Reteaching Lessons

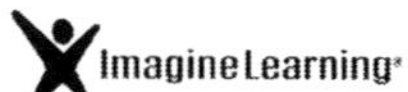

ew	blew
flow	bug
few	view
how	when
chew	stew
saw	wet

ew Word Cards

ue	true
cut	bead
clues	glue
lump	goal
blue	due
trust	much

Reteaching Lessons ✓

Made in the USA
Columbia, SC
23 December 2021

52645052R00150